Imogen Edwards-Jones is the co-author of the best-selling *Hotel Babylon* and *Air Babylon* as well as author of *The Stork Club* and *The Taming of Eagles*. Her fiction includes *My Canapé Hell*, *Shagpile*, *The Wendy House* and *Tuscany for Beginners*. Her new book, *Beach Babylon*, is now available from Bantam Press. Imogen lives in west London with her husband and their baby daughter.

Anonymous is a collection of high-profile insiders from the fashion industry.

FASHION
BABYLON

IMOGEN EDWARDS-JONES
& Anonymous

CORGI BOOKS

TRANSWORLD PUBLISHERS
61–63 Uxbridge Road, London W5 5SA
a division of The Random House Group Ltd
www.booksattransworld.co.uk

FASHION BABYLON
A CORGI BOOK: 9780552154437

First published in Great Britain
in 2006 by Bantam Press
a division of Transworld Publishers
Corgi edition published 2007

A CIP catalogue record for this book
is available from the British Library

Addresses for Random House Group Ltd companies outside the UK
can be found at: www.randomhouse.co.uk
The Random House Group Ltd Reg. No. 954009

The Random House Group Ltd makes every effort to ensure that the papers
used in its books are made from trees that have been legally sourced from
well-managed and credibly certified forests. Our paper procurement policy can
be found at: www.randomhouse.co.uk/paper.htm

Typeset in 11.5/15.75pt Sabon by
Falcon Oast Grahic Art Ltd.

Printed and bound in Great Britain by
Cox & Wyman Ltd, Reading, Berkshire.

2 4 6 8 10 9 7 5 3 1

Every effort has been made to obtain the necessary permissions with reference
to copyright material, both illustrative and quoted. We apologize for any
omissions in this respect and will be pleased to make the appropriate
acknowledgements in any future edition.

Mixed Sources
Product group from well-managed
forests and other controlled sources
www.fsc.org Cert no. TT-COC-2139
© 1996 Forest Stewardship Council
FSC

For Allegra

With very grateful thanks to the wonderful Eugenie Furniss and the handsome Doug Young and all at Transworld for their fabulousness.

And to all the people whose time and patience I called upon during the hours and days I spent interviewing them in wine bars, restaurants, private clubs and the insane sweaty confines of backstage during various fashion weeks; I am extremely thankful as I could not have done this without your humour, trust and kind co-operation.

Prologue

All of the following is true. Only the names have been changed to protect the guilty. All the anecdotes, the stories, the highs, the lows, the scams, the drugs, the deals, the rivalries and the insanity are as told to me by Anonymous – a wide and varied collection of people who all work at the heart of the fashion industry. The designer is fictionalized; however, the incidents are real, the celebrities play themselves, but the stories now all take place within six months of a designer's year. Narrated by Anonymous, all the stories have been condensed into this time period. But everything else is as it should be. The rich buy the clothes, the poor make them, and everyone else thrives on the heady and rarefied atmosphere. It's just another six months in the life of the fashion industry.

1

Today is the morning after the night before, and if I look closely at Alexander's upturned nose I can see that both his nostrils are frosted like a margarita glass. He's been at the jazz. But then we all have. It's the end of another long and exhausting London Fashion Week; how else are we all supposed to remain funny and fabulous without a couple of grams of Bolivia's finest in our Chloé leather Paddington bags?

Not that we are this morning. Lying flat on his back, fully clothed, clutching an empty bottle of Grey Goose vodka tightly to his chest, Alexander looks like he is barely capable of speech let alone an amusing anecdote or witty quip. And I couldn't feel less fabulous. It was my sixth runway show last night, and lying here, staring at the ceiling of this overpriced hotel suite which we booked ourselves into to carry on the after-show party, I can't help thinking things might not be going my way.

It won't be anything to do with the show. I mean, considering my lack of financial backing, all the time constraints and the fact that two of my stitchers walked out at the last minute, my collection wasn't actually that bad. I'd really gone to town with my tailoring skills. Well, that is my signature. I'm known for my cut. I love it. You can take pounds off people with a well-placed seam. My jackets were tight and short, my skirts skimmed the hips and pinched in the waist, my trousers were wide legged and my shirts had leg-of-mutton sleeves. I'd gone for a nautical theme, with stripes and sailor's hats. Lots of white. I think there was one killer white and silver dress in the show. I was actually quite pleased with the way that it all turned out. It arrived on time and in the right order. I didn't have a moment like one designer did, whose collection, entirely of navy blue, fell off the hangers and all he was left with was a pile of crumpled blue clothes and no idea as to which order to put them in. He apparently then sat on the cat-walk and burst into tears saying that he would never design again. But my clothes did arrive. As did the models. A couple were late and a few more were a little worse for wear. They'd been at the champagne early but they were still capable of walking in a straight line; those who weren't had a line to straighten them up. Even the famously flatulent model who guffs her way up and down the runway managed to put a cork in it for my show. Perhaps she'd laid off the beans in my honour. So the smiles were genuine. Even if some were a little rictus.

However, on the whole I thought it went well. Everyone made it there and back. No-one keeled over like Naomi Campbell in her heels, the fash pack flocked backstage to pat and preen and pretend, and we all tucked into the booze after the show.

No, the real problem is that my last two shows were deemed hits by the press. Particularly my last Fall collection. Christ, even Anna Wintour liked it. Not that she saw it, of course. She doesn't really do London. We're too small, unimportant and lacking in advertising funds to warrant a visit from Nuclear. She does deign to descend on London Fashion Week occasionally. She is rumoured to be coming next season, but she is always rumoured to be turning up, on her way to Milan and Paris. Much like Madonna is always supposed to be coming to premières and London fashion parties, so La Wintour is always anticipated and fêted and never shows. It was, therefore, one of the worker bees from US *Vogue* who turned up to my last show. Anyway it was deemed hot and happening, on the button, fashion forward enough to have a whole corner of a page in US *Vogue*. They even included a couple of my blouses and a trapeze coat in the round-ups. *Elle* magazine ran a feature. *Marie Claire* asked for an interview. *Harpers* did a shoot. The *Evening Standard* gave me a double-page spread, suggesting that I might be the new Roland Mouret. A hack from the *Telegraph* came to my after-show party. Even Style.com couldn't summon the energy to slag me off. In fact they were nice. Everyone was nice. Which is a dangerous thing in fashion.

A lot was expected of last night's show, and I'm not sure I could ever have delivered. The British Fashion Council were kind enough to give me the slot I requested, 6.30 p.m. on Thursday, which is a first. Every year they ask me which slot I would like, every year I ask for Thursday evening, and every year they give me Tuesday at 9.30 a.m. No-one wants to go at the beginning of the week, as it means none of the US buyers have made it across the Pond after the close of New York. And no-one can face a morning show. Who wants a glass of champagne before they've managed to get a skinny latte down their necks? But this year I was given the best slot, on the best day; I was even scheduled next to Betty Jackson, so everyone could come. My front row was full, my back row was full. I also had a sniff of celeb – an Appleton, that girl from *The X Factor*. There was even talk of Posh, but Alexander stamped his foot. Not that she would show up anyway. But he was certain to make sure.

'She is all tan, tits and hair extensions,' he pronounced at the mere mention that her people might be calling my person for a front-row ticket. 'And to me quite frankly she just isn't fashion.'

'Cavalli is all over her,' I replied.

'Purlease,' he said. 'That old arse. I reckon he's got as much style as a remainder bin.'

Alexander has lots of grapevine stories that frankly I

think are untrue, and he launched into one of his old favourites. A few years back when Tom Ford was still at Gucci, he allegedly called up his PR in London demanding to get 'that woman' out of his clothes. The PR is supposed to have said she couldn't as Posh was buying their clothes. And Ford is said to have paused and then shouted, '*How can we stop her?*'

'So, if Posh is not good enough for Tom Ford,' Alexander continued with a shrug, 'we don't want her skinny arse anywhere near our collection.'

Now, Alexander starts to cough himself awake next to me. It is one of those hacking coughs where you can hear lumps and lungs curdling together. The bed is shaking. Finally there is one loud hack as he sits up, releasing the vodka bottle which rolls off the bed onto the heavily carpeted floor.

'Oh, fuck!' he says, opening his eyes, rubbing his pale face and running his hands through his slick mousey hair. 'I feel shit.' He coughs again. 'You got a ciggie?'

'Umm,' I say, looking out into the room.

I have slept with Alexander twice a year, every year, ever since we got together some time in the last century, and I have to say he isn't any more charming in the morning.

'Jesus,' he says, rubbing his small nose as he surveys the scene. 'What the fuck happened to this place? It's trashed.'

He's not wrong. There are glasses and bottles and fag butts everywhere. There are half-drunk drinks, butts in half-drunk drinks, and one smeared CD case in the middle of the table. Someone's been wearing the complimentary dressing gown. It's lying by the door. The free slippers are out of their plastic, and someone's left a white and gold handbag behind.

'Oh I say,' says Alexander, carefully getting out of bed, holding onto his head. Dressed in his black suit and white shirt he looks like a magpie on a mission as he gingerly picks his way through the debris in his black silk socks. 'Look at this. This looks quite nice,' he says, picking up the bag and sniffing the leather. 'A possible party steal?'

'It looks like a Tanner Krolle to me,' I say, sitting up in bed.

'Oh, you're right,' he says, dropping it straight back onto the floor. 'Suddenly I'm liking that a whole lot less.'

He sits down on one of the two grey felt sofas and starts going through the empty packets on the table until he finds a cigarette. He sparks it up and inhales. He dissolves into a fit of coughing which culminates in a loud snorting of phlegm, which he swallows.

'God,' he says. 'That's much better. Oh, look,' he adds, cheering up no end. 'Look what we have here. My Selfridges card.' He smiles, holding it up for me to see. 'With my name written in coke.' He taps the card out onto the CD packet and gathers together the remainder of the drugs into a thin line. He searches the table and then eventually in his own suit pockets for some money. He finds one squalid-looking fiver, which he rejects in favour of a taxi receipt. He rolls it up. It's poised by his nostril when he suddenly remembers his middle-class manners and private education. 'Want some?' he asks.

'No thanks.'

'Righty-ho.' He smiles before he snorts the CD clean. 'OK,' he says, clapping his hands together and rubbing the sweat down the front of his Dior trousers. 'How are you feeling?'

'Not terribly confident,' I reply.

Actually, that's a bit of an understatement. I feel sick, scared and deeply unconfident. This has to be the worst moment in any fashion designer's year. You've worked your arse off. You've done your best. Had no sleep for weeks. Nothing to eat or drink other than Haribo sweets and full-fat Coke for days. Yet this ordeal is nothing compared to the reviews. They can make you or crucify you in one morning. They can close your business. Make sure no-one places any orders. Wipe the floor with you. And send you back to fashion ignominy with one swift slip of the pen.

My heart is racing, my mouth is dry, and I can barely breathe. I have had two good shows and one great season. I'm sure they are all queuing up to knock me down. That's the thing about the London shows: they only really like you if you are really new, really young and really really poor. They like to discover you and give you your first break. They love it if someone like

Isabella Blow swoops in and buys your entire collection. Or if Kate Moss walks off in all your clothes. But if you are already doing OK, chugging along nicely with a rack in Harvey Nichols and some Matches orders under your belt, then they have nothing to write about. There's no story. They are looking for the next fashion forward freak with Perspex frocks and feather knickers to put on their front page. If you have been around the block once and collected your British Fashion Award for Best Newcomer, like I did last year, then there is nowhere to go. Except down.

'Do you want me to go and get the reviews?' asks Alexander. 'Or shall we go together?'

'I need some air. Can we go to some internet café around the corner?' I suggest. 'I need to see what Style.com has said before anyone else. After all, that's the one that is going to be beamed all around the world.'

'OK. Squeeze yourself into your skirt and let's get cracking.' He looks at his knock-off watch which he bought on a beach in Sardinia. 'It's gone ten.'

Fifteen minutes and £438 worth of hotel bill later we are walking through Soho looking for a café. It's early September and the weather is gloriously sunny and the sky is bright and clear. Alexander hides his hangover behind a pair of retro shades. He looks a little odd in his black Dior suit and Gucci shoes. Most of the street is still doing the tail end of spring/summer wearing drippy boho skirts, coin belts and gypsy tops; yet he has already moved on. Although I suppose I can talk. I'm in a tight grey pencil skirt and tight-fitting shirt that went down so well in the Fall show back in February.

Just off Wardour Street we find a small café that does coffee and buns and is full of foreign students checking their email.

'We're not far from the office, why don't we go there?' says Alexander, looking around the place, curling his top lip slightly. He doesn't enjoy mixing with real people.

'I'd rather do it now,' I say. 'Before we get back to the office and the phone starts going.'

'OK.' He nods. 'You sit down, I'll get the coffees. D'you want the usual?'

'Thanks.' I smile. I must be the only one left in fashion still to have full-fat milk in their latte.

Alexander slips off towards the back of the café and I go online. In the seconds it takes for Style.com to appear on the screen, all I want to do is throw up. Vodka, coke, stress and three hours' sleep in as many days is enough to make anyone want to hurl all over their keyboard. And then suddenly there it is. The site comes up. I type in my name; a photo of the flatulent model comes on screen. She is swinging towards the lens in a sharp white skirt and sleeveless shirt with a large white collar. I inhale and start to read the copy. 'There is only one way to sum up what went on last night: it was dull. For a designer that we had all hoped was about to hit her stride with her sharp looks and

19

excellent tailoring skills this really did not hit the spot. While you would have to applaud the effort and imagination that went into the collection, the execution was just not cutting edge enough. I had hoped to be blown away by the talent and the ideas that have always abounded in her clothes, but the dresses were too derivative, the trousers were just not daring enough . . .' And it goes on and on. My ideas are not interesting enough, the styling is heavy-handed, my shoes are clunky and ugly. It ends: 'Let's hope this is just a seasonal glitch.' I stare at the review in disbelief. Shit shit shit.

'Oh dear,' says Alexander, inhaling sharply through the back of his teeth. He is leaning over my shoulder reading along with me. He sits down, putting the two mugs of coffee on the table. 'Well, we could always tap into the tranny shoe market.'

'What?' I say, in a daze.

'Like Vivienne,' he continues.

'Westwood?'

'Of course.' He rolls his eyes. 'Her shoes sell like hot cakes in the States.' He smiles. 'But only in enormous men's sizes. They go down a storm in the tranny clubs of West Hollywood.'

'Well, by the look of things and this bloody Louise bitch, I'll only be dressing trannies by the end of today.'

'They're very discerning,' he replies.

'They are?'

'Absolutely.' He smiles again. 'Honestly, don't worry

about Style.com.' He takes an enormous slurp of his coffee. 'Who reads it?'

'Only everyone.'

I slump forward, pick up a teaspoon and start stirring my coffee. I sigh. My whole world is collapsing. The business I have spent nearly six years building up is going to go under. Like so many other British fashion designers before me, I am going to arrive with a bang and leave with a whole load of CCJs and bad bloody debts.

'Do you want some chocolate on that?'

'Please.'

Alexander really does know me very well. He is my friend, my inspiration and my partner. Business not sexual, obviously. We met eight years ago in a pub in Soho. He was a graphic design graduate with a dodgy third-class degree in his pocket and I was not so fresh from Central St Martin's. I had been styling a *Face* magazine shoot and had a few frock designs pencilled on a postcard, and he said he had a mate with a spare room/studio off Berwick Street. We drank some lager, smoked four packets of Marlboro Lights and discovered a mutual love for tailoring. We obsessed about Hussein Chalayan's wooden skirt, gossiped about Vivienne Westwood and shared our Sunday afternoon fixation with the Victoria and Albert Museum. Suddenly it was dawn. And we have been together ever since.

He is brilliant at all the things I hate. He is great with

figures, good with people in the business. He walks the walk and talks for bloody England. He butters up the right folk, gets us deals left and right, and actually enjoys talking to all those frosty females who seem to run the world of fashion. He has only ever really fucked up once, when a couple of seasons ago he tried to re-invent the front row of our show. We had a large white space and he decided we would make the thing very democratic. We made the runway extra long and wound it around the place, placing chairs all the way along it, thereby making every seat on the front row. No-one liked it, not one little bit. Editors were jostling with fashion directors who were shouting at assistants who were arguing with students. No-one knew their place. No-one could work out which was the better seat or who had the better view. You should never under-estimate the egos of these people. Vivienne Westwood's people once made the mistake of handing out more tickets than there were seats for a Paris show. It ended in a riot.

'Here you go,' says Alexander, returning with a latte heaving with chocolate powder.

'Thanks,' I say, taking a teaspoon, scooping up the powder and shoving the whole lot in my mouth. 'I suppose the next port of call is Suzy Menkes.'

An institution in her own right, Suzy Menkes has been writing for the *International Herald Tribune* ever since fashion was invented. A bit boho around the edges, she has a signature curl-fronted hairdo and is one of the best writers around. Known for her fairness, accuracy and love of fashion, a good review from her could turn the whole sorry collection around.

'She won't be out till tomorrow,' says Alexander. 'Or even the day after that.'

'Just the UK media then,' I say, taking another teaspoon of chocolate.

Alexander nods.

'Well . . . our life is over.'

'Maybe not,' he says, rubbing his hands together. 'There's always the *Telegraph*. The *Telegraph* likes you.'

'Yeah, but we need *The Times*, the *Standard*, I need . . . oh God . . . the *Sunday Times*.'

Alexander and I look at each other and start to laugh. It is not happy laughter. It is hysterical and hung over and resigned.

'They are never going to give you that,' giggles Alexander. 'They've never liked anything you've ever done. Ever!'

'I know.'

'They've been rude about you even when everyone else liked the collection.'

'I know.'

'And now you're hoping that they might come through for you this time.'

'I know!'

My voice is so high and strained and loud that the foreign students are beginning to look at us like we're insane. Which I suppose we are.

'Let's get back to the office,' says Alexander. 'Before we make total tits of ourselves.'

Back in the office next to a bookie's off Berwick Street and it looks like we've been burgled. There is stuff strewn every way. Each and every one of the three floors of the building has been trashed. The ground floor where we have a semblance of a reception area with a desk and purple velvet sofa plus a large fitting room to the right with racks and racks of clothes is covered in paper and patterns and tiny bits of off-cut material. There are buttons and trim and pads of pins and needles on every surface. There are single shoes and piles of bracelets and necklaces lying all over the dark pink carpet. Next floor up, where I have my desk plus mood wall and Alexander has his office, is slightly tidier. But there are still rolls of fabric and discarded toiles all over the place. The floor above, where the pattern cutters and seamstresses work, looks like a sequin-stuffed mattress has exploded in it. There are hardly any sequins in my collection, in fact there are only two evening dresses trimmed with the things, yet the whole of the top floor is covered with them. There are also great swathes of silver silk everywhere – remnants of the silver parka jackets I had suddenly decided to make after seeing something rather similar in the Marc Jacobs show the week before.

One of the perks of following New York is that you get to see what all the other designers are doing. It is always worth looking at Marc Jacobs, Anna Sui,

Michael Kors, Calvin Klein, Ralph Lauren and Tuleh, and getting the occasional glimpse of Oscar Pay My Renta, as the girls call him, just to make sure that we are on message. As a small company it is important to get a few items that are similar to what the fash pack are hailing as the trends for the season – a Russian-inspired skirt here, an Edwardian-meets-modern- looking shirt there, a sharp jacket, a silver coat. If everyone else is going red and you're the only one insisting on turquoise then you won't make the pages and pages of round-ups at the end of the season. Those 'essential things for summer/autumn/winter' sections that grace the front pages of the glossies are bread and butter to us new kids on the block.

So three days ago, after seeing something silver and sexy swishing down Marc's catwalk, I sent Trish, our seventeen-year-old work experience student, out down Berwick Street market to get yards of the shiny grey stuff to make up some coats. Alexander barked that she should not come back until she'd found it, and he wanted receipts.

I always feel a bit sorry for Trish, but Alexander says I shouldn't. She gets her train fare in from somewhere way out east, wherever she lives, and £10-a-day expenses. I have no idea what she actually lives on, but I suspect it is Haribos and atmosphere like the rest of us in fashion. Whatever it is, she looks very thin and very good on it. She's always got the latest pair of Chanel sunglasses or a Balenciaga belt that her friends have pinched from the fashion cupboards of the various magazines they work for. The rest of her stuff is usually of her own creation teamed with a T from Top Shop, or something similar.

Anyway, she did eventually return – after, I suspect, fifteen fags and a few coffees in the local caff around the corner – and then all hell broke loose. There was much Portuguese and Polish shouting and screaming from my stitchers, and some surly sighing and Japanese attitude from my pattern cutters, but after a night of smoking, swearing and downing copious cans of Red Bull, they produced three half-decent-looking silvery silk anorak coats with large hoods and pale pink linings. They never made it into the show in the end. My stylist Mimi said she wasn't feeling them, and that was that.

Actually, standing here, gagging slightly from the smell of the old, dank fag smoke that curls down the stairs from the sewing room, I can see one of the coats hanging up on the back of my chair in the office. It looks rather nice, soft and light and strangely elegant. Maybe I should have put them in my collection after all? Or perhaps I'd better just flog them off in the sample sale at the end of the month?

'Hiya,' comes a voice from the bottom of the stairs.

'Hello there, Trish,' replies Alexander.

'Hi, Alex . . . ander,' she says.

'You're learning.'

'I've got the papers,' she says.

'You're in early,' I say, coming down the stairs.

'I slept here.'

'Oh?'

'Yeah.' She nods towards the purple sofa in the reception area. 'Missed the night bus home. A mate suggested I come and sleep with them over in Southwark but I thought I'd save myself the effort and come and kip down here. That pink fun fur coat from last season is ever so warm.'

'You slept in something from last season?' jokes Alexander.

'I know.' She giggles. 'Ma-jor! It was a toss-up between freezing my tits off or making a fashion faux pas, and I thought no-one would know.'

Dressed in a pair of homemade dark grey, high-waisted trousers and black T-shirt with large white Chanel glasses perched on her head, Trish isn't really joking. She would genuinely rather freeze than wear last season. I smile. The girl will probably go far.

'Have you looked at the reviews yet?' I ask her.

'None of the others have got theirs in yet. But I've had a little look at the *Standard*.'

'And?'

'It's not too bad.' She shrugs her shoulders. 'They picked out a few things they like.'

'A few?' says Alexander, sounding deeply dubious.

'Shall I read you a bit?' asks Trish.

'Go on,' I say. I can feel my hands beginning to sweat as she opens up the paper.

'It's on page three?' asks Alexander.

'Yeah,' she replies with a nod.

'That's good,' he says to me.

'OK?' asks Trish.

Alexander and I both nod.

'Blah blah blah,' she starts. 'I'm just skipping the boring bit . . . "Having said all that, if you take away the stiff creations she has managed to put together a very wearable collection that will no doubt please the fashion-conscious career woman."'

'Wearable?' says Alexander.

'Yeah,' says Trish, her mouth hanging open slightly.

'You don't want a collection that is bloody *wearable*. Jesus Christ,' he says, slumping down on the purple sofa. 'Wearable . . . Is that all she can come up with? Fucking wearable?' He is doing the quotation-marks-in-the-air thing. 'Next she'll be saying that our skirts are "pleasant" and our trousers are fucking "nice". Wearable,' he huffs. 'No-one wants to be fucking "wearable" in fashion.'

'Yeah,' agrees Trish, wrinkling up her nose. 'That's almost as bad as being commercial.'

'Well, no, actually,' says Alexander.

'Really?' says Trish. 'But everyone hates commercial.'

'Can I have a look at that?' I ask, walking towards her.

'Sure,' she says, handing over the paper.

I open it to page three and nearly drop the thing.

'Oh God,' I say, folding it back and showing it to

Alexander. 'Have you seen this?'

' "Ted Nicholls Reclaims His Fashion Crown",' reads Alexander. 'Fuck. That's all we bloody need.'

'You're the small piece underneath that,' adds Trish, helpfully.

'Yes, thanks, I can see that,' I say.

'That twat's back from the dead,' says Alexander. 'How the hell did that happen?'

2

Over the next couple of days the rest of the reviews come in. They are mostly negative, mostly uninspiring and mostly all saying the same thing – that my bubble has burst, that I'm a busted flush and that I'm no longer cutting edge. I have to say that I am a little depressed that six months' hard work can be dismissed so easily. Actually, Suzy Menkes was good. God bless her. She talked about my turning a corner and being a little bit more experimental. She liked the stiff skirts and tight shirts. But by then it was all a bit too late. The other broadsheets were dismissive. The *Telegraph* wrote a lot of description, which is what they do when they don't really like something that much. We're still waiting for the *Sunday Times*, but it doesn't really matter what they say. The damage has been done. The collection is not going to be a critical hit.

Alexander is being brilliant about it all. He hasn't stopped chain smoking and pacing between our two offices. He is high as a kite on Fair Trade espressos and spitting feathers that Ted Nicholls is apparently having some sort of comeback. 'It's only because the stupid queen went bust that they love him now,' he says, pacing and coughing and tugging at his bottom lip. 'Bloody play gay. If he'd been successful and had then produced that show they wouldn't have written so many nice things. He was successful, then he failed, and now they love him again. It is so typical. Wouldn't it be great if the fashion world suddenly surprised you?'

Ted Nicholls and I were at St Martin's together. We were in the same year and were lovers for a while. We planned to start a label together when we left college, but then he dumped me, decided that he was gay and moved in with the hardcore Hoxton fashion crowd. He now worships at the altar of Katie Grand, so I don't really see much of him any more. Katie's a bit too cool for school and she wouldn't let someone like me in her gang. Actually, if I am being honest, she has never and would never even speak to me. She's never put any of my clothes in her zeitgeist-embracing fashion magazine, *Pop*. In fact, I would hazard a guess that she would rather die than wear any of my clobber.

And anyway, her court is rather full these days. Lee McQueen, Roland Mouret, Giles Deacon, Luella Bartley, the performance artist Johnny Woo, the DJ Richard Batty and the new head of Mulberry, Stuart Vevers, are all her mates. I know Ted drinks at the George and Dragon on the Hackney Road and spent a lot of time last summer hanging out at Golf Sale, a special fashion club night in a place on Hoxton Square. Sam Taylor Wood used to DJ there, along with a bloke called Gregory Wilkins, and they all knocked back the VLSs (vodka, lime and sodas) and sambuca shots while getting down to some groovy tunes. Kate Moss turned up a few times and even threatened to DJ once, but she never did.

One or two of the liggers and nobodies in that crowd are jazz mad – and I don't mean the music. So I have to say that I wasn't surprised when the last time I bumped into Ted it was on a hot Monday morning in the middle of June and he was sporting a straw fedora and a flip-flop and hadn't been to bed. He'd been to an illegal drinking den off Old Street – some bloke's penthouse flat where you pay for your drinks. He had a terrible summer cold, was chewing his own cheeks off, and was dragging some heavily pierced specimen in his wake.

'Darling!' he exclaimed. 'How the hell are you?'

'I'm fine,' I remember saying, pretending very hard not to give a shit.

'Vince,' he said, gesturing to the pierced person, 'this is the only woman I have ever shagged.'

I smiled. They both looked me up and down and then burst out laughing.

So you can imagine how pleased I am to see him back on the scene and doing so well. Unfortunately for Ted, Golf Sale has closed down. Its popularity had extended to real people, so it was killed off. I have no idea where he hangs out these days. I imagine he is still trying to befriend Samantha Morton at Sunday Social in Islington or frotting up Sadie Frost in the Engineer in Primrose Hill. Ted's a sucker for the famous and will go to almost any lengths to get a celeb in his frocks. He's not quite at the Julien Macdonald and Kelly Brook level, but he is not far off.

Alexander and I don't really have time to dwell on the resurgence of Ted Nicholls's marvellousness, much as it would pain him to hear it. We have a long list of sales meetings to deal with before we pack up the collection and take it over to Paris.

As a small independent company we don't have a sales agent, so we have to meet all the buyers ourselves. Normally in the days following London Fashion Week Alexander and I lock ourselves in a hotel suite in the centre of town and receive buyers from all over the world. We ply them with alcohol, fill them with chicken salad and funsize bits of pizza, and pay some poor sod of a model to parade in front of them in our stuff, crossing our fingers that they might actually put in an order. It's an exhausting process. I sit and smile so hard I need botox and fillers by the end of the session in order to look normal. And Alexander spends most of his time biting his tongue in an effort to appear pleasant. We could farm it all out to a sales agent and put our stuff in with a whole lot of other designers, but quite frankly, after they've taken their cut of between

5 and 10 per cent, the profit I make on the year would disappear altogether.

The large labels, or those who have been bought out by huge conglomerates, like the big daddy of them all, LVMH (Louis Vuitton Moët Hennessy), do it a bit differently. They sell out of permanent showrooms or warehouses in town. For the next five days after each of the London, New York, Paris and Milan fashion weeks buyers from the likes of Harvey Nichols, Harrods, Saks Fifth Avenue, Bergdorf Goodman and Neiman's will all turn up to sexed-up warehouses to view, choose and purchase the clothes. All of the Gucci Group clobber is in permanent showrooms. So Stella McCartney, Alexander McQueen and Yves Saint Laurent, Bottega Veneta, Balenciaga, Sergio Rossi, and, of course, Gucci all have their own people and spaces. The same goes for LVMH, so Chloé, Pucci and Louis Vuitton, Celine, Marc Jacobs, Fendi, Givenchy and Donna Karan all have their own warehouses and selling teams. With over a billion euros' profit for the first half of 2005, LVMH have got a lot of selling to do. Even smaller companies like Club 21, who own Luella Bartley and Mulberry, have permanent showrooms all over the fashion world.

With so much money at stake, the warehouse/ showroom set-up is extremely professional, manned by about fifteen to twenty sales staff. The buyers turn up at their allotted time and are walked around the showroom with a clipboard. Each of them is given markers or plastic discs in their own particular colour so that their choices can easily be seen. They are checked in by a sales rep when they arrive and their last order is called up on the computer. They are logged in and their budget is agreed in advance. If, for example, they spent £50,000 last season, they are asked if they are planning to spend the same, or if they want to increase the budget by 10 or 15 per cent for this season. So while Alexander and I are genuflecting to the left and right, singing for our supper and prancing around for our pounds, the big guns are getting straight down to business. Their profit and budgets are so huge, you're either buying or you're not. They're just keen to get on with it. Occasionally some buyers need to see the clothes on a model, and there is a coterie of stick-thin smiley girls sitting around in thongs backstage, waiting to see if Harvey Nichols wants a quick reminder of that Marc Jacobs skirt before she makes up her mind. They may not be the most beautiful models but they are certainly all perfectly proportioned, with large, shiny smiles on their thin faces.

This year, in an attempt to familiarize the buyers with the brand, we have decided not to hire a hotel suite but to have them come to the studio. It was Alexander's idea really. He said that it would be a good way to net-work the buyers, to make them feel part of our family; perhaps they might feel compelled to spend a little more as a result. With most of the big-store fashion directors and buyers on their way to Milan or already there,

Alexander also suggested that instead of spending money on a house model, persuading Mimi to do it might be a good idea. Strangely for someone who is loath to put herself out for anyone, Mimi has agreed. Perhaps, like most stylists, she has always wanted to be a model, or perhaps she had nothing better to do. Either way Mimi turns up half an hour later than she was told and half an hour earlier than we want her. Lying is the only way to get her anywhere on time.

Posh, pretty and plummy, Mimi is six feet tall, rake thin and a mass of red curls. She once did a foundation course and a year of textiles in Newcastle, but it was far too far away from London, so she couldn't stay the course. She is fabulously well connected, summers in the south of France, and is best friends with everyone at *Vogue*. She doesn't just work for me. She styles endless magazine and advertising shoots and could make plenty of money if she weren't so disorganized, lazy and fond of smoking pot. She does have a sideline in celebrity styling, mostly LA actresses promoting their films over here. She spends a lot of time sewing famous people into frocks and has had her nose in so many celebrity armpits she can tell you who's got a hygiene problem, a fat arse, or been under the knife.

'Hi, hi, hi,' she says as she breezes in in a pair of black drainpipe skinny jeans and an enormous pair of reflector shades, looking a little like a fly. She is carrying a large leather handbag/shopper, a phone, a latte, an umbrella, three plastic bags and a huge Gucci carrier. 'Darling!' she says to me. 'Alexander,' she adds. 'Just fucking come and take a look at this.' She drops everything in a pile on the floor and pulls an apple-green handbag out of the Gucci carrier. 'Honestly,' she says, sniffing the bag, stroking it. She is practically salivating. 'It's the new It bag for the season.' She grins. 'I can't believe it.' She squeals, and holds it up so that we can all bask in its reflected glory. 'Wouldn't you go down on your grandmother for that?'

'My grandfather,' says Alexander, walking over to touch it. 'It's fabulous. What do you think?'

'It's fantastic,' I say.

'Isn't it?' says Mimi, so pleased with herself.

As we all gather around the handbag, something leaps out from between our feet.

'Jesus!' screams Alexander, throwing himself back against the wall. He is not a man noted for his bravery. 'What the hell is that?'

'Oh, don't be mean,' says Mimi, bending down and looking around under the sofa. 'It's Mini Me.'

'Mini what?' asks Alexander.

'Mini Me,' says Mimi, gathering up a very small black dog. 'She's a toy poodle.'

'Poodle?' says Alexander.

'A poodle,' repeats Mimi. 'Everyone's doing dogs.'

'I thought dogs were last year,' I say.

'No, last year it was babies,' she says.

'I thought this year was knitting,' says Alexander.

'It is,' says Mimi. 'Knitting and dogs. Sienna's got two. Porgy and Bess.'

'Well, we'd all better get one,' says Alexander.

'We all have,' says Mimi. Bringing the pooch to her mouth she lets the dog lick her on the lips. 'Give Mummy a kiss. Kissy kissy kissy.'

'Oh God, don't,' says Alexander. 'You're making me feel sick. It's just been licking its own arse.'

'She hasn't,' protests Mimi.

'Of course not,' he replies. 'And it doesn't crap either.'

'Well, I think she's lovely,' I say, scratching its head and shooting Alexander a look. Mimi is, after all, doing us a favour. 'Just no peeing on the carpet.'

'She's perfectly house trained,' declares Mimi. 'Go on then, sweetie,' she says to the dog and with one click of her fingers the dog jumps into the large leather shopper bag. 'See!'

Alexander ushers Mimi and Mini Me next door and gives her a couple of cans of Coca-Cola, an ashtray, a place to plug in her mobile phone and enough copies of *Heat*, *Grazia* and back issues of *Vogue* to keep her busy for the rest of the day. In the meantime Trish goes upstairs to sort out the mess. I busy myself with the front of house, puffing up the purple velvet sofa, straightening the framed magazine covers we have behind the reception desk, and making sure we have enough champagne, fruit and water.

Just like with front-row etiquette, there is an art to

and a hierarchy in selling. The more important you are, the longer your appointment, the more sociable your time slot and the more likely you are to be offered champagne. Flossy from Essex with her hubby-bought-it shop who places orders of under £2,000 is usually offered a crisp and a glass of water; she has a 5.30 slot and is kicked out on the stroke of six. Saffron from Net-a-porter, on the other hand, can stay as long as she likes. She is given at least one glass of champagne and possibly lunch if she wants it. Actually, whatever Saffy wants she gets, with knobs on, a brass band and plenty of bunting. Net-a-porter is one of our biggest clients. Our orders with them have gone from £5,000 three years ago to over £25,000, such is their success and ever-expanding client base. When we broke through the £20,000 mark, I'm afraid Alexander and I booked dinner at the Ivy and got absolutely rat-arsed on good champagne.

If you're not listed on Net-a-porter you aren't really in the fashion business, so to do so well on their site was a real affirmation that we were on the right track. They are extremely discerning buyers. They know how to pick the piece or It dress or bag of the season. They have sharp staff who know their stuff and always seem to pick off the cream of the crop. After a couple of days' selling you can begin to work out what are going to be the big sellers of the season. Your Roland Mouret Galaxy dress, your Luella Bartley Giselle bag, your Stella McCartney over-the-knee plastic boots –

Net-a-porter have always picked them and have always ordered more of them than anything else. These key items then fly off the website in one afternoon. And the one terribly addictive thing about Net-a-porter is that you can log on and see how well your sales are doing. Rather like the pop music charts or the *Sunday Times* bestseller list, you can type in your password and see how well you are doing against the rest of the competition. I catch Alexander at it all the time. I think he logs on between ten and fifteen times a day just to see if our stock is selling.

Net-a-porter is not the only fish in our pond. Harvey Nichols, Selfridges and Harrods all have quite healthy amounts of our clothes. This year we are hoping to have a shop-in-shop at Harrods. Harrods never used to have that much fashion credibility – they were seen as very Arabic and not very hip – but all that has changed recently. They have really embraced the shop-in-shop culture that is very Bergdorf Goodman. Dolce have a boutique, so do Prada and Gucci. They are sort of miniature versions of the original shops. They are branded to the hilt and are a much more effective way of shifting clothes than a few racks along a wall. We are really after what is known as a soft corner: two walls that are branded with the pale yellow and black motif that you get on our bags and they'd have the same wooden racks and hangers on which we have all our stuff. The idea is to hammer home our urban yet organic brand as much as possible. It gets everyone feeling the same sort of thing as they are trying on our clothes. If you have a soft corner, a three-walled boutique or a shop-in-shop you want the same branding wherever you are in the world. So every Stella McCartney shop or corner or boutique will have the same marquetry, pink flexi features and cream wall, whether it is Printemps or Bergdorf. Marni has the same crazy rails, space-age hangers and metal cages for their clothes in New York and the Far East. It is all about trying to control your environment as much as possible.

The ultimate controlled environment for any fashion designer is to have their own shop. Alexander and I are desperate for one. It would solve so many problems, but it is rare that a good property comes up on Sloane Street or in and around Bond Street, and when they do they rent for something like £400 per square foot a month so you have to be pretty sure that things are going to go your way. And when you see Jil Sander closing down and you hear just how empty McQueen and McCartney are even on a Saturday afternoon, you have to ask yourself, is it worth it?

But fashion is all about mark-up, and the great thing about mark-ups is that if you have your own shop your cash flow improves no end. Shops mark designer clothes up by multiplying by 2.9, so a skirt that we sell to the shop for £100 is sold by the shop for £290. The shop, therefore, makes more money on a garment than the designer. The skirt costs me £30 to produce, so if I sell it in my own shop for £290 then I am making £260 profit (minus overheads), as opposed to the £70 I make when I sell to another store. With figures like that you can see not only why designers are always broke, but also why they would all kill to have their own stores. It is even worse if you sell to the States. They mark up by a factor of 3.1, making even more money for themselves. The argument is that they take all the risks so they should make the money. But I don't see that much risk in buying clothes from an established designer and putting them out there. It is not as if they go out breaking new talent. And if they do find someone new, some of them try it on, offering to buy the collection on a sale-or-return basis. My advice to any budding designer who is offered this sort of deal is to tell the buyer where to get off. It will ruin your company and make it go under.

Not that they are that generous when you're an established brand, or one that is going places, as we were until this week. The orders they place are much smaller than you might think. Bergdorf Goodman, for example, spends on average £40,000 a year with us and they are a very important client. But it doesn't end there. In order for, say, Bergdorfs to be happy they must sell through 65 per cent of their stock. So they buy, say, $90,000 worth of stock, which they sell for $279,000; they need to shift $181,350 in order to justify their position, their choice and themselves at the morning meeting. We don't get another big order if the collection doesn't sell. Also, about a third of the stuff gets pinched during shipping. The big stores with outlets all over the US have a central depot where all the stock is held before distribution. The temptation for their staff to half-inch the clothes is clearly too great because I have lost track of the number of times I have counted something like thirty dresses into a box only for twenty-four to arrive the other side. And there is nothing you can do except smile, bite your tongue and make some more.

Alexander is all of a whirl. Two girls from Net-a-porter are in and they look like they are enjoying themselves. They've each got a small glass of bucks fizz on the go with some mini croissants Trish collected from Patisserie Valerie, which are being served on some golden plates I've never seen before. Alexander's handed them a line sheet and a couple of posh-look books that are hot off the press. The line sheet is a catalogue containing neat black and white line drawings of each of the garments in the collection; it states the sizes and colours the piece is available in and also the cost prices. Look books are much more glamorous affairs: photos of models in each of the forty looks from the collection that were in the show are mounted and attractively bound using stiff card. But, as with everything in fashion, there is even a look book/line sheet pecking order. The look books are expensive to produce and are therefore only handed to important clients. Other less important souls have to make do with a simple line sheet and order form to make their choice.

I try to keep out of the selling process. I find it nerve-racking, and I also think I put the clients off. It is hard to dismiss a dress, or a shirt, if the creator is sitting right next to you. It is also impossible for me to keep a straight face when I hear Alexander lying like he does. 'Now this one is going to fly off the shelves,' he insists. 'Keira Knightley has requested that for her next première.' He smiles. 'We've had Cameron's people calling up about this.' I'm not sure if anyone actually believes all the bullshit, but he's a hell of a lot better at it than I am. I remember the days of dragging my beautifully hand-cut and -crafted collection around the shops in the back of a small van, and all I can think, as I sip my latte upstairs in the office, is thank God those days are over.

Come lunchtime and Alexander still has a smile on his face. Two hours with Net-a-porter and he's still jovial.

'I think they like,' he says as we all sit around on the floor of the fitting room eating sushi. 'You know, I can normally tell what they are thinking, and they seemed happy.'

'Fucking hell, darling,' says Mimi, lying flat out on the carpet. 'Now I know why I never became a model.' She stretches out like a cat and lights up a cigarette. 'Everyone asked me and I just couldn't bring myself to do it.'

'My mate Lydia seems to enjoy it,' I say, my mouth full of Californian roll.

'Yeah, well, she's a supermodel,' says Mimi, snorting smoke out of her nose.

'She isn't,' I say. 'She's a top model.'

'Anyway, there isn't such a thing these days,' says Alexander. 'There aren't any names any more.'

'Tell *them* that,' says Mimi. 'Just last week I was shoving some strumpet into a frock and she was giving me such a lot of attitude. And I thought, fuck off, you're twelve and from fucking Siberia or some such shithole. Just because she was the face of Gucci or Prada or whatever, and Steven Meisel has used her in a couple of shoots, she thinks she can lord it about.'

'Oh *her*,' says Alexander. 'My mate booked her for some shows in New York. Turns out she can't walk. Anyone who booked her for anything only let her come out in one look, so they could say they had her in the show. But other than that she was shit. She can't get down the catwalk. Imagine not being able to put one foot in front of the other. How tragic is that?'

'I know,' agrees Mimi, smoking and feeding Mini Me salmon sashimi using chopsticks. 'Tragic.'

'Are you sure your dog likes that?' I ask, watching Mini Me chomping away on the thick pink £45-per-square-foot carpet.

'Dogs love fish,' declares Mimi.

'Isn't that cats?' asks Alexander.

'Oh?' says Mimi. 'Really?'

We all carry on eating our sushi. I'm shovelling it down, like my hangover depends on it. Mimi is feeding all of hers to the dog and Alexander is picking at his. He is on another one of his fad diets – the F Plan, the Cabbage, the Pomegranate, the GI, the Atkins, the Wheat-free. Every week there is something new that he is allergic to, something he can't have, or a new superfood that will protect him from all the cancers he is obsessing about. For a man who pumps himself full of an inordinate amount of chemicals over a weekend, chopping out lines on the filthiest of toilet seats and other flat surfaces, he does seem rather fussy about what he puts in himself the rest of the time. It has to be organic, happy and from a very good family. It has to have had enough room to play and breathe. In short, if it's been treated better than the assistant serving it, he might let it pass his lips.

'Who have we got in this afternoon?' I ask through stuffed cheeks.

'Oh,' says Alexander, picking off individual pieces of rice with his chopsticks, 'it's changed a few times since you last looked. The guys from Matches and the girl from Ko Samui have got a couple of hours each. And then that brassy thing that runs Pandora's Box in Alderley Edge.'

'Isn't that where Colleen Rooney goes?' I ask.

'Urgh,' says Mimi, pulling a face like someone's just farted. 'That walking talking fashion disaster.'

'She's always in and out of Dora's Box,' mumbles Alexander, looking down at the list. 'Anyway, Dora's a big fan of your work.'

'Only the stuff she's seen on the back of celebrities,' I say, picking another Californian roll. 'Get that Scarlett Johansson in another dog-tooth pencil skirt and she might double her order.'

'Bring it up to, oh, er, two grand.' Alexander whistles through his teeth.

'Don't knock it,' I say. 'That'll keep us in fags and Haribos for months.'

'Yeah, well, that's a lot of blood, sweat and tears for fuck all,' mutters Alexander. 'And she's at the end of the day so I won't be able to get rid of her.'

It's nearly eight p.m. when I finally come down the stairs after a hard day reading model blogs, Style.com and looking up my sales figures on Net-a-porter. I can hear Dora's loud flat-vowel voice and smell her menthol cigarettes from the landing. Alexander is sounding increasingly curt. I walk into the room to see that Alexander is ashen-faced, Dora is surrounded by mugs and butts, and Mimi is slumped against the wall in a £2,000 dress.

'Anyway, then I says to Jamie Redknapp, your wife looks amazing in that Julien Macdonald outfit, you should get two of them at £1,800 each. And guess what?'

'What?' spits Alexander.

'He does!'

'Great,' says Alexander. 'Now, listen, I'm afraid that you have been here for nearly two hours and we have to get off.'

'Oh, sorry,' says Dora, gathering up her things. 'Um, you may as well have this. Save on stamps.' She hands over one of our order forms that, even from here, looks remarkably light on ticks.

Alexander smiles and looks down at the paper. He frowns slightly. He jerks backwards as he tries to make sense of what she has done. He looks up. He looks down again. His cheeks turn slightly pink.

'Call that an order?' he bellows suddenly. 'That's not an order. Fuck off! That's an order!'

Dora looks horrified. She huffs and splutters and protests and complains while Alexander pushes her out of the door. He walks back in, dusting down his Dior suit.

'Not to worry,' says Mimi, lighting up another cigarette, 'you've got your revenge. I've just seen Mini Me puke into her bag.'

3

Alexander and I are on the Eurostar to Paris. We're travelling second class along with all the other fashionistas. Only editors and supermodels go first. The rest of us, as there is no such thing as expenses when one owns the company, have to suffer the ignominy of sitting with the hoi polloi. Some of the collection is wrapped in layers of plastic and tissue in the overhead compartment; the rest we've had shipped to the Hotel Bristol, where we've booked a suite for five days of intensive selling. We are hoping to buttonhole all the buyers and fashion directors who were too busy to make it to London Fashion Week, anyone who couldn't quite fit us in. Anyone who is anyone. Well, anyone who is anyone is in Paris.

Paris is full of big hitters. It has the biggest designers, the biggest advertisers and the buyers with the biggest chequebooks. London, on the other hand, is a bit of an inconvenience for the big swingers. Some of them force themselves to come out of loyalty, or old times' sake, in search of some sort of fashion confetti to jolly up their pages or pad out their stores. But the majority of them wait until the fashion circus comes to Paris in order to stock up on young groovy pieces.

New York has its own players – Marc Jacobs, Michael Kors. It has its big advertising brands – Ralph Lauren and Calvin Klein. The same is true of Milan with Prada, Versace and Dolce. But Paris is the mother of them all – it has Chanel, Dior, Galliano, Valentino, Balenciaga, Lacroix, YSL, Louis Vuitton, Ungaro, Givenchy, McQueen. While a thousand will queue to get into a Marc Jacobs show in New York, double that amount will jostle and elbow their way into Dior. The British Fashion Council fights for its three days between Milan and Paris. Every so often it asks its big-hitting talent, the likes of McQueen and Burberry, to return. But in the end, everyone just looks to Paris.

As a designer it is your dream to show in Paris. Here you are taken seriously. Here they give you palaces to show your collections. Here there is history. Here you are an artist. But the competition is so fierce that unless you have huge financial backing, like McQueen, and can afford something like £1.2 million for your first runway show, you have to be so avant garde, like Hussein Chalayan or Sophia Kokosalaki, to get any attention at all. Otherwise, like a fart in a wind tunnel, you sink without trace. No wonder, then, that most British designers when they get too big for their London boots end up going to New York. Even famous people like Luella, Matthew Williamson and Alice Temperley would find it hard to cut a dash in Paris.

Squashed in next to each other, with a bag of size seven evening shoes at our feet, Alexander and I have been discussing which shows and which parties we want to attend. Alexander's desperate to see Dior. I'm keen on Chanel. And we're both prepared to kill our grandmothers for a third-row pew at Galliano. Although Alexander is considering patricide if it means he can see Viktor and Rolf, the groovy new kids on the block. I, on the other hand, am desperate to see McQueen and Chalayan. I also fancy a peek at Balenciaga, if only to see what all the ingénues will be wearing next season.

'We should go to Vivienne's after-show,' he says. 'There are always some models in cages for us to enjoy. Oh, and we've got to go to Galliano's,' he insists, sitting up and whacking me on the knee at the same time. 'He's always got strippers and gimps and things running around for your entertainment. And everyone gets trollied.' He smiles. 'And I just love looking at him.' He swoons. 'Johnny's so fit and brown it looks like he lives in a gym under a sunlamp.'

'If you want brown,' I say with a smile, 'there's always Valentino.'

'Purlease,' he says. 'Not that old satsuma. I reckon he must be quite scary close up.'

I sit back in my seat. 'Let's just see what happens

when we get there, shall we?' I suggest. 'We'll have to see what stuff Lydia has managed to blag for us.'

'OK,' he says sulkily, shifting petulantly in his seat. 'Shhhh,' he adds suddenly, leaning forward and covering his face with his *Telegraph* newspaper. 'Is that one of the bitches from Top Shop?'

I look up to see a bright red bob and a tight pair of skinny jeans disappear up the aisle. I shrug.

'Wonder how many other rag-trade hags are on the train,' he whispers, rather loudly. 'How ghastly!'

Paris Fashion Week also coincides with one of the biggest cloth trade fairs in the world – Première Vision. In an exhibition hall just outside the city, the great and the good in the global rag trade business converge and set out their wares. Indian silks, Swedish cottons, Scottish tweeds, lace, rainwear, and a thousand shades of Lycra are all for sale under one roof; high street and high fashion mix as they choose their cloth for the next season. It is an extraordinary cocktail of Hennes and Hermès, of Whistles and Westwood, Monsoon and Moschino. And Alexander and I are not looking forward to it one little bit.

Just as we come through the tunnel into France, my mobile rings. It's Lydia.

'Hi darling,' she says. 'How's tricks?'

'Fine,' I say. 'I'm here with Alexander and we're looking forward to meeting up.'

Turns out that Lydia has a few fittings this evening but will be free after ten p.m. She suggests that we meet at the Hotel Costes for a flute in order to plan the rest of our evening. She has tickets, she has addresses, she has mobile phone numbers, she has names on lists. It promises to be a big one. Just what we need before we go to Première Vision tomorrow.

'All we need now,' says Alexander, rubbing his hands together, 'are some drugs.'

'Lydia doesn't do drugs,' I say.

'I know,' he says, rolling his eyes. 'Thing is, I do.'

'I'm well aware of that. I'm sure you'll find some low-life hanging around the Costes where you can feed your habit.'

I'm looking forward to seeing Lydia. She and I go back a while. She is one of the dying breed of models and is pure class. Well, she isn't actually classy at all. She is Camden born and bred. She has poker-straight blonde hair down to her bosom, baby blue eyes, lips like marshmallows and an accent that could cut through the Lock crowd on market day. She tones it down for interviews, but give her a few glasses of pop and there is no mistaking that she is a North London girl. Discovered at fifteen shifting clobber on her cousin's stall, she didn't start earning her keep until she was nineteen. Up until that point she was turned down by *Just 17* magazine nine times and lived in model accommodation for so long that she ended up owing her agency £30,000. I remember once asking her if they put her up for free. 'Free?' She laughed. 'Nothing's for free, darling. Not the phone calls, the tube passes, the head shots, the call cards. They're all invoiced for, they're all totted up, and they're all expenses pending.' Maybe that is why she is so nice, because it took her a while to get there. She wasn't handed it on a plate like most of these jumped-up teenagers.

She and I became mates when I met her hanging around St Martin's one afternoon. I persuaded her to do my graduation show. She gave me her time and her fabulous figure for free; I gave her some clothes, and I have continued to dress her ever since. She now favours Marc Jacobs, Azzedine Alaia and Lanvin, like all the glamorous girls about town. But she does wear my stuff more often than most and she is sort of my muse. I always think of her when I am designing and she always comes in to check the collection before the show, flying in especially from wherever she is in the world. She has promised that I can design her wedding dress whenever that happy moment might be. However, working in an industry dominated by super-skinny women and gay men, that moment is looking increasingly far off. Nice men don't make passes at girls in advertising campaigns. So as far as I know she is desperate and dateless. Although, I could find out differently tonight.

In the meantime there is the small matter of some selling to do first. Alexander and I make it to our rather small yet expensive hotel suite with about half an hour to spare. We have Sheikh Majed al-Sabah coming over to look at the collection and we need to order up champagne, orange juice and a selection of delicacies for his amusement. Our sales break down to 35 per cent UK, 22 per cent USA, 24 per cent Europe, and the remainder is made up of the Far East, the Middle East and Australia. Sheikh Majed buys nearly all our Middle Eastern stock, so he, along with Katya X from Russia, who has the biggest buying budget in the world at the moment, are our most important foreign clients. Known as the Sheikh of Chic, Sheikh Majed, nephew of the Emir of Kuwait, owns Villa Moda, a huge fashion powerhouse that has vast malls in Dubai and Qatar. He's also recently opened a 100,000-square-foot emporium just outside Kuwait City, and has projects in Mumbai and Singapore. He is a discerning buyer with large pockets and only just started buying our stuff last year. He is usually accompanied by Isabella Blow, and, as he turns up on time, with some woman dressed in a Philip Treacy hat, I see that today is no exception.

Alexander is out of the blocks quicker than an Olympic sprinter. He has them in their seats and refreshed within three minutes of their arrival. He's also booked some sixteen-year-old fresh in from Russia to model for us, and she is working the Persian rug for all it's worth. I'm all smiles and gushing remarks while totally transfixed by Isabella Blow's ruby red lips. With the rest of her face covered by her hat, they are her only visible feature, and they appear to talk as if disembodied from the rest of her. The effect is disconcerting to say the least. Sheikh Majed doesn't appear to notice. He is his usual delightful and entertaining self. He says the collection is 'beautiful', he says everything is 'beautiful', and he leaves promising a 'big, big order'. Alexander is so overjoyed that he finishes off their untouched champagne.

The rest of the afternoon is spent in meetings with Lane Crawford from the Far East and Harvey Nichols Hong Kong. Although they have yet to stock our stuff, these guys have the potential to become our biggest buyers if we get the pitch right. The Far East, Russia and China are the emerging markets of the moment. Everyone is excited about India, but China is the one that is really about to go. The Chinese have built these huge malls, most of which stand empty with big brands like Prada and Louis Vuitton waiting to move in. Russia has proved a strange and lucrative market. Most of it is run by Mercury, a Russian company owned by two entrepreneurs, Leonid Friedland and Leonid Strunin, that has an annual turnover of something like £300 million. Owners of a rundown arcade, the Tretryakov Projezd, they managed to transform it into the glitziest piece of Moscow real estate for the biggest and best luxury brands. Armani, Prada and Gucci are already well installed. Although the luxury goods market over there is worth something like $720 million, business is unpredictable, with shops remaining quiet all week only for a car to draw up outside and disgorge an oligarch's wife who drops $500,000 in half an hour. No wonder, then, that Alexander is talking about buying in some caviar for Katya X when she shows up tomorrow.

'I think it was a good day,' says Alexander on the way to the Hotel Costes in a cab. 'Everyone was very positive.'

'No-one is ever negative in fashion.' I yawn. 'Honestly, they can hardly come in, sit down, drink our champagne and say they think our stuff is shit.'

'Well, I think they liked it,' he insists.

'Maybe.'

'You'll see,' he says. 'This collection may not be fashion forward, but the consumer likes it.'

The courtyard of the Hotel Costes is crammed. This is *the* place to be during Paris Fashion Week, and it shows. There are models packed and stacked onto every available surface; they all have a flute in one hand and a fag in the other. The noise is overpowering, the number of languages in operation worthy of the lobby of the United Nations.

Alexander and I stand around at the entrance feeling like a couple of right arseholes. We are both frantically scanning the crowd for Lydia. It doesn't do to look lost and uncool in this tough crowd. I am beginning to wish that I'd worn my sunglasses. I can see a couple of fashion hacks holding court, shrieking at each other across the table, and the last thing I want is to be caught out.

'Can you see her?' I ask.

'No. Fuck. Can you?'

'No,' I mumble out of the corner of my mouth. 'Can you see anywhere to sit?'

'Fuck, no. You?'

'No.'

'Shit.'

'Yeah, shit.'

'How much longer can we stand here?'

'Thirty seconds?'

'Jesus Christ! Are you two twats deaf or something?' The vowels come flat and fast. 'I've been shouting and waving like a drowning bloody whore. Honestly. Over here, over here.'

Alexander and I turn around to find all six feet one inch of Lydia standing right next to us, flute and fag in hand. She looks stunning, glowing and airbrushed. Up close, she doesn't really belong to the human race. She belongs to the model race, who refer to the rest of us as 'civilians', and you can sort of see why. Everything about her is longer, taller, thinner and more languid than anything my gene pool could ever produce. Even the shitty little beanie hat she's shoved nonchalantly on her head looks fabulous. On anyone else it would look like a boiled egg. On Lydia, it is a style statement.

'Champagne? Champagne?' she asks each of us in turn. We both nod. 'Oi, garçon,' she shouts at a passing waiter. 'Deuz coops.' Her accent doesn't allow for anything resembling French. 'Sit down, sit down.' She continues to stand, scratching vigorously at her crotch.

'Fucking hell,' she says. 'I am sorry, but I've got some sort of bloody thrush from this couture dress I had on the other day. I should have known it was dodgy. There were great big blobs of period in the gusset. You know, it was one of those corset thingies. Anyway, I usually carry panty pads with me because you pick up all sorts in these clothes. You know, they go from model to model, and shoot to shoot, in the same day. Five at a time when the dress is hot. *Vanity Fair*, *Harpers Bazaar*, *Vogue* . . . you're always catching stuff. My mate Natalaya got lice from some sixty grand dress last year. Models are filthy bloody things. If I catch who gave me this I'll give her a smack around the face. I'll wait till the glossies come out in six weeks and I'll work it out. Skanky bitch. Anyway, how are you guys?'

'Oh, fine,' I say. 'Um, the show went OK.'

Alexander and I talk her through the collection and the reviews. Lydia says 'bitches' at all the right moments and 'fabulous' at all the others. She says again how much she loved it all and how she'll model for me next season if I want her to. I am about to lean in and ask her advice on what she thinks my next collection should be about, as she flits from studio to studio and knows exactly what everyone else is up to, when I feel a tap on my shoulder.

'Dudes, dudes,' says a voice. I turn around to be shot twice by Max Davies' index fingers. 'Hey dudes,' he says again, shooting Alexander and Lydia one after the other. 'How's it hanging?'

Max Davies is a photographer famous for always wearing leather trousers and his rather bad coke habit. For such a jerk, it is amazing that he is such a good photographer. Lydia always maintains that he is so busy talking about himself and his conquests that he makes the models feel so unselfconscious that they perform.

'It's hanging well,' says Alexander. 'And you?'

'Oh man,' says Max, who talks like he is from across the Pond even though we all know he comes from Solihull. 'I've got this bollock problem,' he says, putting his hands down the front of his trousers. 'I've been flying commando all day and I've got this fucking hideous chafing.' He hauls his balls over from one trouser leg to the other. 'I've come back to change.'

'You staying here?' asks Alexander.

'Course, man, doesn't everyone stay here?'

'Er, no,' says Lydia. 'Anna Wintour's always at the Ritz.'

'Anyway, man,' says Max, 'I've got to go.'

'Bye.' I smile.

'Catch ya,' he says with a wink, like I might possibly fancy him in some way. Which I don't.

'Catch you,' says Alexander.

And Max moves on to the next table. He offers out his recently bollocked hand to a couple of fashion boys, who duly kiss it.

'Does everyone have a genital problem today?' asks Alexander.

'Actually,' says Lydia, 'I've got a bloody liver problem.' She drains her flute. 'Shouldn't really be drinking this stuff. I went to a homoeopath a month ago who told me I had the liver of a fifty-five-year-old alcoholic.'

'That's fashion for you,' says Alexander, knocking back his glass.

'No,' says Lydia, 'it's Roaccutane.'

'What's that?' I ask.

'You know, the stuff my agency put me on because of my bad skin.'

'You have bad skin?' asks Alexander, leaning in for a closer look.

'Not any more,' says Lydia. 'But do you remember that stuff I was taking last year? Well, it made me so depressed I was on Prozac.'

'It did?' I ask.

'Yeah. It's lethal stuff. You're made to sign a contract every four weeks when you're on it to say that you will try not to get pregnant otherwise you have to have an abortion because you'd have some sort of mutant child. It really messes with your hormones. And they put young girls on the stuff. You know, whose hormones aren't balanced or anything. What they need is time to go through puberty, but because of some stupid ad campaign they can't. So they get dosed up with this stuff. It dries your body out totally. Your eyes, your nose, your mouth. The lips to your vagina are all cracked and sticky.'

'Jesus,' says Alexander. 'I'm gay, I don't need to know

about your vagina. Or anyone else's for that matter.'

'Shut up,' I say.

'Yeah,' says Lydia. 'Anyway, we all get it from doctors in New York and it costs $600 a pack and no-one bloody checks up on you. I'd been on it for a year before I found out that you are only supposed to be on it for about six weeks at a time.'

'Shit,' I say.

'I know. And now my liver and kidneys are fucked. I've got to do this detox thing in order to sort everything out. I've got to drink three litres of water every day to rehydrate. It's a nightmare.'

'It sounds awful,' I say.

'I know. People think Kate taking coke is bad. If they only knew the shit we take for our skin. I think it's dreadful.'

'I agree,' says Alexander.

'Anyway, I can have a few drinks now that I'm off the stuff. Bottoms up. Shall I go to the bar?'

Lydia makes her way over to the bar and is hailed and high-fived by about six or seven people on her way. Alexander and I sit back in our seats. For all the hideousness of the scene here, it does make great viewing. I spy a couple of *Vogue* fashion assistants comparing Chloé handbags at the bar. I can see a stylist I can't stand laughing her head off in the corner. There's the notorious blond German party boy called Marco wending his way through the mêlée, a mobile attached to his ear. And there are more models than you can shake a *Glamour* front cover at.

'God!' huffs Lydia as she puts three flutes down on the table. 'Look at my bloody foot!'

She shoves a large flat black ballet pump in my face. For a beautiful girl, Lydia has amazingly unattractive, unkempt feet. But then so do most models. Inundated with free manis, pedis and makeovers each and every time they do a shoot or a show, they let their feet and hands get filthy, allowing them to return to their natural cloven state between jobs. I suppose if you have everything done for you, all the time, what is the point of doing it yourself?

'Can you see?' she says. 'Look at the red bore hole.'

Sure enough, as Alexander and I look more closely there is a red mark on the top of her foot.

'There's some black tranny at the bar,' she says, 'who thought that I was trying to encroach on his territory. Why do I always get the trannies after me? I suppose because I'm six foot one they think I'm one of them. Anyway, he—'

'She, darling,' interrupts Alexander. 'Trannies are definitely girls.'

'Well then, she, instead of warning me off, saying get off my patch you fellow tranny prostitute, trod on my foot very hard and very slowly.'

'Ouch,' I say. 'It looks sore.'

'It is. Does she know how expensive this foot is?'

'Oh, at least five grand,' says Alexander, somewhat sarcastically.

'Actually,' says Lydia, turning around, 'quite a bit more than that.'

'Oh, er . . . six?' Alexander whistles through his teeth.

'I earned £106,000 last week in Milan,' she informs us with a smile. That shuts Alexander up. 'Sixteen grand from the Prada show alone. But it was hard work.'

'What? Walking?' says Alexander, sounding not terribly sympathetic.

'Well, if you want to parade up and down in your G-string and stilettos with another fifty girls at a time while a line of homosexuals look you up and down and work out if you are the right look for the show, then be my guest.'

'Fifty at a time?' I ask.

'Yup. Mr designer is that busy.'

'The blokes have it much worse,' says Alexander. 'I know a menswear designer who makes his models strip off totally naked and try on the same pair of pants. Can you imagine how crusty those knickers are at the end of the day? After thirty or forty backsides have been in them?'

'The blokes don't seem to mind that much,' says Lydia. 'I know all the menswear designers want fresh young naive things who they try and put into a 28 trouser when they see that the bloke is a 32. Just so the young chap from Illinois can come out of the changing room and say, "The little old pants are a bit too small."

And the designer's saying, "No kidding. Are they tight over the butt? Turn around so we can take a look." '

Alexander is laughing. 'I know, I know,' he hoots. 'Isn't it terrible? But you girls get naked too. Don't you remember that lovely story about Kate Moss and her first show in Paris for Vivienne Westwood?'

I nod. 'When they all stripped off in a row?'

'That's right. And they're all there, naked, and the only one with a full bush is Kate. All the other models have pubes like landing strips or lines of Velcro.'

'And come the next show,' I add, 'hasn't she had a full fannicure like the rest of them?'

'By that afternoon,' says Alexander. 'Sweet.' He smiles. 'She must have been all of sixteen.'

We sit and sip our champagne, while Lydia fills us in with the gossip about which show has been good and who has died on their arse. She talks about who has been misbehaving and that two Russian girls from her agency are up the duff. 'You can tell,' she says, making a round gesture around the stomach. 'It always happens at the end of every season. Four weeks of drinking, travelling, being away from home for so long . . . most of them don't know where they are sleeping, plus the fact they are all seventeen. It's a recipe for disaster. Chantal's got her work cut out for her.'

Chantal is Lydia's booker. She not only books all her jobs and sorts out her cabs, hotels, skin and flat, she also takes 20 per cent commission on her jobs. And now, so it seems, she also sorts out abortions.

'Oh,' Lydia says, 'did you also hear that Suzy Menkes fainted on Anna Wintour at the Lee McQueen show?'

'What!' says Alexander. 'That's like the Queen Mother passing out on the Queen!'

'I know. Apparently the music was so loud and the place was so hot that she just keeled over. Anna got her carried out and left the show with her.'

'God,' I say. 'Who wrote the reviews? Did they stop the show?'

'No, they couldn't,' says Lydia. 'Backstage it was a nightmare.'

'Really?'

'Oh yeah. Everyone was running around like headless chickens. What to do? But the show went on.'

'Of course it did,' says Alexander. 'As it always does.'

'Oh look,' says Lydia, 'there's DeeDee.'

'DeeDee?' I ask.

'Yeah, you remember, that model I shared a room with when I first came to London.'

'The one who rocked the bunk beds shagging the waiter she'd just met when you were asleep above her?'

'That's the one. Deborah from Essex, now known as DeeDee from London . . . Hiya!' She waves across the courtyard. DeeDee waves back. 'Fuck. She looks rough.' Lydia smiles. 'No wonder she's lost that high-street campaign. Such a shame. Couldn't have happened to a nicer girl.'

Alexander's giggling.

'I think we should get out of here,' I say.

'Yeah,' agrees Lydia. 'We've got parties to go to. Who do you want first? Westwood, or Stella McCartney?'

Alexander and I look at each other. 'Westwood,' we both say at the same time.

'Yeah,' agrees Lydia. 'Who fancies drinking cruelty-free champagne watching one model whip another with leather substitute?'

4

I'm meeting up with Alexander for some coffee and a croissant at Les Deux Magots. We're steeling ourselves to take the overland train to Première Vision, otherwise known as the Rag-Trade Hag Express. It's better to have some sort of solids and caffeine inside you before attempting to jostle your way on board. There is nothing more aggressive than a rag-trade hag, except perhaps one that is hung over, dehydrated and trying to cram two days' worth of buying into the next five hours.

Alexander is late, of course. He picked up some boy at the Westwood party and left me for some dirty sex halfway across town. I stayed up quite late. I think it was about three a.m. before I got to bed. Not terribly responsible behaviour for someone who is supposed to be in charge of their own business. But Lydia is hard to resist, especially when she insisted that Puff Daddy would be at Les Bains Douches, as would a whole load of other stars who I must meet so that I can dress them. In the end, I stood in the corner, stuffed against the wall, the wrong side of the red-roped-off area, unable to hear a thing. I saw some shortish bloke who might well have been Puff Daddy, or P Diddy as he is called these days, but I can't be sure. Lydia introduced me to an American singer who looked a bit like Gwen Stefani. She was in town doing fashion week and I pretended to care. I nodded at a few models I know, drank a lot more champagne that I managed not to pay for, and gleaned that Sharon Stone is rumoured to be coming to town for the Louis Vuitton party at Le Petit Palais tomorrow night. The fashion party to close the week, and therefore the season, it will be the biggest bash, hosted by the biggest company, and they will hurl cash and caviar and champagne at it. And everyone'll go crazy. Even Anna Wintour will come and show her face just so long as she can be in bed by ten p.m. Well, the woman is in the gym by five a.m and having her hair done at seven, so you can sort of understand her need for an early night.

Looking at Alexander sloping along the street towards me, his hair fluffing all over the place, I kind of wish that he'd had a Wintour moment and gone to bed early last night. Grumpy queens are difficult enough as it is, but grumpy queens without their hair gel are a nightmare.

'Can you believe it,' he says, slumping down next to me, 'I shag the only gay man in the western hemisphere who doesn't have any hair products in his bathroom.

Look at this shit.' He runs his hands through his hair which fluffs up like a small duckling. 'Just when you have your stereotypes sorted, this happens. Who's ever heard of a gay man who doesn't have the whole of bloody Space NK in his bathroom? And he's a fucking hairdresser!'

'Maybe it's a coals to Newcastle thing?' I suggest. 'He doesn't like bringing his work home with him?'

'I don't care what it is,' he says. 'I'm not seeing him again.' He knocks back the remainder of my café au lait and picks up the other half of my croissant. 'And I need a chemist.'

An hour later, a gelled, perfumed and altogether more pleasant Alexander is sitting next to me on the overland RER train to Parcs des Expositions. We are both hiding behind various bits of fashion press – he *Womenswear Daily*, me *International Herald Tribune* – avoiding all eye contact, our ears trained for any gossip. And the two girls in the row in front do not disappoint.

'Did you hear about the US *Vogue* lot last night?' asks one voice.

Alexander leans forward to try and find out who is speaking, but can't see her face.

'What?' says the friend.

'Well, there was this huge queue for the Dior show last night,' she says. 'And there were loads of people there. You know, UK *Vogue*, *Vogue Italia*, Nippon, loads of big buyers, and then the US *Vogue* contingent turned up and they just queue-barged the lot of us. One of them muttered something like, "Coming through!" And the PR just buckled and let them all in way ahead of anyone else.'

'Who do they think they are?' asks the friend.

'I know,' says the voice. 'I mean, the UK *Vogue* lot were just standing there.'

'Really?'

'Yeah.'

'How embarrassing.'

'I know.'

'How about Elizabeth Saltzman?'

'Oh, I didn't see her.'

'She's gorgeous, isn't she?'

'Yeah.'

'Old money, you know.'

'You can tell.'

They both sit there for a minute, shoving cheese baguettes into their mouths.

'I hear your ex-pal the photographer is in town.'

'Oh yeah?' the other girl mumbles through the bread.

'He demanded that he be sent a navy or black BMW with camel interior for the shows.'

'Right . . .'

'He said he would only have camel interior.'

'Right?'

'The car's been in the Ritz car park all week. He only hasn't touched the thing!'

'Americans . . . I tell you . . .'

'This the stop?'

Alexander and I shuffle out with the rest of them. Every year I regret coming to Première Vision and every year I think I should be important and glamorous enough to send some sort of assistant. But the idea of Trish wandering around this enormous industrial estate with the company credit card is enough to make me get out of bed and get on the train. The only person who really need not be here is Alexander. But he is coming out of politeness and moral support. Plus, he knows I'd kill him if he left me to do this on my own.

Having said that, we've worked together long enough for him to understand what the label stands for and who we're aiming at. I'm not one of those fresh, young, feminine designers with frills and frou-frou. We're more of a sharply tailored brand with an eye on the older, more sophisticated market – more Roland Mouret than Chloé. I'm keener on the silhouette than on the details and the trimmings, so we tend to buy good quality, simple fabrics and Alexander does have quite an eye for those. He can spot a good jersey at twenty paces, so when I'm being indecisive and un-focused, he's incredibly useful to have around.

We queue up to collect our passes and numbers and cards, filling in forms, flashing our IDs wherever we go. There is a hierarchy even in fabric. Some stalls won't accept certain customers. Say, for example, you are pure high street, there are some jersey suppliers who won't let you anywhere near their stands. You have to go through security, smile at the bouncers who man the stand, sign in, show your ID, explain who you are, and only then are you allowed to touch the fabrics. Nylon makers from Hong Kong are begging for Top Shop to grace their stands, but some producers won't let them through the door. Primark, Mark One and Morgan are all also treated with the same disdain. As an independent designer I am welcomed more or less everywhere, but the bigger the mill and the larger the corporation, the less keen they are on collecting my little order.

If this weren't stressful enough, there is also the small matter of motivation. Having just put the spring/ summer collection to bed, as it were, the last thing on earth I want to do is to have to think about another show. It is the beginning of October and I am already thinking about next Fall. A whole year from now. What will women want to be wearing then? How can I come up with the must-buy colour or fabric for next year?

There is supposed to be a science to it. In the middle of this huge place, the size of five football pitches, there is an atrium where they predict the news and the colours for next year. Black always seems to be in with a chance, and every spring/summer someone will suggest yellow and green. Turquoise occasionally rears its head. But for Fall or autumn/ winter there are usually some browns, dark greens and dark blues. There is always gold or silver for evening wear. And, with an eye for the Christmas market, some sort of red. But I always think you can't go wrong with purple. Anyway, whatever they are saying in the atrium it is usually a good idea to ignore it. After all, who wants the same colours as Mark One?

'So, what are we feeling for Fall?' asks Alexander, his voice jaded and resigned.

'I'm feeling . . .' I think about it. 'Luxury . . . opulence . . . decadence and, um, sexy?'

'Oh,' says Alexander, pretending to be impressed. 'Not stressed and downbeat, then?'

'No.' I smile. 'We don't want anything that says boho.'

'Oh Lord no!' he says. 'We've all had a Miller Meltdown. Even Sienna's cut her hair off and gone all sixties. Anyway, that's not your thing. Whoever's heard of tailored boho?'

'True.' I nod.

'Shall we just get some black and purple velvet?' he asks.

'Good idea. And some silk? A splash of tartan? We haven't done patterns for a while. I think we should move away from the plain monochrome minimalist look a bit and soften up. And you know I love a tartan.'

'Yup,' he confirms. 'And a coffee?'

We sit down at some shitty table for a cup of coffee, which actually tastes quite nice. Then, just as we get up to leave, Alexander notices one of the designers from Gucci who sets off in the same direction as we do. Like a game of grandmother's footsteps, we follow her around the exhibition hall looking at the same materials, sourcing same product. We pass Siulas, a

Lithuanian linen company, and Berlaine, a purveyor of French knitwear, in Hall Five. In Hall Six we both pause at Idealtex, an Italian silks supplier for the top end of the market, before moving on to Hokkoh Co., a Japanese textiler that specializes in Japanese prints inspired by 'handcraftmanship' – or at least that's what their flyer says. We both then move on to Jackytex to sniff around their very smart knits. To begin with, we are not doing it on purpose. But after stopping together for the sixth time at a stall selling a gorgeous purple silk from India, she starts to look round, getting increasingly pissed off. Alexander thinks it is hilarious to follow her, particularly as we are getting such a rise out of her. I, on the other hand, think it makes rather wise business sense.

Eventually she gives us the slip. She sits down and orders a café au lait and it takes all my powers of persuasion to stop Alexander from doing the same. We really have to get this job done before getting back to the centre of Paris for some more selling appointments this afternoon, and I want to see if I can arrange for a Scottish mill to mix me up some Black Watch tartan with a bright pink stripe running through it, for some fitted jackets I think I might be making. I have a bit of a thing about Black Watch – it's butch and traditional and reminds me of gentlemen's clubs and cigars. If we give it a modern pink twist it should update the fabric and make it a tad ironic at the same time. Or at least that's what I'm hoping. We spend over an hour with a

Scottish mill that say they will only make me up the tartan just so long as I order 200 metres. I hate it when they do this. This is one of the reasons why small fashion houses like mine go under. Bloody manufacturers. I only really want 60m of material, but the minimum order is 200m. Sometimes they might take pity and give me a deal for 100m, but even then I only want to make twenty jackets, so what the hell am I going to do with the extra 40m? In the end, I manage to haggle him down to 150m. Alexander thinks I am mad. Maybe I am. I'm hung over certainly, and perhaps that's why I capitulated so soon. But we need to get back. I can't stand the bright lights in here or the salmon-pink section walls. What else am I supposed to do? Anyway, now Black Watch with a dash of bright pink is not only going to feature in the new collection, it will be the signature print of a collection of clothes I haven't even thought about designing yet. I hope I haven't made a dreadful mistake.

I come out in a cold alcohol sweat on the train.

'Do you think I've fucked up?' I ask Alexander.

'Well, we're certainly taking the high road this winter,' he says with a smile.

'Shit.' I start to scratch the back of my hand, which is something I always do when I am extremely nervous. 'Shit. Oh shit.'

'It's lovely,' says Alexander, grabbing my thigh determinedly and giving it a squeeze. 'We're feeling Scotland this season . . . which is good . . . because we haven't felt Scotland for a while. Not since . . . Fuck, when was *Braveheart*? Please God tell me *Braveheart* was twenty years ago. When was it?'

'I have no idea,' I say.

'It's got to be twenty years ago,' he says. 'Or nearly. If it is, we're in the clear. It's the twenty-year rule.' He looks very pleased with himself.

I sit back in the seat, cross my fingers and hope to hell that *Braveheart* was a mid-eighties production. Fashion famously works in cycles; what goes in must come out, and vice versa. And this process usually takes about twenty years. So, if you are ever stuck for what to do for your next collection, just dig out a *Vogue* from twenty years ago and you won't be far off. Hence, everyone these days is doing fitted and tight and pinched at the waist. Think Robert Palmer videos. Think the return of the shoulder pad, the legging. Everyone is doing Versace except, it seems, Versace. Oh Jesus, when the hell did Mel Gibson paint his naked backside blue? Or something to that effect.

Alexander and I make it back in time, only to have our first appointment at the Bristol cancel on us. The woman is from some bloody boutique in Sydney; she bought two jackets and a couple of skirts from us last time, so I don't mind that much. She phones to say she's got flu. Alexander and I know she has a hangover or is too 'tired' to make it. Fashion people are always tired. It is the standard excuse for all bad behaviour, all hissy fits, all tears and tantrums. Either that or it's IVF. Only four weeks ago I had a girl on the phone from *Elle* magazine asking about a pink skirt from last season. When I said that I no longer had a sample, that we had moved on and that we were just about to show the spring/summer collection, she burst into tears and told me all about her latest bout of egg collection. I couldn't get her off the phone. She shared for forty-five minutes. Honestly, just because I am one of the few female designers around, does she really think I am interested in her vagina?

'So Kylie, or whatever her name is, is too tired to make her appointment?' I ask, lying back on the bed and lighting up a cigarette.

'Yup,' says Alexander. 'And she hasn't bothered to reschedule.'

'Fuck her,' I say.

'I agree,' he says.

Alexander stands up and snaps open a Coke from the mini bar. I smoke and worry that the reason Kylie has cancelled has more to do with the collection and less to do with her hormones or alcohol habit. Meanwhile, the fit model booked by Alexander, who we have found out is called Irena and is from St Petersburg, mooches over and sits down on a chair next to me. Dressed only in her flesh-coloured thong and silver heels, she asks for a light.

'You OK?' I ask, handing over my pink plastic bic. 'Do you want something to eat?' She looks thin, even for a model.

'No thanks.' She smiles, running her hands through her thin brown hair. 'I prefer cigarettes.'

'Oh right.'

'Eating is a waste of money,' she adds.

'Right.' I smile. We both sit and smoke. 'Um, you enjoying Paris?'

'It is fine,' she says, taking a deep drag on her cigarette. 'Much better than Milan. Milan is a fucking meat market.'

'Oh.'

'There is this one club where there are pimps picking up young Russian girls trying to get them to make prostitutes.' She shakes her head. 'Horrible. Young girls. Fourteen, fifteen. From Poland. And Russia. They think we are easy prey . . . But you know, the Americans. They are not shy about sending their girls away to the other side of the world to pay for a trailer back home. I meet one girl who had her mother on the phone all the time. Calling up. Shouting. She has bought herself a new trailer and can't make the payments. The daughter is not making the money quick enough. So she spends the night in the clubs. Her mother is happy.' She takes another drag on her cigarette. 'Paris is much better.'

'Good.' I smile. 'You're happy doing this?'

She nods. 'Milan you feel like they rent you for the hour. They shout at you in Italian. They are rude about you to your face. I have a degree in university in English in St Petersburg. I am not stupid. I can see what they do. No matter how much money they pay you, you lose your dignity, you have nothing. I learn this early in life. I don't like to parade naked with lots of other women.'

'No.'

'And the mafia is everywhere. They control the model agencies. You don't get paid for nine and ten months after the shows. They all play poor. They say they have nothing, they say they will pay you a couple of thousand dollars extra next time they book you, and they never book you again. The kickbacks delay the cheques. My agent does not conform.'

'Right,' says Alexander, suddenly pricking up his ears. He likes this sort of subject.

'You know she has bombs through her letterbox, death threats, she struggles all the time but she won't be bullied. I come from this bullying culture. I know what it is like.'

'I'm sure,' I say.

'Yes,' says Alexander.

'That is why I like her.'

'I'm sure,' I say again.

'So, no, I don't like Milan very much.'

'I can see,' says Alexander.

'And there is one fashion house that gives its front-row celebrities some phials of cocaine with their dresses.'

'I've heard about that,' says Alexander. 'A gram and a dress at the same time. It's—'

'Terrible,' says Irena.

'Fabulous . . . ly awful.' Alexander corrects himself quickly. 'Can you believe it?'

'I can't believe they've got the money to do that,' I say.

'It's all about being part of a club,' says Alexander. 'Saying you are in our gang and here, have a good time on us.'

'I'm sure most of their front row is AA and NA these days anyway,' I say.

'I don't think they do it any more,' says Alexander.

'Really?' asks Irena.

'I think so,' he says.

There's a knock on the suite door – our next appointment is very unfashionably early. Irena stubs out her cigarette and goes into the bathroom to slip on her first look, while I rush over to open the window. The last thing I want is for the collection to stink of cigarettes. Although, I have to say, nearly everyone in fashion still smokes. But then, it is an industry that thrives on image over everything. You might be starving, drunk and high, with dried-up kidneys and the liver of a fifty-five-year-old alcoholic, but just so long as you can make it down the catwalk looking fabulous, who cares?

Alexander and I spend the rest of the afternoon and early evening selling our hearts out. We smile at the woman from Hamburg who is thinking of adding another dimension to our corner in her store. We butter up Katya X from Russia with some obscenely expensive champagne that she takes two sips of. We are nice to a

couple of Italians who tell us that our look 'inglese' is
going down a storm in Rome. Even Printemps turn up
on time, and are pleasant, and seem interested enough
to get Irena in and out of eleven outfits before they disappear off round the corner to Viktor and Rolf.
Alexander says that we should feel pleased with ourselves. He says that things are looking better than last
season. He thinks we should order ourselves a big fat
cocktail when we arrive at the Ritz for a drink with
Lydia. We should look like big players even if we aren't.

Lydia is looking long, lean and gorgeous when we
find her perched on a stool at the bar. She is in full
make-up and her hair is up in some complicated-
looking chignon.

'You look fabulous,' I say as I kiss each of her earlobes. I contemplate sitting next to her but realize that
would be an error. Who wants to sit next to a top
model? They only make you feel bad about yourself. So
I push Alexander forward instead.

'I have been to a fitting for Mr Valentino,' she says,
taking a sip of her raspberry martini.

'Oh yeah?' says Alexander, corkscrewing his backside onto the stool next to her. 'Hence the make-up.'

'Absolutely. Mr Valentino doesn't do models unless
they have full make-up, hair and jewellery.' She smiles.
'Poor bloke, I think he has no concept of real scruffy
women. He likes us to be presented to him on a podium
so he can admire his creation at its most lovely.'

'He does make exceedingly good dresses, though,'

says Alexander. 'Who are you to ruin the fantasy?'

'I suppose so,' says Lydia. 'And anyway, he pays between nine and twelve grand a show, and I've been on a bloody diet for two weeks to get this casting, so what do I care about a bit of lippy?'

We all nod in agreement, and Alexander and I concentrate on the tricky task of ordering a drink while trying not to appear to be celebrity spotting. Eva Herzigova struts past. Anna Wintour sails through the lobby. Jean Paul Gaultier is holding court in a corner. Naomi is looking glamorous down the other end of the bar. She must be opening or closing for Valentino. The model world not only divides into super and not so super models, but also into the lifestyle models who fly around the world doing commercial shows like Chanel or Valentino, and those who don't. The lifestyle models do a couple of adverts and then turn up like wild horses to the respective fashion weeks. Some will behave badly, get trollied and get papped with inappropriate people; the rest of them just do the shows, get on with it, and collect their cash. They don't stay up late drinking, they stay up late in fittings. They work until two in the morning, and get up at six. They can make a lot of money and have a very good career, but very few people will ever know their names.

'Seen Kate this week?' asks Alexander.

'No, not so far,' says Lydia. 'But you know she hates the catwalk. She's too sexy to do the shows. She oozes sex appeal, and sometimes that just gets in the way.

Don't you remember I told you about Marc Jacobs last year?'

'I think so,' I say.

'You remember,' she says. 'They told me off because my bottom and arms were moving too much. I was breaking the uniform. They wanted these clones, and I was standing out too much. We were all given the same hair and the same make-up. We were androids. But he's so hot. It's a shame I can't do his shows any more.' She shrugs. 'I'm too well known now. He doesn't use names. They detract from the clothes. But actually he doesn't pay that much anyway. D'you know, some designers pay you with last season's clothes, and who wants those?'

'The cheapskates,' says Alexander, sucking on the straw in a banana daiquiri he insisted on ordering.

'*We* hardly cover our models in riches,' I point out, referring to the £200 we pay them for their efforts.

'Yeah, but you're not a world-renowned fashion label, are you?' says Lydia.

'I am sadly well aware of that,' I say.

'Oh, I didn't mean . . .' She covers her mouth with her pink-tipped hand.

'Don't worry.'

'But I love your stuff,' Lydia says, smiling.

'Don't look now,' says Alexander, leaning in, 'but I've just seen two of the hacks who slagged off your previous collection come into the bar.'

Lydia, Alexander and I all put down our drinks and

stare at the two women as they walk towards the bar. Squeezed into unforgivingly tight jackets and slim-fitting skirts, they both look hot, bothered and hugely uncomfortable. I smile. There is something deeply gratifying about two women who are clearly too fat for fashion trying so desperately hard to be fashionable. I would not normally enjoy such discomfort so readily were it not for the fact that they are both a couple of bitches who have taken my reputation to the cleaners and back.

'Evening,' I say, smiling and lifting my glass in their general direction.

'Darling!' they reply. I can see them both frown slightly as they try to remember what they wrote about me. The assistant does have the decency to blush, but the editor grins away like a certified lunatic, thinking she has got away with it.

'Lovely to see you both.'

I'm smiling away. They are smiling back.

'And you,' says the editor.

'Great,' I say. 'Having fun?'

'Oh yes,' says the editor. 'Excellent. Really good stuff.'

'Excellent,' parrots the assistant.

'Any favourites?'

'Oh,' says the editor.

'Oh,' adds the assistant.

'All terribly good?'

'Terribly,' the editor replies with a nod.

'Good,' adds the assistant.

'Oh look!' says the editor. 'There's Glenda Bailey. I must go and say hello.'

'Glenda,' says the assistant.

'Do you mind?' asks the editor.

'Oh, do,' I smile.

'Lovely to see you,' says the assistant.

'We must have lunch,' says the editor as she turns on her heel to walk away. 'Very soon.'

'Love to.' I raise my raspberry martini. 'Look forward to it.'

'I don't know why you don't tell them to fuck off,' says Lydia, turning her back on them. 'I can't stand those two, and their magazine sucks.'

'I don't want them to think I care,' I say. 'Anyway, things have got an awful lot worse for them now.'

Further down the bar the editor and the assistant are now stuck in a queue. Circling like old jumbos over Gatwick, they hover in some sort of holding pattern, waiting to meet the editor-in-chief of *Harpers Bazaar*. They lurk, grinning, hopping from one foot to another, trying to catch her eye, while Glenda stands talking to Viktor. Or is it Rolf? I don't know which is which.

'What is more painful, two porcupines having sex, or watching this?' asks Alexander as he drains his banana daiquiri. 'Reminds me of last Paris Fashion Week when I went up to that twat at *Dazed and Confused*, who I thought was my friend. I walked up, said hello, and they turned around and said, "I'm busy at the moment. Can you come back in ten minutes?"'

'It always gives me immense pleasure watching the hacks in fashion week,' says Lydia, lighting up a Marlboro Light. 'They spend all year bitching about each other, trying to do each other over. Honestly, the shit I hear on shoots about who hates who, and who's done what to who. They are so horrible about each other. I always think that fashion week is as if all the bullies have been forced to go on a school trip together. One of the things that keeps me amused, going down the catwalk, is all the animosity they feel towards each other and they all have to sit with each other. Then they're worried about who has got the better seat, who is more important, who is looking better or thinner, or who is more successful. It makes me piss myself laughing.'

'Oh, she's talking to them now,' says Alexander. 'Oh, and she must have cracked the best joke in the world. Look how they laugh!'

'Shall we go?' asks Lydia.

'OK,' says Alexander.

'We've got three parties, dinner at La Coupole with Missy Raider, and I've got a Lanvin fitting at ten thirty.'

'Shit,' says Alexander, noisily sucking up the last of his cocktail. 'It's all bloody go in fashion.'

5

Back in the UK and Alexander and I are exhausted. Selling and partying do not exactly go hand in hand. But I have to say that I wouldn't have missed the Louis Vuitton party for the world. The end of Paris Fashion Week and the end of the season, it was like everyone had finally been let off the leash. The Petit Palais looked incredible, the champagne flowed, the supermodels posed and the portaloos outside rocked to the sounds of fashionistas doing jazz. Never have outside facilities been so popular. While waiting in line, legitimately I might add, I was privy to the most ear-piercing scream. Turns out some unfortunate stylist was so keen to trough down that he swept the stash of coke off the toilet seat with his fringe. The angry hell he unleashed from his fellow snorters, the spitting and the swearing, was hilarious to hear.

But it really was a great party. Eva Herzigova, Dita Von Teese, anyone who is anyone was there. I got plastered on expensive bubbles, Lydia copped off with some smooth-looking Italian who insisted he was a prince, and Alexander stole three goodie bags and then promptly left them all behind in the cab. Needless to say, the next day's meetings were a write-off. Irena failed to turn up, Alexander called in sick and retched down the phone just to prove a point, and I was left holding the fort with the only two buyers (German) to make their meeting.

'It was great,' says Alexander, sitting on the edge of my desk, blowing smoke in the face of Damiano, one of his pals who's dropped by the office for a coffee and a fag on his way nowhere.

Alexander has a group of pals who are constantly popping in. He refers to them as the 'A Gays'. There is, however, very little of the A list about them, so Lydia, Mimi and I refer to them as his 'fash trash' gang. Nick is perhaps the most powerful of them all. He works for a men's magazine as a deputy fashion assistant. He is funny, handsome, up with the gossip, and is always dressed in next season's clothes. Patrick is the kindest. An Alexander ex, he works as a shop assistant for Versace and always looks immaculate. He usually has an Elton John story, has met Donatella more times than he can shake a tango-tanned stick at, and is the best person to know come Christmas, as he is a big fan of the five-fingered discount – otherwise known as stealing. A DJ and fashion booker with a voice like a girl and the body of a small child, Damiano is the least busy of the three, so he is often lying on the sofa downstairs, sitting at Alexander's desk or cadging free water from the cooler just outside my office.

'Yeah,' sniffs Damiano, 'I heard it was a good night. I had a ticket.'

'Oh yeah?' says Alexander. 'I didn't know you were at fashion week.'

'Yeah, well, that was it,' says Damiano, relaxing back into the armchair in my office, swinging his legs over one arm. 'I couldn't be bothered to get over there. The agency were given a few tickets but, you know, I had stuff to do.'

'Yes,' I say, getting increasingly annoyed by Damiano's inertia. He keeps yawning and stretching, looking like he is bedding in for the afternoon. 'We have a bit of stuff to do at the moment.'

'So have I,' says Damiano, picking the fluff off his Dior jeans.

'What are you doing?' asks Alexander.

'I am meant to be scouting in Top Shop.' He looks up. 'It's our week. Select gets it one week, we get it another. Models One the next. And it's a fistfight for half term.'

'What?' says Alexander. 'You are all in Top Shop? Where? Oxford Street?'

'Yeah,' says Damiano, like Alexander is a moron. 'Only the flagship store. But you know, that's where all the young girls are. The ones who like fashion anyway. There, and Covent Garden on a Saturday. I spend the whole time walking up to women asking the time. Mainly to check if they've got nice skin.'

'Haven't you got a drug for that these days?' I ask.

'What?' He looks at me. 'Yeah, we have, but it is easier without it.'

'I bet,' I say.

'We've got a new Russian at the moment,' he continues, 'who looks like she might be the next Kate.'

'Another one,' says Alexander.

'Yeah.'

'I thought there was only one Kate, and she seems to be doing OK.'

'That has to be the quickest rehab and comeback in the history of jazz,' snorts Damiano. 'Have you ever heard of anyone kicking the bugle that quickly? What was it?'

'Three weeks.'

'Three weeks!'

'Where was it?'

'Meadows.'

'The rehab clinic of choice.'

'We send all our girls there,' says Damiano. 'For exhaustion.' He does the quotes-in-the-air thing with his fingers.

'Maybe she didn't have a problem?' I suggest.

Both Alexander and Damiano look at me and laugh.

'Purlease,' says Damiano. 'Don't you remember that *Vogue* cover she did when she was dressed in a crown, holding a sceptre?' We both nod. 'Well, rumour has it that she was so out of it for that shoot they had to prop her up, and the people supporting her were airbrushed out of the picture.'

'Bollocks,' I say. That is definitely one of the crazier grapevine stories.

'Well, that's what they say,' says Damiano, hands in the air, looking innocent. 'I'm just saying what I heard.'

The phone goes on my desk. It's Trish from downstairs.

'Hiya,' she says. I can hear her munching gum down the phone. 'An order for you. Alexander's not at his desk.'

'It's an order,' I say, handing over the phone to Alexander. 'Listen, Damiano, do you mind? I've got work to do.'

'No, sure, man,' he says. 'Don't mind me.' He leans further back into the chair and slides his Converse All Stars up the wall. 'Go ahead.'

'But I do,' I say. 'Can't you both go next door?'

I don't really have anything to do except stare at the wall and try to think up designs for the next collection. The thing is I am so dog tired and full of old toxins all I really want to do is look up how my stuff is doing on Net-a-porter and sink my teeth into the enormous BLT sandwich that is in a drawer in my desk. There is no privacy in this place.

Alexander and Damiano slope off next door, and just as I am poised to sink my teeth into my sandwich, Trish walks in with a copy of *Grazia* magazine. Dressed in a

pair of the skinniest jeans I have ever seen, with a blue
and white striped French top, she's bobbed her hair, just
like Sienna.

'Hiya,' she says. 'Seen this?' she asks as she pulls the
chewing gum out of her mouth, stretches it, snaps it
and nibbles it back in with her two front teeth.

'What?' I ask, putting down the sandwich.

'This.' She slaps the magazine down on my desk.

I look down. There is a huge photo of Ted Nicholls
relaxing at home. He looks smug, at ease, and
fortunately a little fat around the middle. 'Ted
Nicholls Is Back' claims the headline. There's three
pages of the guff. Ted lying on a sofa. Ted grinning
like a jaunty twat by a bar. And Ted sitting in a
bath in a black suit, white shirt and shades, trying to
look like James Bond. 'I design clothes for real
women with curves and attitude,' he is quoted as
saying.

'Like you know anything about women, real or
otherwise,' I mutter, pushing the magazine across the
desk.

'There's a photo in *Heat* as well,' says Trish. 'He's at
some première with Kelly Osborne in his dress.' Trish
spends her whole day reading these magazines while
pretending to answer our phones, type my letters and
send out clothes from the press rack to shoots. So
nothing gets past her. 'And he's done Sofa Supper in *ES*
magazine.'

My heart sinks. I think I might just have to slash my

wrists. Ted Nicholls deserves a slap, not a bloody triple-page spread in *Grazia* magazine.

'Good news,' says Alexander, waltzing back into the office, swigging a full-fat Coke. 'Selfridges have doubled their order from last season. Matches have been on the phone asking about the white shirts, and Ko Samui have asked for nine of the white and silver dresses. In fact, quite a few people have been asking for the white and silver dress. It could be the hit of the season.'

So the buyers have gone through their budgets, consulted their line sheets and look books, and orders are beginning to come in now. Alexander and I are beginning to see the fruits of our six months of hard work. And so far so good. Although, because we are not a large label, the numbers are much smaller than you would think. Its twenty jackets here, fifteen shirts there. Even our largest clients don't go above thirty, and that's including the full range of sizes.

Talking of sizes, we only go up to a 14, and that's a normal 14, not Marks and Spencer sizing. Marks size 8 is equivalent to a Chanel size 12. I often get berated by larger women about why we only go up to a 14 and don't take into account the fuller figure. There are numerous reasons for this sizing decision.

Firstly, it comes down to cost. Simply in material terms, it costs me twice as much to make a size 16 dress as it does to make the same garment in a size 8, and I can't pass the cost on to the shop and therefore the customer. If size 16 clothes were nearly twice the price of size 8 clothes, then I might be tempted. But sadly they are not. And when my profit margins are as slight as they are, I can't afford to cater for the larger lady.

Secondly, there just isn't the demand for big designer clothes. Maybe it is a vicious circle: we don't make them large, therefore large girls feel too fat for fashion and aren't even tempted to go designer shopping. But all I know is that at the end of the season I am left with more 14s than any other size. Come to our sample sale, or staff end-of-season sale, and all we have are 14s. Granted, we have a few shop-soiled 10s, but it's normally large sizes that are left. So we concentrate on the 8–10 market, because that is where our client base lies. In fact, if anything, designer clothes sizes are shrinking. The standard small clothes size recently went down from an 8 to a 6. In the USA sizes are decreasing from 6s to 4s, with some women coming into stores demanding the new size 0. The skinny jeans fetish has recently highlighted the difference; a mate of mine at Matches told me that they sold out of their Sass & Bide jeans in 4 and 6 before any other size. It seems that while the rest of the country is getting more and more obese, the rich and the fashionable are getting thinner and thinner.

There is also a third reason for a lack of size 16s, and it is probably a lot less diplomatic and a little more prejudiced. Fashion is a business that deals in fantasy, dreams and illusion, and who fantasizes about being a size 16? Unless of course you are a 20, then 16 probably looks rather good from where you are sitting. But on the whole, no woman sits down in the hairdresser's, flicks through a *Vogue* magazine and wishes she were the large girl in the advert. Designer clothes look better on skinny bodies. I have one designer mate who, when rather drunk at the *Vogue* drinks before London Fashion Week, once admitted that if he could get his clothes to walk down the runway without anyone in them, he would be a happy man. 'The lines hang in the right places without tits and arses,' he slurred. 'If only a flat piece of paper could move down the catwalk on its own. To be honest, as a designer, the last thing you want is anyone wearing your clothes.'

And I'm afraid I kind of understand what he means. Dresses, shirts and skirts look so perfect when you draw them on pieces of paper in the studio. You colour them in and hang them on the wall and they are design-perfect. It's only when the fabric flaws are introduced and the pattern cutter says that the dress won't hang properly – in short, when other people get involved – that things get fucked up and I start having to compromise. Real women get in the way of the art and true aesthetic of fashion, and that's the problem. So the thinner they are, the closer they are to the piece of paper the dress was designed on, and the better it is for me or any other designer.

It is fortunate, then, with an attitude like that, that anyone wants to buy our clothes at all. But they do, and

Selfridges have doubled their order. I have to say that I am slightly amazed. Perhaps this collection might be a critical flop but a popular success? The only problem that all these orders leave us with now is, how to get the stuff made?

At the moment, all my clobber is made in the UK. Well, as anyone in the business will tell you, this, of course, is strictly not true. You can have your stuff made up anywhere in the world, but just so long as the last hook and eye is put on in the UK, or the zip is finished off here, you can shove 'Made in the UK' on your label. Since the demise of manufacturing in the north almost nothing is made here any more. Even Marks and Spencer have moved most of their stuff to the Far East. Ten years ago, being British-made and carrying the British quality mark actually meant something; these days it just means that someone's put a button on before it went on the shop floor. And if you look closely enough you can tell it wasn't made here. The tension might not be right in the stitching, the seam might be crooked, the garment won't be steamed or folded correctly. But there is not much you can do. Where are we supposed to go to get anything made here any more?

I have a small manufacturing deal in Hungary, just outside Budapest, where I get most of my jackets and shirts made up. The quality control is a bit of a problem. I have to check 15 per cent instead of the usual 10. That means when a shipment of a hundred jackets arrives at the office, I take fifteen of them randomly out of the boxes and check the seams and the finishes. If they are OK, straight, smooth and problem-free, I have to assume that the rest are too. I simply don't have the time to check the whole lot.

For the remainder of my stuff, I have a small deal in Portugal, and for the rest I rely on a team of mostly Polish and Portuguese stitchers who work out of a studio in Shoreditch. They are lovely women – some are here legally, others are not – and they all work their backsides off for £8.50 an hour. They are the mainstay of the company. I don't know all their names, but when I pop into the studio to check quality control, I am sure to be extremely pleasant to all of them. Some actually take their work home with them and sit in front of the TV running up jackets and skirts. But at best the set-up is, as it sounds, rather amateur. It is the one great sticking point for the company. If we get any bigger, if any more orders like the Selfridges one come in, I am going to have to rethink how we do things.

I sit and listen to Alexander talking about orders while eating my BLT sandwich. If only someone would buy me out, I could get myself a sexy licensing deal and things would be very different.

One of the main advantages of being owned by the Gucci Group, LVMH or Club 21 is that they organize the manufacturing of your clothes. The Gucci Group have their own factories in and around Milan and Florence, as well as a few in Hungary, where they make

McQueen, McCartney, Balenciaga and Yves Saint Laurent. LVMH have a similar set-up. There are also other licensing manufacturers such as Gibo, Aeffe and Onward Kashiyama who look after the larger labels like Paul Smith, Westwood, Gaultier, Alberta Ferretti and Hussein Chalayan. It is a simple deal: you, as the designer, get between 10 and 15 per cent of all sales, while they take the risk, make the product and maintain the quality control. As a designer you merely supply the ideas; they do the rest. They also sell your clothes in the sexy warehouses across town. It is a delightfully simple system, and the designer can sit back, relax and get on with designing, leaving all the boring bits to someone else. Quality is assured, as are numbers, so your buyers are confident that you can deliver the correct number of clothes to a certain standard, on time.

That's the idea anyway. Of course, the system is not without its pitfalls. First of all, I always think 10 to 15 per cent is not very much for all the creative input, for putting yourself out there and having your name above the door. Secondly, there is immense pressure put on the designer to deliver the sales that are dictated by the licensor, so if you don't hit your targets you are out on your ear. And thirdly, they don't always deliver on time. Just as with everything in fashion, the big boys go first. The larger your order, the more likely you are to be at the front of the manufacturing queue. In a system where we all have to deliver our clothes at the same time, this puts the small-time player at a huge disadvantage. Deliver late and some shops will cancel their order. If you can't get your spring/summer collection in by January, then they don't want it at all. There is some unquantifiable critical mass that has to be reached before you get a place in the queue that is anywhere near the front. Otherwise there is the awful possibility of going the way of Clements Ribeiro, who went into liquidation last year because their licensor failed to deliver on time. They were at the back of the queue and could not fulfil their orders. They filed for bankruptcy in August. When it goes wrong, it goes horribly wrong. They have since put a small show together that looked fabulous, but they are currently not manufacturing. It's enough to send shivers down your spine.

The other great problem is cabbage. Cabbage is the stuff that falls off the back of a lorry, or indeed out of the factory gate, and ends up on a market stall next to the cabbage – hence its name. Cabbage doesn't come from the factory short-serving the client, i.e. delivering 2,000 handbags instead of 2,200. It comes from the leftover product that the factory hasn't used in the making of the bag/dress/shirt. When ordering material for your bag/dress/shirt you have to add on at least another 10 per cent for mistakes. If the factory is careful and doesn't need this extra material, they are left with another 10 per cent of your product that is unaccounted for. It disappears out the back of the factory and ends up in a Florence or Milan market. The bigger the order, the larger the amount of cabbage. The Gucci handbags in Florence market look just like the real ones, simply because they are the real ones. The Pucci scarf is the Pucci scarf, and the Dior wallet is a Dior wallet. We are extremely wary of cabbage and order all our material to the exact metre rating for all our clothes in Hungary. So there is very little margin for error. We are a small company and can't really afford cabbage.

Fake goods are an entirely different story. Made of sub-standard product with poor stitching and often to never-produced designs, fakes are a Far Eastern speciality. Profits from their sale help to fund organized crime and terrorism, and they are the bane of the fashion industry. However, there is some recourse. Only recently Chanel, Prada, Burberry, Louis Vuitton and Gucci sued Beijing's Silk Market for a couple of hundred thousand pounds for selling fake goods with their names on. They found boxes and boxes of bags with their labels all over them. This sort of stuff is so substandard it is easy to spot. Cabbage, on the other hand, is something the big companies can't do very much about.

Alexander is still talking. He is running through the orders. He's right about the white and silver sequin dresses – they are going down a storm. It is around the ordering stage that you begin to work out what is going to be the star of the collection and what is not going to work at all. No-one's put in a single order for the orange jacket that also comes in apple green. Somehow the orange has put everyone off to such an extent that they haven't even considered the apple green option. That garment took me days to think about and hours to design, but it won't go into production at all. At least everyone has gone for the white dress. Small boutique shops like Ko Samui will usually take what they perceive as the key pieces from the collection as a money driver, plus a couple of the other more obscure pieces to make sure that they keep their more off-the-wall image alive. Selfridges and Harvey Nichols obviously order bigger and more safely. Even the old bag from Pandora's Box Alexander shouted at a couple of weeks ago has confirmed her piss-poor order and gone for a few white dresses.

'Clearly everyone is feeling white and silver for this season,' says Alexander, looking up from the list.

'If you look closely,' I say, 'you'll find that it resembles the *Some Like It Hot* dress worn by Marilyn Monroe.'

'Shit, I knew I'd seen it somewhere before.'

'It appeals to the slut/whore in every girl,' I say. 'It is also burned into our collective consciousness as something we are programmed to find attractive and sexy.'

'And who says you're just a pretty face?' says Alexander.

'Do they say that?' asks Damiano, sounding puzzled.

'You still here?' I ask.

'Yeah, well, now I have bunked off for the whole afternoon I have got to make it look convincing. I may as well wait for Alexander to go to this party tonight.'

'What party?'

'Oh, some *Pop* magazine thing,' says Damiano.

'You're going to fraternize with the enemy? Where's your loyalty?' I ask.

'Mimi invited me,' Alexander says.

'Mimi.' I sigh. 'I might have guessed.'

'She's been styling for Louis Vuitton,' he explains, 'so she's become mates with Katie Grand.'

'Katie's career has always amazed me,' says Damiano through a yawn. 'How can the woman who started out styling PJ and Duncan end up doing Miu Miu?'

'Who the fuck are PJ and Duncan?' I snap.

'Ant and Dec,' say Alexander and Damiano together, their eyes round with surprise.

'Don't you know anything?' asks Damiano.

'Clearly not,' I say.

'Anyway, so I thought you wouldn't mind,' says Alexander. 'You never know, I might win her over, get her to put your stuff in her magazine.'

'And hell might freeze.' I smile. 'Honestly, what do I care?' I add with a shrug.

'All's fair in love and fashion,' breezes Alexander as he makes to move next door. 'Oh, by the way,' he adds. 'I've had a call from Neiman's and they are sending back 10 per cent of the stock that didn't sell.'

'Have we got to buy it back?' I ask.

''Fraid so,' says Alexander. 'That was the condition on which they tried us in the first place.'

'Shit.'

'It's not very much,' he says. 'Nothing to worry about.'

'Any more coming in?'

'A few bits, but nothing hideous.'

Alexander walks back into his office and I sit and stare at Ted Nicholls's smug face grinning out at me from the glossy pages of *Grazia*. I hate it when we get our old stock back. There is something deeply depressing about clothes that don't sell. All that effort, all that tender love and care, and no-one wants them. Although actually, I have to say that is not totally true. Some of them find a home. If after the stores' end-of-season sale, or our sample sale, or staff sale, or friends and family sale, the clothes still haven't sold, they end up in TK Maxx or Century 21 in New York. We have a deal with both of them that they take between 50 and 60 per cent of our leftover stock for which we get very little in return. Well, the stuff is nearly two years out of date by the time it gets there. It's been on the shop floor for six months and we have tried to flog it twice before it ends up on the TK Maxx pile. And then they only come twice a year to collect our stock. It takes them three months to process the order and another three to get the stuff out onto the shelves, so stuff I made nearly two years ago is now selling in an out-of-town store near you.

The rest of it gets cut up and burned. Criminal, isn't it? Thousands of pounds of expensive, beautiful clothes get destroyed every year by their own designers rather than being sold somewhere that might tarnish the brand. Fashion may be about beauty and aesthetic and aspiration, but it is also about the brand. Brand is everything. Tarnish the brand and what are you left with? Why pay £1,000 for a dress that you know costs less than £100 to make? Why buy a Chanel bag when there is one at Accessorize that is just as charming? So, rather than helping out those less fortunate than ourselves, we guard our image and burn the lot.

'You two off then?' I ask as Alexander and Damiano poke their heads around the door.

'Yup,' says Alexander, looking even more sheepish than before.

'Send everyone my love,' I say, my voice loaded with sarcasm.

'Will do.' He smiles, buttoning up his black Margiela coat.

'Oh, and if you see that Ted Nicholls, give him a firm kick in the bollocks.'

6

I have been staring out of the window for the past two days. I'm looking for inspiration for the new collection and it just isn't coming. This is a nightmare. Unlike composers, painters and writers who can sit around for months at a time, twiddling their thumbs, knocking back the pastis and pulling fluff out of their navels, waiting for the muse to find them, fashion designers have to deliver a minimum of two collections a year, every year, otherwise they go out of business. You can't arrive at the beginning of London Fashion Week and throw your hands in the air and say, 'I am terribly sorry but there's no spring/summer this year.' Fashion is a strange business. It claims to be an art, but really it is all about business. If you don't conform to the rules you are dead in the water. And the rules dictate that no matter how devoid of ideas you are, no matter how knackered and uninspired, you still have to get models into frocks and, twice a year, shove them down a catwalk.

My mood wall is a joke. Something along the lines of a student collage, it has photos and swatches and carefully torn out bits and pieces stuck to it and is supposed to tell you something about what we are feeling at the moment. Not dissimilar to what a very rich woman might give an interior designer to tell them what she fancies in her sitting room. The mood wall sets the tone of the collection and is there to inspire me as I sit here, smoking and soaking up more coffee than a slops tray at Starbucks.

And judging by what I've got up there at the moment, I'm devoid of any ideas and feeling fuck all. I have a couple of old *Vogue* tears stuck up there from the early sixties with demure-looking women in twin sets and tulip skirts. I like the skirts and the wide belts. I'm feeling that waists are back. We've had tits and bare tummies for long enough. An elegant waist with a cinched belt is what I'm thinking we might all be feeling next season. I am also feeling that it's legs, it's décolleté. Now that we are all loving the Mouret. It's simple. It's to the knee. A turn of an ankle. A nice shoe. It's cleaner, less frou-frou and ra-ra. It's just a shame that there is nothing up there that says any of that. Instead I have a photo of Audrey Hepburn in *Breakfast at Tiffany's*. I have a mocked-up swatch of that huge amount of tartan I'm having specially made in Scotland. I've got a bit of lace that I found on the King's Road. And I have a few grabs of handbags, shoes and boots that I half-heartedly tore out of a 1986 *Cosmo* I found at my mum's. Well, it conforms to the twenty-year rule, and I couldn't believe my luck that she still had one hanging around. I initially thought that it was serendipitous. But then I remembered that's all we used to get down in Exeter – very out-of-date *Cosmopolitan* magazines.

Growing up round there, it was hardly a hotbed of fashion. I always find it strange that most of this industry's biggest movers and shakers come from very unfashionable, usually provincial beginnings. Katie Grand is from Birmingham, Luella Bartley was born in Stratford-upon-Avon. Christ, even Roland Mouret was born in Lourdes. Is it something to do with being starved of cool and cred as a child that drives most of us in adulthood?

'Feeling inspired?' asks Alexander, leaning on the doorframe. He is dressed head to foot in black except for a bright orange Hermès belt.

'Not really,' I reply, slumping forward at my desk and doodling on my silhouette pad.

A ready-drawn collection of naked lovelies printed for me, the silhouette pad is where I design all my clothes. Its pages are full of sketched outlines of the sort of women who wear my clothes. I change them from season to season. This Fall's is whippet thin, with heels, attitude and an Emma Peel haircut. She is supposed to be inspiring. Sadly, today it is going to take more than line drawings to get me going.

'Is Mimi coming in?' Alexander asks.

'Yeah.'

'Well, she'll have a few bits and pieces,' he says, smiling encouragingly.

'I bloody hope so.' I sigh.

'Do you have any idea what you are feeling?'

'Waists and ankles . . . shoulders?'

'There you go.' He smiles again. 'No bums?'

'Bums?' I look at him like he's a total arse. 'Bums are so Jennifer Lopez and so last century.'

'OK,' he says. 'Lucky I'm the business and you're the talent then, isn't it?'

'Question is,' I mumble, 'what would Miuccia do?'

'If we all knew that, we too would be millionaires.'

I sit at my desk and call up Miuccia Prada's latest collection on Style.com. I play the slide show of every look from the collection and enlarge each of the photos. It does feel rather pathetic to spend one's time looking at other people's shows, trying to work out what they have done and where they might go next season. But there are some designers you would be a fool not to check out.

Miuccia Prada is probably one of the most fashion forward designers. She is a designer's designer, and we all look to her as some sort of visionary. Balenciaga is also always worth casting one's eye over, as is Phoebe Philo at Chloé. Although since boho is over, she is a little less important than she was. Alaia is also worth looking at, and obviously Marc Jacobs. As a cut freak, it is always good to take a look at McQueen and Chalayan. One must always keep an eye on those who are perceived to be ahead of the curve. If only so that one might attach oneself to their well-cut coat tails.

But in the end a lot of it, sadly, comes down to resources. I don't have the team of cutters Valentino has, or an atelier of seamstresses like Karl Lagerfeld at Chanel. Karl can order changes and dresses and new toiles to be made right up until the night of the show. He can have dresses remade six or seven times, moving hems by millimetres to satisfy his every whim. Miuccia's collection only comes together at the last minute. She too can go right to the wall. She can think about grand ideas and themes. She will take something like the war in Iraq and while the rest of us are shoving khaki combats down the catwalks she'll come up with a bunch of young innocents dressed in white, wafting like lost souls down the runway. She is so ahead of herself. She is already feeling what the rest of us are barely smelling.

Mimi arrives to catch me copying a Prada shirt design off the net. I am concentrating so hard that I don't actually hear her coming up the stairs. It is not until Mini Me yaps its toy poodle way into my office that I realize she has arrived. Dressed in a fabulous tight black fitted jacket, a floor-length skirt and big biker boots, she looks fantastic, flustered and exhausted.

'Fucking hell,' she says as she dumps six large

designer bags at the foot of my desk. 'I have had such a shit couple of days. And I have such a hangover.'

'Hi to you too,' I say, leaning back into my chair. 'Where were you last night?'

'Oh, God,' she says, holding her head gently with remembered pain. Or is it shame? 'I went to this première, for the new Scarlett Johansson movie. I spent the morning putting her into dresses, sewing her up for interviews and a couple of shoots, and let me tell you, she is quite pleasant to start with, but come two p.m. she seems to get tired rather quickly. Talk about grumpy pants.'

'Hasn't she just done that new Louis Vuitton shoot for a million pounds?'

'A million lire more like. D'you know, she's not that pretty in the flesh,' declares Mimi, emptying out one bag after another on the floor.

'Really?'

'Honestly,' says Mimi. 'Give me Sienna any day. At least she's entertaining. Anyway, last night was not much fun. The after-show party sucked. Scarlett ignored me all night. Pretended I hadn't spent the whole bloody day with her. Simon and Yasmin Le Bon were there, so that was good. She's gorgeous. But there was no vodka, just champagne, which is why I feel so shit today. Anyway, I left with a whole gang of us and we went to Café de Paris.'

'Is that still open?'

'Course it is,' she says, frowning at my stupid

question. 'This other stylist was dancing on a glass table, fell through it and landed on about forty wine glasses. I had to take her to casualty and we ended up sitting there until six in the morning. I'm shagged.' She lets out a great big theatrical yawn just to make her point. 'And I've got to go out tonight. A shop opening. Urgh.'

'I didn't think you did shops.'

'My mate Amy is doing the goodie bags and she says they're giving away Jimmy Choos.'

'Right. She OK?'

'Who?'

'The stylist?'

'Oh, yeah.' Mimi nods, and pulls out some more clothes from one of the bags. 'She does that sort of crazy stuff all the time. Oh fuck off, Mini!' she says, leaning across the pile of clothes to hit her dog, which has just made a nest in what looks like a silk suit. 'That's bloody vintage YSL!' Like the dog is supposed to understand quite how fabulous that is. 'Right,' she says, looking up at me. 'Let's check all this stuff out. Shall I start with the amazing Dior dress I found?'

A designer's relationship with their stylist is a strange, abstract and unquantifiable thing. There are some who are hugely instrumental in the shaping of the collection, and others who simply tweak the models just as they are about to step out onto the catwalk. The influential ones are there every step of the way, discussing seams and shapes, and telling the designer exactly where they are going wrong and how much they must take the shirt up, or let the trousers out, in order for the silhouette to work. Some are more like muses. Their essential style is what the designer is after. Their essence of cool is what inspires them. So the stylist only has to turn up to a party in a fabulous frock for the designer to be excited. The dress will not be discussed but it will subconsciously influence what goes down the catwalk next season. Then there are the super stylists, like Katie Grand is to Giles Deacon. Mate, muse and key adviser on the collection, she has a tremendous influence on the models who appear in the collection. She styles so many magazine shoots and advertising campaigns that she is owed many favours and can pull them in left and right. She is an important and useful person to have on your side.

Mimi is neither useful nor important in that way, but she is rather good. She has an excellent eye and great taste. Her mother was one of those glamorous sixties women who married well and was photographed by Bailey. A great society beauty, Carmen is more reclusive than she used to be, but she can still be seen inhabiting a villa just outside Villefranche, smoking brown More cigarettes, rolling very thin, very strong joints, and sporting a Pucci kaftan. Mimi did once seek her assistance when styling a bikini shoot for *Vogue*. Her mother arrived late two days in a row, drank most of the on-set refreshments before midday, and then spent the rest of the day moaning, 'Darling, Mummy needs drugs,' when asked to do anything remotely taxing. She did rather let the side down.

'So, what do you think?' asks Mimi, flapping out a stunning black Dior dress. Sleeveless with a square neck, fitted bodice and full skirt to the knee, it looks modern and classic at the same time. 'Fifties.' She smiles. 'Isn't it fabulous?'

'It's wonderful,' I say, getting out of my chair. My heart is beating slightly faster. It could be all the coffee, but I'm hoping it's the pitter-patter of inspiration. 'Where did you get it?'

'I found it at the back of my sister's wardrobe.'

'Really?'

'Yeah. I was rummaging through it last weekend with her. She was looking for this old gold Ozbek jacket she had, and we found this. It had fallen off its hanger and it was in the back on the floor. I remember her wearing it to some party in the mid-eighties when she was about fifteen and being voted the sexiest girl in London in *Tatler*.'

'It's silk taffeta,' I say, stroking the material and fluffing out the underskirts.

'I know. Like it?'

'Love it.'

'Shall I put it on the rail?'

'Definitely.'

'That's nice,' says Alexander, running his hands through his mousey hair as he stands in the doorway. 'Sending that down the runway as is?'

'I thought I might,' I say.

'Good idea,' he says. 'Don't forget to take the label out.'

Mimi starts to laugh.

Designers steal other designers' clothes all the time. We are always picking up little vintage dresses in Portobello, taking out the old label and shoving our own in before sending it down the catwalk. Sometimes it's so obvious you can't believe no-one notices. A Dior dress here, a Balenciaga jacket there, even something that is screamingly distinctive like Azzedine Alaia – and no-one seems to spot it. Last season I had an old Pierre Cardin skirt that I pinched in its entirety. Mimi found it on the Portobello Road and we just snipped out the label and sent it down the catwalk. Another time I just copied the design in a different fabric. Most audaciously, two seasons ago I found a black and white swimming costume in an Oxfam in Chelsea and shoved that on the runway. We sold twenty-five of them in Harvey Nichols alone. Look in some designers' windows and you will see so many Portobello frocks it's embarrassing. The other day I was with a mate who runs a stall on Fridays in the market and she spotted one of her dresses in a window that she'd flogged the week before for £35. It was unchanged, dry-cleaned and popped on a mannequin, marked up at £1,350.

As well as Portobello market, there are another couple of places we all go to seek inspiration. The most important is Relik. Hidden away in West London at the foot of the Trellick Tower, just off the Golborne Road, Relik is a veritable treasure trove of vintage goodies. Owned by Fiona Stuart, Claire Stansfield and Steven Phillip, all ex-Portobello stallholders, it basically sifts through the shit for you, and only stocks fantastic pieces from the 1920s to the 1980s. Yamamoto, Malcolm McLaren, Bodymapp, Westwood – they are all ripe and ready for the ripping off.

Last time I went there, a few weeks ago, it was really rather embarrassing. All I can say is that the fashion muse was clearly out of town. I walked through the door and bumped into one designer, who was over from Italy on a fact-finding mission. He recognized me as I walked through the door but didn't say anything. I silently followed him around the shop for a while, feeling increasingly tense and uneasy. We were both rather keen on a couple of Alaia dresses, but neither of us wanted to put our cards on the table. Then another UK-based designer walked in. I could see he was a bit sheepish, because he is normally quite a friendly chap. I have met him a few times before and we are on speaking terms. We also once shared a pattern cutter. But he put his head down, pulled his collar up and headed for a couple of Westwood frocks that were hanging towards the back. He was finding the whole situation as uncomfortable as I was. The first designer could stand it no more and left, opening the door for another as he went. It was like some bloody French farce. No sooner had one international designer left than another one arrived.

While Relik is the artistically-blocked fashion designer's first port of call, you can often find us in Virginia in Holland Park, Steinberg and Tolkien in Chelsea, Appleby on Westbourne Grove, One of a Kind in Notting Hill and Palette London in Islington. For accessories it is a little bit harder to predict. However, for sunglasses there is only one place to go – Arckiv in East London, favourite hangout of the head designers from Louis Vuitton and Gucci accessories, both of whom are rumoured to buy up to fifty pairs of shades at a time. Anyone who is after a vintage look for film, TV or commercials always ends up there. All the specs for Steven Spielberg's movie *Munich* were sourced there, and nearly every shoot in *Pop* magazine features something from Arckiv. It's a great place. Considering the amount of time I spend in there, trying on enormous butterfly shades or frames last seen on Elton John when he had no hair and crocodile-rocked the house down, it's a shame I don't do accessories. It is one of my favourite ways to waste an afternoon.

'What else have you got?'

I lean in and light up a ciggie. Mimi really has been doing her homework. I am beginning to feel quite excited.

'OK,' she says. 'This is fan-fucking-tastic. You're going to love it.' She grins as she flaps out a long black dress for my approval. 'It's Ossie Clark.'

'Wow,' says Alexander.

'It's beautiful,' I say.

'I know,' she squeals. 'Relik.'

We all nod. Of course.

'I know it's not quite your thing but I thought it was such fun that if you don't want it I'm going to have it myself.'

It's a floor-length black dress with a fitted top, puffed sleeves and a plunge front. It looks very *Abigail's Party*, but at the same time it exudes sophistication. The navel-length plunge rescues it from the twee and makes it incredibly sexy.

'Do you think it works like that?' I ask Mimi.

She takes a drag of her fag and thinks. 'If we made it to the knee?'

'I think it might upset the balance,' I say, taking the dress and hanging it on the rail. 'How about if we lighten the material and take the weight out of the skirt?'

'Good idea,' she says.

'OK, OK, OK,' I say, feeling my palms growing clammy with excitement. 'What about this?'

I grab hold of my silhouette pad and start to draw. I steal the top half exactly, walking over to the rail to check the lines and the seams and the way the fabric has been cut. I alter the bottom half. I make the skirt slimmer and less diaphanous. Floor-length dresses are hard to wear these days. No-one really likes the sort of large cupcake effect they went for in the seventies – it's a bit too prim and proper. But give it a bit of a Roland Mouret, cut it well, slim the skirt down and brush it over the hips, let it skim the buttocks, and you have a red-carpet show-stopper.

'Not bad, not bad,' says Alexander, looking over my shoulder. 'I can see Cameron Diaz in that.'

'I've got shoes,' says Mimi, pulling out a pair of black geometric heels in suede with silver piping. 'Terri Havilland.'

'They're gorgeous and lovely.' I smile over the desk. 'But we don't do shoes.'

Not doing accessories is one of the nightmares for my brand. Bags and belts are a licence to print money. They are the holy grail of fashion, and they send your profits into the stratosphere. Of Louis Vuitton's £6.4 billion revenue last year, only 10 per cent was made up of ready-to-wear. The rest was accessories. If you get the right bag, an It bag, a hit bag, your label moves into a different league. The UK market is now worth £350 million; it has doubled in the last five years. Some 60 per cent of women own at least ten handbags, and a further 3 per cent own over twenty-five. And the mark-ups are fabulous. Even if your bags cost you about £80 to make, you can shift them for anything from £800 to £3,000 retail. More usually they are about £30 to manufacture, and they go for about £150 wholesale and between £450 and £500 retail. And the great thing about bags is they are properly mass market. Your size 16, 18, hell, 24, can all buy a bag at no extra cost to the designer.

Once your bag is so sought after that there's a waiting list, you can smile all the way to the bank. Buyers go crazy for them. I remember Matches had Chloé Paddington bag evenings where only the most loyal customer was allowed to purchase the bag under the counter, like some very special blend of fashion crack cocaine. It sold out worldwide without ever making it onto the shop floor. A couple of seasons ago, Luella Bartley managed to clean up with her Giselle handbag. Fendi has recently closed the waiting list on its £1,010 B Bag with new stock not expected until some time next year. The current must-have is the YSL muse bag, which I understand is still available in the shops. But sadly, we have never managed it. I have designed a couple of bags that we always send down the catwalk, but no-one ever seems prepared to kill someone else or go down on anyone in order to get their hands on them. They sit and gather dust in the sample cupboard and end up on the shelves of TK Maxx some twenty-four months later.

There is an art to handbag design, and I haven't got it. I have had long conversations with Alexander about trying to get a handbag designer to join the company, but they are hard to come by and they are some of the most expensive stars in the fashion transfer market. Perhaps one of the best and most talented is Stuart Vevers. Formerly at Louis Vuitton, helping to amass that £6.4 billion fortune, he went off to design Luella's hit Giselle bag, and has recently been made head of

Mulberry accessories and ready-to-wear. I rather wish Alexander and I had managed to lure him to us when he was thinking of moving on. But we don't exactly have very much to give. I suppose I would have given him shares in the company. We would've had to give quite a lot away to attract someone who is capable of making that much money for the company. I can't help but think that accessory designers are a little bit like the drummers in a rock band. They get all the money and none of the fame. The band couldn't function without them, but no-one knows who the hell they are. Sometimes that seems a rather enviable position.

If handbags are the holy grail, shoes are a little bit more problematic. At the end of the day, I think you have to have the perfect licensing deal for shoes to work for you. It costs over £7,000 to make a last, or shoe template, and even then you have to make the shoes in every size and colour from 36 to 41. You also have to have good distribution otherwise you end up with three pairs of shoes on a shelf, and that just looks sad. Whereas three handbags looks exclusive. And there is so much competition in the shoe market. What with Messrs Blahnik and Choo, the luxury shoe market is rather sewn up. I did think of going on a cordwainer's course when I came out of St Martin's, but quite frankly, unless we get bought out by Bernard Arnault I shall have to stick to customizing a few pairs of shoes with a splash of diamanté for most of my shows.

God, I think with a sigh as I look at Mimi's shoes, I dream of being bought out. It would change my life. It would be the perfect answer to all my problems.

'I know you don't do shoes,' says Mimi, holding up the fabulous pair of Havilland heels. 'I thought you might use them for the mood wall.'

'Good idea,' I say. 'I like them and I think we are all feeling black and silver and a bit geometric for this season.'

'We are,' agrees Mimi.

'We are?' queries Alexander. 'Look, actually, could you tell me about your ideas, because I just want to check we are all feeling the same woman for next season.'

I get up from behind my desk and go through the few ideas that are on the mood wall. Inspired by Mimi's Dior dress and the fantastic Ossie Clark silhouette, I explain to Alexander that it is about waists and ankles and sexy decorum, and he seems to be getting it. Although I'm keen to keep all the slim, slick shapes we've done before, I think we need to soften our look this season. The jackets will still be sharp and shaped but we'll add a bit of colour instead of just using black and white and the primaries. I warm to my theme and, because of all the tartan we have on order, we're going to be about northern nights full of stifled sex.

'Christ,' says Mimi. 'Rather like some sort of Scottish Hogmanay night in a castle where you all have to play sardines because there is shag all else to do?'

'Yeah,' agrees Alexander.

'Where you have loads and loads of buttons to undo,' adds Mimi, who has clearly been in this very scenario a few times before.

'Buttons I like,' I say. 'Buttons on sleeves, all the way down backs of dresses. All covered in tartan.'

'I love it,' declares Mimi. 'There is nothing sexier than a covered button.'

This may sound mad, but I have to say I kind of know what she means. This has been a productive afternoon. I am now feeling inspired. I am feeling that I might have the energy to get cracking. Fall is a really lovely collection to work on. It is all about textures and layers, and now covered buttons are on the agenda. I'm feeling really quite excited.

'Hiya, sorry to bother you,' says Trish as she lopes into the room. Her Sienna bob is looking a little greasy. 'Um, I have just had a call from *Elle* magazine.'

'Oh yes?' I say.

'And they are really keen to do a shoot with the white shirt that is in the collection?' Her voice is raised expectantly.

'What white shirt?' I ask.

'You know the one. Like here.' She points at a page in the look book that shows the flatulent model on the catwalk in a white shirt and shorts combination. 'But I can't find it downstairs at all.'

'Ah,' I say.

'Ah,' says Alexander.

123

Mimi starts to laugh.

'They want it for nine a.m. tomorrow,' says Trish.

'Shit,' I say. 'Isn't that the one we got from Marks and Spencer?'

7

Dorota, my head seamstress from Poland, stayed up all night to make the Marks and Spencer shirt. I frantically called her in and she arrived at about seven p.m. She finished about four in the morning and passed out on the sewing table as it was too late for her to get back to West Hampstead. I came in at eight and found her face down in some satin, her pincushion band still attached to the back of her wrist. She'd smoked two packets of Lambert cigarettes, and as far as I could work out she'd drunk three Red Bulls and two Diet Cokes and chewed her way through a family packet of wine gums. But she'd done it. The white shirt, all steamed and pressed, was swinging on a hanger in my office, smelling slightly of fags with an acrid afternote of body odour. But it was ready.

It wasn't the most difficult of jobs for Dorota to do – she's used to making clothes at short notice – but it was perhaps one of the least productive. I was tempted just to take the Marks label out and sew mine in. But the quality of fabric didn't feel quite up to scratch. If you are going to charge £350 for a shirt it has to feel a little bit more expensive than something you can pick up for £25 in Marble Arch. Even if the design is exactly the same.

Trish packed the shirt up with a whole lot of other stuff that *Elle* had called in. She layered it all in tissue, wrapped it in plastic, marked it all up in one of our large carrier bags, popped it all on a bike, and no-one, I hope, was any the wiser.

Two days later and I have just spent the morning in St Martin's library. Mimi's hunting and gathering exploits have inspired me into thinking Ossie Clark for the new collection. I have to say I have always liked his stuff. I loved the recent exhibition at the V&A, and I've had a postcard of the David Hockney painting of him and his wife and Percy the cat on my fridge at home for years. But, although I was familiar with his work, I hadn't really explored the coats he did for the French outfitters Mendes in the early seventies. Ossie was always known for his Celia Birtwell prints and for putting women in trousers, which was a taboo in the sixties. Amazingly, some of the major hotels still only admitted women in skirts to their receptions. If they only knew what went on in those five-star establishments these days, those uptight concierges would turn in their graves.

Anyway, I found the coats in the library, and they

were stunning. Their amazing pleats and sharp sleeves with buttons all up the cuffs were truly inspiring, and just what I was after. I sat down among the sweaty, starving students to trawl through the images and sketched for a couple of hours. I was interrupted by a few passing students who wanted to talk about their collections and ask for advice, but mostly it was a very productive morning.

I have to say, despite the library, I find it kind of hard going back to St Martin's sometimes. It reminds me what a hideous time I had there. None of the tutors particularly liked me. I wasn't trendy enough, I was a bit too middle class, and let's be honest, my work wasn't weird enough for them. I also didn't have the Stella McCartney connections. There were no supermodels at my graduate show. Unlike Lee McQueen, there was no Izzy Blow declaring my genius. It really pisses people off that I now have a turnover of £2 million. The fact that very little of that is profit is never mentioned in the press. But it does make a few of the bastards who wrote me off right at the beginning a little short when I see them.

You'd be surprised how many grudges, feuds and future hatreds are born at St Martin's – some of them famous, others less so. I only wish I hadn't wasted so much of my time in love with a man who was prepared to change his sexuality in order to get ahead. There is a saying that if you aren't gay before you go to St Martin's, you are when you leave, and Ted Nicholls is a case in point. Maybe he did always bat for the other team. But I saw little evidence of that when we were going out. Hell, he didn't even have a moisturizer in his bathroom cabinet. These days, however, he is coiffed and groomed like the best of them. I wouldn't have minded if he'd actually told me first. That he had seen the light, that he had always known he was gay, that he'd had some sign, that he'd remembered as a child covering his cricket stumps in silver foil and making them into wands. He could have said he loved me and that he was sorry. Instead he just tipped up, wrapped around the waist of star pupil Jeff Arseface, who went on to work for Givenchy, have his own label, and thankfully go bust within eighteen months. They flaunted it, showing off and snogging in public all the time. All anyone ever did after that was look at me with pity in their eyes and think that I must be totally shit in bed. I was the woman who turned men gay. No-one wanted to go out with me after that.

Despite my mixed feelings about St Martin's, I walk back to the office feeling invigorated and inspired. Trish is on reception, reading *Closer* magazine and eating Green & Black organic chocolate biscuits. Quite how she can afford them on the wages we pay I don't know.

'All right?' she says as I walk in.

I am clearly not commanding enough respect in my establishment. When Karl Lagerfeld enters the Chanel building there are a list of people who are called in advance by the girl on reception just to warn them that

'Monsieur Karl est arrivé'. And all I get is a sniff and a mumble over the top of *Closer* magazine.

'Any messages?' I ask, in an effort to engage.

'Oh, right,' she says, taking her Lanvin flats off the desk. Where did she steal those? She sifts through loads of pink Post-its that are stuck to various surfaces. 'Well, Damiano called. I'm not sure if it was for you or Alex.'

'Ander,' I add.

'What?' she says.

'Alexander,' I repeat. 'He doesn't respond to Alex.'

'Yeah, right, course,' she says. 'Um, Lydia says she's in town if you want to meet?'

'OK.'

'And Kathy Harvey is upstairs with that girl Robbie Williams fancies?'

'Oh shit, right,' I say, suddenly realizing I am over half an hour late for this meeting. 'Can you hold all my calls?'

'Sure,' she says.

'And can you bring me up a latte?'

'Yeah. Only thing is, I don't have any money.'

'Isn't there some in petty cash?'

'Not the last time I looked.'

'Oh, don't bother,' I mumble on my way up the stairs. I must get myself another bloody assistant.

I walk into my office to find Kathy Harvey going through my designs, which are stuck up in a line opposite the mood wall. Loud, clever, powerful, with a thick Essex accent and full of gossip, Kathy Harvey is in her early fifties and leaves little to the imagination. All highlights and cleavage, she has it all racked up and laid out on a platter like an all-you-can-eat buffet. A PR who specializes in celebrities, she knows everyone who is everyone and has been in the business for over twenty years. I have known her for five years, and we seem to have packed rather a lot into that short time. We have danced in Regines in Paris, run topless down the Fontanka in St Petersburg, and been thrown off a yacht in Cannes. She has a fondness for tequila and a penchant for older men with plenty of money. I like her very much, although there are times when I admit I am a little afraid.

'There you are,' she says, flicking fag ash on my floor. 'Like the look of the new collection. It looks very sexy. This dress is great.' She points to the Ossie Clark rip-off with the plunge neck and puffed sleeves that is flapping on the wall. 'It would suit Vanessa here down to the ground.'

I turn and look around the door to see a stunning dark-haired urchin of a girl sitting in the armchair. With delicate sharp features, long, elegant eyebrows and an impishly short haircut, she is striking and reasonably familiar-looking.

'This is Vanessa Tate,' says Kathy. 'Only the hottest new star in town.'

'Hi,' I say.

'Hello,' she says, getting out of the chair. Dressed in a tight-fitting black calf-length skirt and black V sweater, she is a sweet, sexy ingénue with a touch of Bardot styling.

'Vanessa has a huge film coming out in ten days with Joaquin Phoenix and George Clooney, and we were wondering if you wanted to make the dress,' says Kathy, her red mouth puckered up around her cigarette. 'World première in London. It's going to be huge. Trust me.' She smiles. 'I'm in PR.'

'What's it called?'

'It's *War and Peace*,' she says, looking slightly shocked that I have to ask. 'Fortunately it is more Peace than War, and Vanessa plays Natasha.'

'Right.' I smile. 'I'm presuming that's the lead.'

'That's right,' says Vanessa. 'It's my first big part.'

'You've done a couple of *Midsomer Murders*,' insists Kathy.

'Hasn't everyone?' she replies.

'Anyway,' says Kathy, 'she is going to be huge. There's a whiff of the Oscars about it.'

'You really do do PR,' I say with a laugh. Vanessa looks offended. 'Although I'm sure it is good.'

Kathy smiles weakly. 'You'd better believe it. It's *The English Patient* all over again.'

'Sounds fantastic,' I say.

'Anyway,' says Kathy, 'I like the look of this.' She waves her short, bloated fingers in the direction of the puffed-sleeved plunge dress.

'I think it looks fabulous,' says Vanessa, who I have to say has a figure to die for. Long legs with a flat stomach and a small bosom – exactly the sort of girl you would want in your clothes. Although I'm not entirely sure I want to waste this design on an unknown like her.

There are really only about ten women in the world who can actually shift frocks: Nicole Kidman, Gwyneth Paltrow, Madonna, Kate Moss, Cameron Diaz, Sarah Jessica Parker, Sienna Miller, Uma Thurman, Scarlett Johansson and then, in a league of her own, Paris Hilton. Because of the amount of free press she generates, it is always worth shoving a few things on her back. There are a few, like Kylie Minogue, Chloé Sevigny and Gwen Stefani, who speak to the trendy end of the market, and there are also plenty of ingénues like Mischa Barton, Kirsten Dunst and Reese Witherspoon who get the odd front cover or two and who can help your campaign along. Then there are the pap fodder girls, like the Olsen twins, Nicole Richie and Lindsey Lohan, who have gone a bit more upmarket recently. Everyone else likes to think that they can sell dresses, but they probably can't. The likes of Rachel Weisz and Keira Knightley might be spotted wearing the Roland Mouret Galaxy dress, but they are trend helpers rather than starters.

The first brand to fully understand the power of celebrity was Versace. Back in the eighties they were the first catwalk show to use all five supermodels – Christie, Naomi, Claudia, Linda and Cindy – at the same time. They were also the first brand to hand out clothes for free. Now everyone does it, except for Prada. Anyone who is seen photographed in Prada has paid for it. Miuccia, as a good communist, does not worship at the altar of fame. One designer was so keen for Madonna to be seen in her clothes that during the singer's latest tour of the States she was said to have left a rack of clothes in every single hotel Madge stayed in. Only thing was, they were a nightmare to pack up and take with her. What's a girl to do if she is playing twenty-eight dates? As a result, Madonna left the racks behind every time, leaving the clothes to the maids. Which I'm sure was not quite the sort of image the designer was going for.

So, is Vanessa Tate the sort of girl who is going to shift my dress? She is certainly pretty enough. But is the film good enough? Will it be a hit? I have seen her face around town a bit recently; she has been turning up at all the right parties, dressed in all the right kit. However, she is not yet an It girl, or a trendsetter; if she were, she would probably be going to a bigger, better-known designer than I. Kathy and I could well be mutually scratching backs.

Vanessa wanders over to the mood wall and starts stroking the swatches and checking out the handbag tears.

'Listen,' says Kathy, leaning over and whispering in my ear. 'I know she's not that well known yet, but the film is fucking good. She is stunning in it, and she is already being seeded by some cool brands.'

Seeding is one of the more profligate pastimes of the big-label brands. Each of their enormous PR departments is given a budget with which to give product away for free. Seeding budgets can be enormous, and the results are rather intangible to say the least. Each PR has a list of about a hundred famous people to whom they give, say, a free handbag, in the hope that they will be photographed holding it. If one person out of the hundred is photographed with the bag, this is considered to be a hit. It's not exactly a very cost-effective way of getting publicity, but when your revenue is £6.4 billion a year, I suspect you don't mind that much.

The lists obviously differ from product to product. Joss Stone gets seeded by teen brands, whereas someone like Cat Deeley gets seeded by more grown-up brands like Celine and Fendi. Style makers, like stylist Bay Garnett, get Chanel. Madonna doesn't get handbags because she rarely carries one. Sienna Miller gets seeded by nearly everyone. In fact, the girl gets something like twenty-six handbags a month, and they are worth between £2,000 and £30,000 each. An estate car comes to her house every week loaded down with dresses, bags, coats, hats, make-up, body products and, more weirdly, candles. Gwyneth Paltrow can't cope with all the stuff she gets sent. She often has parties at her house where she invites all her mates over to go through the piles of freebies on the instruction that they can take what they want. And if Gwyneth and Sienna are inundated, just think how much stuff trend diva Kate Moss gets sent. Her agent, Sarah Doukas at Storm, must be guarding the gateway to fashion's most fabulous treasure trove. There is no way on earth that Kate, or indeed Sarah, could wear all that stuff. But I have to say, nothing drives a seeder more crazy than seeing a mother, or a sister, with the £10,000 crocodile bag. Someone who only makes the list by the skin of their teeth could get themselves struck off for a faux pas like that. It doesn't do to hurt a seeder's feelings.

There is also social as well as celebrity seeding. On a different list from actresses, supermodels and stylists, there is a sort of lunching ladies set – Tara Palmer Tomkinson, Laura Bailey, Yasmin Mills, Donna Air. They are each given the £500–£800 handbag in the hope that they have it hanging around their necks when they are papped coming out of San Lorenzo.

The nature of the paparazzi shot affects what is actually seeded. There is very little point in seeding shoes because the photos are normally cropped around the waist. Necklaces are more useful than bracelets, which is why every girl worth her gown at the Oscars has something huge and expensive around her neck, rather than her wrist. Hats and earrings do well. They usually don't seed something useful like a smart black jumper or a white shirt. It will be some sort of eye-catching piece, like a pom-pom cardigan. Or a yellow mac.

When you think that Sienna Miller has been snapped

over 800 times carrying her Balenciaga handbag, and there are something like 600,000 fashion hits using her name on the web each day, you can sort of see the point of it all. It's just that the big brands have to back a few other loss leaders on the way. Oddly, celebrity endorsement is worth more than model endorsement. It is something like thirty to forty times more effective for Cameron Diaz to be pictured in a dress than for either Elle or Naomi to be wearing it. The public perception is that the model has been asked to wear it, whereas the actress has chosen it.

I find it a fascinating part of fashion marketing. Even though we can't afford to do it. Weirdly, it has to be said that overseeding can be just as damaging to a brand as not seeding at all. If every two-bit celebrity can get their hands on the latest It bag, then it loses its cachet. Spot ex-*Big Brother* contestants Jade Goody or Makosi with a Chloé Paddington bag and it instantly loses its appeal. You'd suddenly find that the Kates and Gwyneths of this world start to leave theirs at home. Worse still, you'd see their nannies using them around Tesco.

Fortunately, Vanessa Tate looks nothing like Jade Goody, and I do sort of trust Kathy's instinct on this. She would not be wasting my time with Vanessa if she didn't think something mutually beneficial could come of it. She wants to break a new star as fabulously as she can, otherwise it doesn't reflect well on her and her PR skills. And I want someone to give good red carpet in what I hope will be my show-stopping dress.

I take the sketch off the wall and lay it flat on the desk.

'What colour were you thinking?' I ask.

'Gosh,' says Vanessa, 'I'm not sure.'

'You're dark so you would suit most things,' I say. 'Blondes are more difficult. Red always makes them look like Princess Diana.'

'Yeah,' says Kathy, laughing and flicking her ash into my coffee cup. 'How does it go around the back?'

'What?' I say, looking at the design.

'The back?'

'Oh,' I say. 'Um . . .'

'Actually,' says Kathy, walking closer to the row of sketches, 'none of these designs has a back.'

'They don't?' I say, knowing that she is right. 'I know they don't,' I lie, trying to recover my composure. 'We always do this when designing a collection. When you're working fast, you don't want to be held up.'

If I were Pinocchio, my nose would be right through the door by now. Truth is, I've forgotten them. Backs are so bloody boring to sketch they are often the last thing a designer gets around to doing. But to forget them entirely is a little bit more than an oversight. I remember howling with laughter when a mate of mine once told me a story about Rifat Ozbek showing his collection to the late Leigh Bowery, and Leigh asking him where the backs were and Rifat realizing that he had forgotten them all. And now I have done the same.

I have to say I've been so interested in the plunge-and-puff combination I actually haven't thought about what it would look like from the other side. I mean, who cares if the front is working so well?

Sometimes, and I have to admit I have done this a couple of times myself, designers get so carried away with the intricacies of the front that they end up with a dress for which it is actually impossible to have a back. And that's when you thank God for pattern cutters. They are usually the ones to point out that a dress is unwearable or unmakeable. The straps don't work. You can't keep it up at all. The back will fall open. The thing will fall off in the car before it gets anywhere near the red carpet. You'd have thought that years at college would have made us understand that you can't design clothes like a child just because they are pretty, that someone does have to wear them, a body has to be able to fit inside them at some point. But it doesn't stop us from trying. Pattern cutters try as hard as they can to come up with a solution – adding an extra strap here, an invisible bodice there. But sometimes you have drawn something that is unsalvageable, and it has to go into the bin.

'So, how do you think this back might go?' asks Vanessa.

'Well,' I say, thinking on my feet. 'If you are showing a lot at the front it usually follows that you cover the back.'

'OK,' she says. 'Because it is quite exposing.'

'Exposing is good,' says Kathy. 'It gets you column inches.'

'But are they column inches you want?' I ask. 'We can all show our arses like Kelly Brook in Julien Macdonald, but has that helped her Hollywood career?'

'We could plunge the back as well,' suggests Kathy.

'If you want a Julien Macdonald, you should go to him,' I say, a little annoyed that she could presume to know my job. 'Or Cavalli. I just don't do the bling-bling kind of stuff.'

'No, you're right,' says Kathy. 'Who wants to look like a desperado out of *Big Brother*?'

'Or Victoria Beckham,' says Vanessa.

'Oh God, yes,' says Kathy, curling her nose.

'So, plunge front and demure back,' I say.

Vanessa nods. 'Sounds fantastic.'

'I am also going to suggest a dark purple. This is for next Fall, and you are going to wear it this Fall, so it has to be a colour that works for both of us.'

'I love purple,' she says.

'I might put something shiny on it,' I add. 'But we can discuss that later.'

'Great,' says Vanessa.

'Sounds perfect,' agrees Kathy. 'Obviously no-one else is going to wear the dress before Vanessa?'

'No,' I reply.

'Shall we put that in writing?' Kathy asks.

'Don't be silly.' I smile. 'The première is in ten days'

time. How am I going to get it on the back of someone between now and then?'

'Just checking,' she says. 'It's my job to check.'

'Sure. Course it is.'

'Do you want to come to the première? I think you should. Be photographed with the dress?'

'Hmm.'

I'm not actually sure if I fancy that. I have to say that red carpets don't make my heart beat faster and my adrenalin run. I hate them. They make me feel sick. I don't like it when they shout my name – or don't, as the case may be. The most-photographed designer around at the moment is probably Stella, then McQueen, then Matthew Williamson, but the rest of us don't really milk it that much. No-one stands in the press pen shouting at Burberry's Christopher Bailey, or at Azzedine Alaia, or indeed at Roland Mouret. Vivienne Westwood still pops a few bulbs. Patrick Cox works it for all it's worth, wrapped around the waist of Liz Hurley. But for the most part I like to stay under wraps.

'I think I might send Alexander,' I say. 'He loves that sort of thing.'

'Think about it,' says Kathy. Her mobile is ringing and she has already moved on. 'Sorry,' she mouths. 'It's the *Sun* . . . Whatever it is, the answer's no comment . . . What? With a dominatrix? Are you sure? But he's happily married . . .'

She has one finger in her ear and is pacing around my office. Vanessa smiles and makes a move to leave.

'When can you come in to be measured?' I ask, looking at my diary containing endless fabric meetings.

I am now rather regretting saying that I would make this dress. I'm also still worried that I am wasting my best design and possible It dress on an unknown. It means I can't get it on the back of someone for the Golden Globes, the BAFTAs or the Oscars. It will have been used and tarnished, and no-one wants to go second. Then again, I can't see a line of potentially nominated actresses queuing up Berwick Street, and with the reviews I've had for this season it's not that likely.

'Tomorrow,' she says.

'Tomorrow?' Tomorrow is packed with meetings with agents from the rag trade.

Alexander and I have to see about 200 fabric dealers in all, calling with samples for the next collection. We did choose a few at Première Vision, including the pink-shot Black Watch, but we still have a hell of a lot more to select. We need jersey for skirts, cotton for shirts, and I am hankering after a strawberry pink silk to line the tartan coats I'm feeling. If I am going to run with the Scottish house party idea I need some really opulent fabrics with a touch of decadence to them. Alexander and I book these meetings back to back in order to get them over with. It is hard to concentrate, because after a while one silk jersey seems very much like another. I have to force myself to stay alert. The constant supply of lattes helps. We look at swatch after swatch. I have the designs in mind when I am choosing. Sometimes a design changes because of a fantastic fabric I have seen, but most of the time I am matching designs to swatches and not the other way around. Once we have chosen something, if it is memorable in some way, and not just a white cotton, we ask for exclusivity. For a small outfit like ours it is extremely important that the rose print we have chosen for our shirts doesn't find its way onto waistcoats at Marks and Spencer. Most of the time, depending on the size of the order, they agree.

'I can only do eight a.m.,' I say.

'That's fine,' says Vanessa.

'Bring a thong and heels.'

'Sorry?' she says, looking a little surprised. 'A thong and heels,' she repeats, standing on the landing, pulling on her fitted coat. She glances towards Alexander's office.

'Don't mind me,' he shouts from his desk. 'I'm totally and utterly gay.'

8

I have spent the last ten days with Vanessa Tate's breasts in my hands. I've had my nose in her armpit, my head up her crotch, and I've smelt her morning breath so many times it's almost as if we've been lovers for the past week. Making a red-carpet dress for someone is an extremely intimate experience and, due to my rag trade meetings, most of Vanessa's fittings have been in the early morning, before either of us has truly managed to find our day faces and wash the night's sleep away. At the end of all this I can truly say that I know the girl. And unlike a few celebs I have dressed in the past, she was lovely, and the dress I made was bloody fantastic.

Last night, when I went to her house in West London and did the finishing tweaks and touches, it looked so stunning, I almost cried. In the end we went for a dark purple silk chiffon. It was a nightmare to sew. Dorota nearly walked out halfway through because the material had 'a life of its bloody own'. It kept on slipping and was incredibly unforgiving to stitch. But she finished with three days to spare. So I called in this fantastic beader I know near Mile End to decorate the bodice of the dress. It is slow, intricate work, and usually costs a fortune. But I have known Anna Maria, an Italian café owner in her late sixties, ever since I moved to London about fifteen years ago, and she gave me a good deal. Her husband died almost twenty years ago and she runs the café by day and beads by night. She loves it, and says that it gives her something to do during the long evenings on her own. The result was a work of art. It clung in all the right places and flowed in others. It was glamorous and demure, sexy and chic, the closest I have come to haute couture. There was nothing ready-to-wear about this dress; it fitted like a glove and shimmered so beautifully I found it hard to contain myself. I was almost tempted to go to the première just to hear people's reactions. But Alexander went instead.

It's 9.30 a.m. I am sitting at my desk in the studio waiting for him to come in. His mobile is off, so it must have been a good night. I have a pile of newspapers on my desk, and Vanessa and the dress are on the front of almost every one. The *Mirror*, the *Mail*, the *Express*, *The Times*, they all have a shot. The *Telegraph* has run the photograph over nearly a whole half page. Vanessa is beaming out, radiating star quality. Her neat short dark hair and her white skin contrast with the luxuriant dark purple of the dress. She looks amazing. The dress looks amazing. I am so excited. I have never had such front-page reaction to something I have made before. She has even managed to eclipse George Clooney, which, bearing in mind how much the press love him here, is really saying something.

The front door bangs downstairs. I hear the slapping of expensive leather-soled shoes on the stairs. Alexander has arrived.

'You up there?' he shouts.

'Yeah,' I shout back.

'Jesus Christ,' he shouts, 'your bloody dress went down a storm. You won't believe the reaction. It stole the night. Vanessa stole the night. It was un-fucking-believable. It was fan-fucking-tastic. She looked incredible.'

He arrives at the door. His face is white and clammy-looking. His eyes are red. He is out of breath and sweating old alcohol and coke. It also looks like he's developing a rather large zit on his chin from all that jazz. It was a good night.

'How are you?' I ask.

'Shit,' he says. 'I feel like a parrot has crapped in my mouth. But that doesn't matter.' He grins. 'Have you seen the papers?'

'I know.' I smile.

'Fucking great,' he says, flopping down in the armchair. 'It went down like a whore's knickers.'

'Is that good?'

'Oh yeah,' he says. 'Kathy was grinning from ear to

ear all bloody night. She was so pleased with herself. She got plastered and kept slurring, "Your partner's a genius," in my ear.'

'So she's pleased?'

'She's over the fucking moon.'

'Really?'

'You know she is.'

'It is always nice to hear,' I say.

'It was a hit, and your name is everywhere.'

'I know. I can't believe they gave me a credit.'

'It's great.' Alexander sighs back into the chair.

'Good night?'

'Not bad,' he says. 'I got to chat to George Clooney.'

'You did?'

'Bet you wish you'd gone now.' He smiles.

'I do actually. What's he like?'

'Well, you know how every Hollywood movie star you've ever met is shorter than you thought, uglier than you thought, and usually a bit of a cunt?'

'Yeah.'

'Well, he is the only one who isn't. He is just as charming as you would have hoped. He is just as handsome and just as entertaining. You see, I have this theory.' He coughs, snorts the phlegm and swallows it. It is one of his most disgusting habits. 'The year you become famous is the year you stop growing as a person. Like, Michael Jackson became famous at five or something, which is why he is permanently five. He wants to play children's games, hang out with kids, build a bloody fun fair in his backyard and eat sweeties. Robbie Williams was sixteen, which is why he is always shagging girls and behaving like a teenager. George, on the other hand, was nearly forty, which is why he is such a delightful, well-rounded individual.'

'Interesting,' I say.

'So on those grounds Vanessa Tate will be permanently twenty-four,' he adds. 'Last night was the night when she became famous, and it was entirely due to you.'

'That's not exactly true,' I say.

'You'll be able to milk it tonight.'

'Oh God.' My heart sinks and my face falls into my hands. 'I'd put that out of my head.'

'What are you wearing?'

'I don't know, something I've made.'

'Obviously.' He smiles.

'What have we been nominated for?' I ask, picking up my pen and drawing devil horns and a moustache on the template model on my pad.

'Best . . . um, I'm not sure,' says Alexander. 'Best Designer?'

'No, I'd remember that.'

'Red Carpet?'

'No.'

'Let me go and have a look,' says Alexander, peeling himself out of the chair. 'Actually, I don't feel like going. Do you?'

'I can't bear the idea,' I reply.

The British Fashion Awards are perhaps the least exciting night out in a fashionista's calendar. There is plenty of champagne, wine and rubberized chicken but very little glamour. Unlike the Council of Fashion Designers of America Awards held in June in New York, which can boast a calibre of guest to rival the Oscars – Renee Zellweger, Sarah Jessica Parker, Nicole Kidman and Lauren Bacall rub shoulders with Tom Ford, Miuccia Prada, Ralph Lauren, Diane Von Furstenberg, Michael Kors, Anna Wintour and the rest of the US fashion industry – we can only get together one designer and a few buyers from Next. It really is a poor show. Sponsored by a champagne company and underwritten by someone like Harrods, it is usually held at the V&A. It is the sort of event you only go to if you are nominated, and even then only if you are fairly sure you are going to win. It is supposed to be full of the great and the good of the fashion industry, but at £185 a ticket, sadly only Top Shop can afford to snap up thirty at a time.

This year some actress I have never heard of is hosting the event, and I know that Suzy Menkes is getting some sort of lifetime achievement award. I imagine Roland will pick up Best Red Carpet, we'll get to watch a couple of crap runway shows, and the rest of us will sip our wine and bitch about the people on the next-door table.

'You're up for Red Carpet,' says Alexander, walking back into the office, looking at the invitation.

'Am I really?'

'Apparently so,' he says.

'How very strange. I only did about three dresses for the red carpet last year and none of them was very memorable.'

'Perhaps they've put you down to keep up the numbers,' he suggests.

'So lovely to have your support,' I say. 'So, do we have a table?'

'No,' he says. 'We have three tickets.'

'So that's you, me and . . . ?'

'Well . . . ?'

'Isn't Lydia around?'

'She's presenting an award and is, I think, sitting with McQueen, who is also presenting an award.'

'Oh,' I say.

'There's always Damiano.'

'Oh God, do we have to?'

'Well, he will come at short notice.'

'That's true.'

'Nick's going already, with his lot from work.'

'Go on then,' I find myself saying. To be honest, my evening can't get much worse.

Alexander goes next door to give Damiano the good news and I sit back in my seat and admire my front pages. Perhaps I should frame the *Telegraph*? I have quite a few magazine shots in frames downstairs but nothing quite this large and flashy. They are mostly pages from *Vogue* or *Elle* where they have teamed something of mine with someone else's clobber. This time it's entirely me and my name they have credited in the picture caption. I should call my mum. This is the sort of thing she can relate to.

I am just about to pick up the phone when Trish ambles into my office with a bunch of flowers.

'These just came,' she says, shoving them out in front of her like a pissed-off bridesmaid. 'Aren't they amazing?'

They are indeed. They are black wax roses, perhaps the most revolting flowers I have ever seen. Someone has actually taken a perfectly normal and very beautiful bunch of roses and dipped them in black wax so that they are stiff and totally scentless. They bring a whole new meaning to gilding the lily.

'Jesus,' I say.

'Aren't they ma-jor?' says Trish, moving in to smell them. 'There's a card from Kathy.'

'Of course.' I smile. Only Kathy could source something that unpleasant. 'I'd better give her a call.'

'Oh, before you do,' says Trish, 'I've been getting calls from people wanting to buy the dress in the papers today.'

'You have?'

'Yeah. About twenty so far this morning.'

'But it hasn't even gone down the runway.'

'I know.' She shrugs. 'And when it does, it will be old hat.'

'It's all moving so fast these days. People want

everything now, they don't want to wait.'

'Yeah,' sniffs Trish. 'Don't worry, it'll inspire a Top Shop collection before you can get it into the show anyway.'

'Don't say that.'

'What do you want me to do with the calls?'

'Take their names and numbers and put them all on a waiting list.'

'OK,' she says. 'Just so you know,' she adds as she turns to go down the stairs, 'they all want it in the purple.'

'Of course they do,' I say, suddenly feeling very depressed.

My mood hasn't improved by the time I'm walking down the sodden reddish carpet on my way into the British Fashion Awards. I have squeezed myself into a black silk knee-length dress that I found on the sample rail downstairs. I'm not normally a size 10, but fortunately this A-line dress only has a sash around the bust so it can more or less fit any size. My hair is pulled back into a ponytail. I am not one to waste a blow dry on this piss elegant event. Alexander and Damiano walk up beside me, working the photographers like a couple of tarts fresh from *Big Brother* success. Alexander throws shapes left and right, trying to give the press what they want, and Damiano sticks close to Alexander and occasionally puts his tongue in his ear. I don't know who they think they are appealing to. They won't even make the round-up in the *Draper's Record*.

Inside, the noise is amazing. There is the loud trilling of models and the nasal drawl of bitching queens. There is some loud dance music playing over the speakers, and the sweet smell of alcohol and perfume hangs in the air. Alexander and Damiano head straight for the large champagne flutes.

'Let's neck these,' says Damiano with all the sophistication of a wino.

Alexander is a little more circumspect and looks around the room, holding out for a vodka. He knows that he and bubbles don't mix terribly well. Finding nothing resembling a Sea Breeze, he grabs at a passing glass of champagne instead.

'Oh look,' he says over the rim of his flute. 'There's McQueen.'

'Where?' asks Damiano, his head spinning around, surfing the room for celebrity.

'Don't look,' says Alexander, 'but he is walking right behind you.'

'Shit!' says Damiano as he paris-turns. 'What the fuck's happened to him? He's lost so much weight!'

'Lipo,' whispers Alexander. 'I thought everyone knew that?'

'Liposuction!' declares Damiano. 'Well I fucking never.'

The two of them stand and stare as the new slimline McQueen walks by. Both their mouths are slightly ajar as they scan every inch of the man.

'Not bad,' they both say at the same time.

'How much do you think it costs?' asks Damiano.

'A couple of grand a pop?'

'I think it's worth it.'

'I know.'

'He looks so much better.'

'Mmm,' they both agree.

I stand nursing my glass of champagne, catching the eye of various fashionistas and exchanging stiff smiles.

'Great dress in the papers today,' says someone as they squeeze past, tapping me on the back.

'Thanks,' I reply.

Alex Shulman, the editor of UK *Vogue*, swans by. Damiano steps forward and tries to say hello but the woman looks so stony-faced that he swallows his smile and shoves his face straight into his champagne glass. Alexander spots the make-up artist Charlotte Tilbury and announces that he is going over to try to persuade her to do our next show. She is up for Best Fashion Creator and is one of the best in the world so I don't really fancy his chances. Will Young walks past, and it is all that Damiano can do to stop himself from screaming.

'He touched me,' he whispers loudly in my ear, spitting over my cheek. 'He fucking touched me.' He downs another glass of champagne to celebrate.

'Hello, sluts!' shouts a familiar voice while someone grabs me from behind and plants a fragrant kiss on my cheek. 'How are you lot?'

I turn around to see Lydia looking stunning in a

golden brocade dress by Burberry Prorsum. Her long blonde hair is messy and curled and sexily dishevelled. Her heels are stratospheric. The effect is that of some golden Amazonian goddess.

'You look great,' I say.

'Bollocks I do,' she says. 'I put this lot on in the back of a cab. I came straight from a shoot where some bastard fucked my hair up so much I just had to shake it out and splash water all over it to get it out of this shit beehive thing he'd done. I've got so much product in it I could hang wallpaper. Anyway, what are you up for?'

'Red Carpet,' I say.

'Oh,' she says, looking over my shoulder. 'Do you think you'll get it?'

'Shouldn't think so.'

'Right,' she says. 'Oh look, there's Lisa!' She waves. Her Chanel bracelet rattles next to my ear. 'I like Lisa,' she says to me. 'Quite a laugh. Although I heard a thing about her the other day. She was given this free dress by this designer mate of mine because she had done his show, and then six months later she tried to send it back, complaining that she didn't like it. After she's worn it a few times I'm sure. Quite cheeky, don't you think?'

'Any big names here?' asks Damiano.

'Fuck off,' says Lydia. 'I'm only here because I've been paid.'

'Oh,' he says, looking disappointed.

'Heard *such* a good story this week,' she says. 'A model apparently went to stay at this country house hotel and walked out without paying.'

'Really?' I say.

'Yeah. So the hotel rings up her assistant and says that this girl's left without paying. The assistant says she'll call her back. She calls back and says that the model says she wasn't there. The manager laughs and says sorry but I checked her in myself and I showed her to the room. She had quite a good weekend, if you know what I mean. The assistant says I'll call you back. She calls back and says the model says she'll pay half. Isn't that hilarious?' Lydia starts to laugh. 'It's always the richest ones who want something for nothing. Honestly, it's like dealing with a child.'

'How are you?' I ask.

'Oh, OK. I'm presenting an award tonight, Best Shop or something.'

'Are you sitting with McQueen?' asks Damiano.

'Think so.'

'Have you seen how thin he is?'

'Has he been at the lipo again?' she asks.

'Looks like it.'

'That's hilarious.' She grins. 'He does it every two months or so. Has the whole lot sucked out. What is it with male designers and their weight? Have you seen Lagerfeld recently? He's lost so much weight all his skin must be loose. I bet the reason he wears those extra-high collars on his shirts is so you can't see the flesh on his neck. I was so shocked when I went to Chanel for a fitting in Paris. Weird. Oh look, there's Liberty Ross. Isn't she gorgeous?'

Liberty Ross is indeed looking gorgeous. Dressed in a floor-length blue satin shoestring strap dress, she is one of those effortlessly chic aristo models in which we seem to specialize in the UK. We have an endlessly stunning line of women who don't really choose modelling, modelling chooses them – Stella Tennant, Iris Palmer, Sophie Dahl, Jacquetta Wheeler, Liberty, and the new face on the block, Rosie Huntington-Whitley. Russia and Eastern Europe turn up loads of lean, lovely, anonymous catwalk fodder, but over here we appear to produce the household names. And unlike the Americans and the Australians, none of them seems to work too hard. While Elle and Cindy churn out fitness videos, Kate and Naomi go out nightclubbing. While Claudia sips her wine and mixes it with two parts mineral water, Sophie stays up till dawn. Although Lydia did once tell me that she heard Kate ordering an artichoke for dinner and contemplating stomach crunches to fit into a catsuit – she says she found it kind of heartening. But on the whole, the Brits don't have to work at it. Which is why they can be rather badly behaved.

Liberty walks past with Saffron Aldridge, stopping to say hello to Karen Elson with her trademark red hair in a pale yellow dress. I see Suzy Menkes in the corner, her hair curled at the front, dressed in a golden Burberry

Prorsum coat. I smile and try to catch her eye but she is deep in conversation with McQueen. Alexander comes up and mutters something about 'Tilly darling' saying no to the show. He adds that dinner is served so we all move through to eat.

I am sat between Alexander and a round man with white hair. An expansive flower arrangement blocks my view of the catwalk. Erin O'Connor, dressed in a red high-neck Russian-looking number, walks towards our table in search of her seat. I engage her with a smile and hope that she is joining us. I have worked with her a few times and have always found her charming. The sort of girl who'll iron her own outfit if you're a bit short-staffed, which we always are. But she doesn't see me. And I'm not in the mood to shout and wave and make a tit of myself.

'You up for anything?' asks the round man.

'Best Red Carpet.' I smile, taking a sip of an enormous birdbath-size glass of wine.

'Had any rehearsal time?' he asks. 'Did they get you in early to walk through the show? Tell you which model's in your stuff?'

'No,' I reply.

'Then you haven't won,' he says.

'Oh,' I say.

Even though I knew that already, I can't help but feel deflated. Of course Roland has won. I couldn't possibly eclipse his moment. His Galaxy dress has been on everyone who is anyone going down the red carpet.

Christ, even Carol Vorderman's squeezed into a Mouret. But to hear it straight out like that is a little disconcerting.

'Well, I thought as much,' I manage to say.

'I've worked on the show here many a time,' he sniffs, tearing his bread in half. 'And if you haven't rehearsed, you haven't won.'

'OK,' I say.

'I remember telling Vivienne Westwood that a few years back so that she didn't have to sit through the dinner. She was quite grateful.'

'So, what have you done for the shows?' I ask, trying to steer the conversation away from my failure.

'Got the models ready, that sort of thing.'

'Oh, right. Anyone nice?'

'Not really,' he says. 'I remember giving that Linda Evangelista her clothes. I gave her a corset and she said, "Linda likes that." I gave her a pair of huge heels and she said, "Linda likes that." You know, talking in the third person about herself. I gave her a pair of shorts and she said, "Linda doesn't like that. Linda doesn't do shorts because no-one knows that Linda's got cellulite."'

'She sounds fun,' I say.

'Yeah,' he says, tucking into his non-specific awards ceremony starter. 'A mate of mine got whacked by a model at these awards. He gave her some Westwood shoes to wear and asked her if she needed to practise in them as they were quite tricky to walk in. She told him to piss off and that she was a professional. Anyway, just as she was about to go on she realized the error of her ways. She couldn't move. Sarah Stockbridge flew down the runway ahead of her in the shoes like she was on air, and he said, "That's how you do it." She goes out, takes three steps, and comes straight back. He says, "Call yourself a professional?" She tells him where to go and slaps him across the face.'

Roland Mouret walks up to the table and starts to talk to someone across from me.

Alexander digs me in the ribs and whispers, 'You should say hello.'

'He can say hello first,' I say.

'But he's more famous.'

'All the more reason.'

'Honestly,' says Alexander, 'you designers. You're all bloody egos. It's pathetic.'

I ignore Roland, he doesn't notice me, and we all take our places for the awards. Needless to say, I don't win and Roland does. But since his parting of the ways with his business partners, Sharai Meyers and her millionaire husband Andre, the question of the night is, does he win for his company or for himself? Charlotte Tilbury gets her Fashion Creator gong, Karen Elson gets Model of the Year, and Christopher Bailey gets the biggest back slap of them all.

'He's a nice bloke,' says the man with the white hair. 'He's worked hard. I remember a story about when he was working for Tom Ford. Christopher flew over from

London to LA with the samples for the new Gucci collection and he put his bags in the hold. The airline mislaid them. He rang Tom Ford to tell him. Tom asked if they were the only set of samples. Christopher said no, he had another collection back in his office in London. Tom told him to get back on the plane and go and get them. Christopher told me that he learned his lesson and he doesn't put his samples in the hold any more.'

'That's learning the hard way, I suppose,' I say.

'I think Tom's a bit of a control freak. He's got a brilliant eye for detail. But he's not a designer, you know,' he continues. 'He trained as an architect.'

'Yes,' I say.

'My mate went to one of those Colin McDowell talks – you know, when you meet the designer – and he said to Tom Ford, you're the only designers whose drawings we never get to see. You know, we know what Galliano's sketches look like; Lagerfeld's are amazing. But no-one knows what yours look like. And do you know what he said?'

'No?'

'They're secret.'

Some more models parade down the catwalk as they announce another award. I think it's Best Shop but because of our conversation I've missed it.

'Jesus,' says Alexander, as they call out the names. 'That person's not popular.'

'Really?' I say.

'Yeah,' he smiles. 'Can't you tell by the clapping? It was like a one-armed-man convention in here.'

'Shit,' I say. 'How was mine?' I ask, feeling paranoid.

'OK,' he says. 'I whooped it up a bit for you.'

The last award is finally handed out, and I'm thinking I might get ready to leave. The fashion gangs are moving around from table to table. Lee McQueen has his own entourage with him – Sam Gainsbury, Guido, Annabel Neilson. They are all too cool for school and stare through me. But then he is hardly alone. Every designer has their entourage. Stella has Madonna and Gwyneth, whom she guards like a Rottweiler lest the rest of us get a look-in. Luella has Giles Deacon, Stuart Vevers and Darren Dan. Patrick Cox is always with Elton, Liz Hurley and Tim Jefferies. Philip Treacy usually has Izzy Blow and some random Russian muse. Matthew Williamson has Sienna Miller, Jade Jagger, Bay Garnett and a few other posh floaty lovelies. I suppose even I have Alexander, Damiano and Mimi. Us designers don't tend to move around very well on our own.

'All right there?' comes a voice and a hand on my shoulder. I turn round. My heart sinks. It's Ted Nicholls. 'Bad luck on the award,' he smiles. He is chewing the sides of his cheeks somewhat. He's been at the jazz. 'For the record, I liked what you did in the paper today.'

'Thanks.' I find myself simpering; my hands are actually mincing in front of me. What the hell am I doing? The man is an arse.

'You're looking good,' he says. 'I like the hair.'

'Great,' I say. 'Who are you here with?'

'You know, the Hoxton lot,' he says, gesturing behind him.

'Cool,' I say. Shit, I think. What did I say that for? 'Business good?'

'Great,' he says. 'I've got someone interested in buying the company.'

9

I have to admit that I don't remember much about my conversation with Ted. The only reason he came over to talk to me was so that he could gloat that someone was sniffing around, thinking of buying his talentless bankrupt arse.

Every designer dreams of being bought out by someone like LVMH or Gucci. You get backing, you get advertising, you get money for your shows, you get to be sold together as a package with the rest of the Gucci designers, so if your collection sucks one year the shops can't turn their noses up because if they want to have Balenciaga, they have to buy you as well. Think of the licensing deal. Think of the accessories. Think of the bags. The money. The support. Who gives a shit if you're just the name above the door? They give you a shop!

Anyway, I got plastered and ended up in some nightclub called Guilty Pleasures where I spent most of the night dancing to Neil Diamond and talking to some very chatty queen who told me some story about how Hussein Chalayan berated the fashion press when he won his fashion award a few years back. He was furious that Maria Grachvogell had got all this press when she used Posh Spice in her show. I remember nodding away. He told me some other story about some supermodel being filmed by a boyfriend shagging another girl with a strap-on dildo, and now they don't speak to each other. He said the film was amazing. I asked him if he'd seen it. He said yes. I had a feeling he was lying. I traded him another supermodel story about threesomes that I know to be true. One model had a rather racy boyfriend, and in order to keep him entertained she used to pick up other young models at shows and take them home to the bloke and they would all get down and crazy together. The queen's eyes were out on stalks.

'No!' he said.

'Yes!' I insisted.

'No!' he said again.

'Yes!' I replied, and was promptly sick all over my shoes.

Now, of course, Alexander won't let me get away with it. Every time I tell him off for something, or ask him to do something that he doesn't want to do, he gently reminds me that I vomited all over my own shoes. Worse still, because they were Alaia and I refused to take them off, I squelched home smelling of booze and regurgitated award ceremony food. Like it was at all pleasant in the first place.

Christmas is fast approaching and Alexander has been juggling orders for cloth for the next season, checking up on all the orders that we have got in for this season, while at the same time trying to find somewhere for the staff Christmas party. When I say staff party, it sounds a little grand, but it is important to have some sort of get-together. I don't pay anyone huge wages so it is kind of Alexander's and my way of saying thank you. Some designers don't seem to see the need for it. One of them is so hip they are not inviting a single one of their students to the Christmas party.

'They were told there weren't enough funds,' Trish said, snapping her chewing gum in my office. 'They are owned by an international for fucksake. There is enough money to keep them in mulled wine and figgy pudding until the next bloody millennium. And it's not as if they get paid. They get fuck all. And I bet they'll get last season's stuff for Christmas or some shit-smelling perfume. And the company wonders why so much stuff goes missing from the atelier. If they were treated better they might not be so light-fingered.'

With her words of warning ringing in my ear, I gave Alexander a gentle prodding and we eventually decided that some wine and nibbles was perhaps not enough, so we booked a long table in the Century club. I also told Alexander to invite a couple of the most important seamstresses, the pattern cutters and a few livewires like Mimi and Lydia to jolly things along.

Mimi could not appear less interested when I remind her of the dinner tonight. She gets Mini Me out of her handbag and checks her Palm Pilot, mumbling something along the lines that she has thirty-five events to get to between now and Christmas and if she is not careful she is going to end up in Meadows with half the fashion industry. She is, however, much more enthusiastic about her trip to 20th Century Vintage Fashion, a farm on the edge of Dartmoor owned by a husband and wife team called Mark and Cleo Butterfield.

'Honestly,' she says, leaning over and handing her dog a small chocolate, 'it was my first trip down there and I've never seen such fantastic stuff. You know it's the place where Steinberg and Tolkien call when they want some choice pieces for VIP clients like Dolce & Gabbana. You've never seen anything like it.'

Mark Butterfield specializes in vintage clothes from the forties through to the seventies and he is said to have the best collection of Ossie Clark in the world, which was the main reason why Mimi went down there. I should have gone myself, but she has such a good eye that I trust her. Anyway, Mark's stuff is supposed to be fantastic. He regularly lends to films and adverts; he supplied costumes for *Munich*. He also rents his clothes to places like Top Shop, who copy his stuff and send it back to the farm. He is visited by designers from all over the world, although some are more appealing than others. There's one designer, for example, who buys from him, gets 'inspired' by the clothes, and then burns them so that no-one can tell quite how 'inspired' he was.

'Can you imagine how upsetting that is?' asks Mimi, lighting up a cigarette and sitting down in my office chair. Mini leaps up onto her lap. 'He and his wife have collected all these clothes from all over the world only to have them burnt. Half of them should be in museums. In fact, he does lend to museums.' She takes a drag. 'Anyway, I've got you a load of forties stuff.'

'Forties?'

'Yup,' she says, pulling out a neat tight black cocktail dress with buttons, a collar and short sleeves. 'Everyone's doing it. They've all been down there getting forties stuff from Mark. He hasn't got much left.'

'Really?'

'Absolutely. Look.' She holds up the dress. 'How can you not feel that?'

I look at the dress and its shape and wonder if she is right. The neat silhouette feels very now. My seventies ideas that I have pasted up in front of me suddenly look a bit old hat. They look bulky, whereas what Mimi has in her hands is very sharp. Maybe she's right. Maybe forties is where we're all headed. The Scottish house party idea full of suppressed flirting that I have been mulling over seems to work better with the forties shapes. It's also so much more up my street. It's all about cut and lines and that's what really gets me excited. I just wonder if I am already too far down the track to change. We have all the material booked. Alexander and I have spent weeks sifting through the stuff, choosing one cotton over another, comparing prices. I smile. Makes me think of one designer I know who made all their shirts out of children's cotton one season just to save on some cash. Children's cotton is of much poorer quality, about 20 per cent of adult cotton, because it doesn't have to last as long. Just three to four months. Anyway, they cut their costs, made more money, and no-one was any the wiser. Alexander and I have not gone that far; let's just say we were quite careful when it came to things like cashmere. We went for something a little less thick and luxurious than I would have gone for a couple of years ago, when I was a bit more naive and willing to please.

But back to the forties.

'Is it what everyone is doing?' I ask.

'That's what I've heard,' Mimi says. 'Can't you see this in a red jersey? A little deconstructed. You know, slim yet soft, tailored but not hard? You must be feeling it?'

'I'm feeling it,' I say, and I'm not actually lying. I think she has a point. My heart is beating faster. Question is, can I really face re-doing the whole lot?

Mimi gets up from the chair – Mini hits the floor with a yap – and walks over to the collection of some twenty-five looks I already have up on the wall.

'I like the Ossie coats,' she says. 'The Mendes ones really work. The pleats and buttons are quite forties anyway.'

'Mmm.' I get up from behind the desk to join her. 'Do you think?'

'Yeah,' she says. 'Are you doing them in the tartan?'

'That's the plan. Here's the swatch.' I pick up a piece of the material and give it to her.

'That really is lovely,' she says. 'Traditional and modern.'

'I've also got this load of pink silk,' I say. 'I'm planning the Vanessa Tate dress in pink silk. I'm feeling pink for next season. All part of the traditional rich stuff. You know, like those rich pant suits Balenciaga did last season.'

'Everyone's loving those,' says Mimi. 'Sien has just done a shoot in one of their pant suits for the cover of UK *Vogue*.'

'Really?'

'I think it's Feb. My mate said it looks great.'

'I'm also thinking lace,' I add. 'You know, I really like those Balenciaga shirts they did with Edwardian collars and lace cuffs.'

'Fuck, lace,' says Mimi, rolling her eyes. 'My mates who own a stall on the Portobello Road can't buy it fast enough. Last week they went to Kempton racecourse and some antiques fair in Cheltenham just to stock up on it. They've had people from Louis Vuitton, Marc Jacobs, Lacroix, Galliano, Alice Temperley and Paul

Smith down there in the last few weeks buying up the stuff.'

'What, all of them?' I say, wondering if the fact that I am feeling what everyone else is feeling puts me on the curve or slightly behind it, as they have all been there and done their buying already. 'From the same place?'

'My mates know their stuff.' She smiles. 'Which is why they do so well and people go there. They always say how interesting it is to see which of the big names still do their own sourcing.'

'Yes?' Is she having a dig at me because I try to leave the office as little as possible?

'You know, Galliano and Gaultier are always down there snuffling around. He says there are a few designers he hasn't seen for years.'

'What exactly did Galliano buy?' I ask, thinking that even if he has gone through a fur-trimmed trouser stage he is still the king of the catwalk, and whatever he is feeling I'll have a bit of it.

'A couple of collars,' says Mimi. I knew she would know. 'And a couple of sixties fur hats.'

'Fur hats?'

'Yeah. They're probably for him, though. You know how much he loves a hat.'

'That's true.'

Mimi and I sit down on the floor and start going through her clothes. She has a couple of lovely little tight jackets that I have my eye on, a dress from Givenchy that I can't believe wasn't grabbed by another designer, and two or three skirts that I take straight upstairs to put on Dorota's table for her to copy. On the way back down I bump into Trish on the stairs.

'Looking forward to tonight?' I ask.

'Oh, it's going to be ma-jor,' she says. 'I hear Lydia is coming?'

'That's right.'

'I think she's great.' Trish is practically swooning.

'Well, perhaps you should sit next to her?'

'Do you think?'

'I don't see why not.' I smile. I am perfectly happy to pimp the services of my friend if it means an improvement in staff morale. 'She'd love it.'

'Oh, thanks, that's so ma-jor.'

'Did you want anything?'

'Oh yeah,' she says. 'We've had some people on the phone wanting to order the orange jacket they saw in *You* magazine at the weekend.'

'What orange jacket?'

'You know, the one that also comes in green that was in the spring/summer show?'

'Oh, that jacket,' I say. 'It hasn't gone into production.'

'It hasn't?'

'No. No-one ordered it.'

'They didn't?'

'No. We don't have any at all.'

This is always bloody happening. Some dozy old tart like Trish sends out a sample to a magazine, and because the garment hasn't been ordered by anyone it doesn't actually exist any more. The orange jacket is probably still at *You* mag, or in the sample sale pile, or even on its way to TK Maxx. All I know is that no-one can buy it anywhere. Most magazines don't care if you can or cannot buy the clothes. US *Vogue*, I know, is a stickler for stockists. But there are some magazines that positively delight in the fact that you can't buy the outfit anywhere. They don't care if the jacket is twenty years old. They don't care if it has never been made. Just so long as their page looks good and the stylist is satisfied and other fashion people think the shoot is achingly fashion forward. It's almost as if they don't give a shit about the reader. But for the most part, when some stylist or fashion editor rings to call in clothes, you do try to send out what you actually have in production.

And it would have to be *You* magazine that Trish sent the orange jacket to. *You* magazine is one of the best mags around when it comes to reader response. You can have a whole page in *Tatler* or a corner in *Vogue* and your phone doesn't even squeak. Put something in *You* mag and the phone will ring off the hook for the whole of the following week.

'What was the piece?' I ask, feeling incredibly annoyed.

'Oh, it was great,' says Trish. 'Alexander's got it in the office. It was on the hottest pieces for the next season. And the orange jacket was one of the twenty things they chose.'

'It's just a damn shame no-one ordered it and no-one's making it,' I say.

'Yeah,' says Trish, not very helpfully.

'Did you not think to send something else?' I ask.

'What?' says Trish. 'No. They said they wanted the orange jacket. I did offer.'

'You did?'

'I thought it was better to get something in than nothing at all.'

'I suppose so.' I grudgingly conclude that she does have a point.

'Anyway, I just thought I'd ask about what to do with the people calling?'

'Right,' I say. 'Tell them there has been a rush on the orange jacket and that they can put their names down on the waiting list.'

'Oh, OK,' she says. 'But there isn't a waiting list?'

'No.'

'Oh, so I'm lying?'

'Yes.'

'Like with the Vanessa Tate dresses?'

'No, because we are actually going to make that dress in the purple silk. It'll go into production with the new Fall collection.'

'But not the orange jacket?'

'No, Trish. There are thousands of fashion victims with their names down for clothes all over town who will never ever make it to the top of the list because the

173

thing they are waiting for so patiently is never going to be made. OK?'

'OK.'

'Got it?'

'Got it,' she repeats. 'Poor bastards.'

'Exactly. Poor bastards.'

I walk back into my office a little exhausted by the conversation. One of the problems with employing students is that they often turn out to be a false economy. Perhaps if I had a proper PR person to deal with the press they might have persuaded *You* magazine that a white dress was better than the orange jacket and we might have sold a few more dresses today. But if you pay peanuts, as the expression goes . . .

'Oh God,' I say to Mimi. 'Did you hear that?'

'I did,' she says.

'Honestly,' I say as I flop to the floor.

'Don't sit down there!'

'Too late,' I remark as I plonk my backside down. 'Why?'

'I think Mini has pissed on your carpet.'

Actually, Mimi knew that Mini had pissed on the carpet, and I sat right in it. Fortunately I had a spare set of clothes which I'd brought in for the Christmas party, so I went off to change immediately. Later, Alexander came in with a couple of bottles of Moët and we all tucked in. Then the four of us, including Mini, walked down the road to Century in Shaftesbury Avenue and took the lift upstairs to the dining room.

Lydia is already sitting at the head of the table. She is of the Kate Moss school of modelling: no matter what you were up to the night before, if you arrive early then you can leave early. She has pattern cutters on either side of her, and there are a couple of seamstresses sitting together on the banquette.

'Hey there,' says Lydia, getting out of her seat and coming towards me. 'Nice of you to show to your own party.'

'We're only ten minutes late,' I say. 'Stop complaining.'

'I'm not.' She smiles. 'I've knocked back a couple of shots of Grey Goose waiting for you, so I'm feeling fine.'

'Excellent,' I say. 'Let's all sit down. Trish?'

'Yeah?' she says, looking up. She is dressed in a black sequin vest with tight black jeans and very high heels that she told me were from Oasis though they look like Jimmy Choo. I have to say she looks great.

'You're next to Lydia.'

'Ma-jor.' She smiles. 'Hiya,' she says to Lydia. 'We have met before, when you came . . .'

Lydia listens politely to all the occasions on which she and Trish have met. She spends her life doing this and has got it down to a fine art. She agrees in the right places, smiles in the right places, and makes the person talking to her feel totally at home. Her diplomacy when talking to unimportant people is, I'm sure, one of the reasons why everyone books Lydia. All the years she and I have been in this business I have never heard any-one being rude about her. And this is a rude business.

That said, Lydia is often rude about other people.

'Guess what?' she says to me as she shoves some buttered bread in her mouth. 'I've been invited to go on Mr X's yacht.'

'No!' says Alexander, abandoning the clearly lame gossip he had been indulging in. 'Fuck me!'

'I know,' says Lydia. 'Only the most glamorous invitation you can get in fashion.'

'There's always Mr Y's yacht,' corrects Mimi.

'Well, which one is better?' I ask.

'Well . . .' says Lydia.

'Mr Y,' says Mimi.

'D'you think?' asks Lydia.

'That's what all my friends say,' she says.

'When are you going?' asks Alexander.

'In June,' she says. 'The invite came through my agency today.'

'OK, will you check for me when you go if the story about him not coming above deck during the day is true?' asks Alexander.

'What story's that?' I ask.

'Oh,' he says, 'that he stays below deck all day in a cooled room so that his make-up doesn't slip and he only comes above deck at sunset.'

'Really?' I say. 'That so defeats the reason for having a yacht.'

'Careful, you don't want to end up in the same

scenario as one person I know,' says Mimi.

'What's that?' asks Lydia.

'Because you stay on the yacht, you end up owing Mr X a favour. That's why she ended up in the front row of his menswear show. Like she gives a shit about menswear! What's she there for? But they called in the favour after my friend had stayed on the yacht, and there wasn't much she could do about it.'

'Right,' says Lydia. 'I don't mind looking at a few blokes' clothes if I get to stay on the yacht. Seems like a good deal to me.'

'Have they all got yachts?' asks Trish.

'Practically,' says Mimi. 'But all these things are used to network people and entertain guests, to keep the illusion of glamour going.'

'I've heard they're all bugger boats,' says Alexander. 'You know, they sail around the Med picking up boys. They moor off somewhere like Mykonos, get the prettiest boys out of all the clubs, take them back on board, have fun with them, then sling them off the next morning.'

'Are you sure?' says Lydia.

'Who cares?' says Alexander. 'That's what I'd do if I had a shiny hundred-foot fucking floating penis extension.'

'Shall we order our starters?' I suggest, as the waiter comes back for the fifth time with his notebook.

Three quarters of an hour later and we are all tucking into a turkey dinner. I don't quite know what made me book a traditional Christmas dinner, but it seems to be going down well with the pattern cutters and Dorota and her gang up the other end. Alexander is not touching his, which I presume means he's been to the toilet to sharpen himself up a bit. Lydia is eating with the unselfconscious gusto of the naturally thin and gorgeous. Meanwhile, Mimi is religiously avoiding her carbs. Trish, on the other hand, is having too much fun to eat.

'Anyway, so I heard this,' says Alexander. His left nostril is running slightly, but he doesn't appear to be able to feel it. 'That Karl, right, only wears Dior because he loves Hedi's designs so much, and thinks his stuff is so fantastic. He also only eats this food that is specially prepared for him and comes all foil-wrapped. Fuck knows what's in it. And if his team is going out for lunch with him, they have to go via Karl's chateau and wait while he eats his lunch, and then they will all go out. They all put up with it.'

'Oh, they're all like that,' I say. 'I don't think I'm anywhere near interesting enough.'

The pudding is served. Only about three people eat it. Drink then takes over. Alexander is getting more and more twitchy, and Mimi appears to have joined him.

'I heard this disgusting story,' she suddenly announces, 'about this designer who went and stayed in a house in Ibiza. They rented it for a couple of weeks for the summer. And guess what they brought with them?'

'What?' asks Alexander. This is already shaping up to be his kind of anecdote.

'Industrial amounts of colon cleansing powder!'

'What?' he says.

'I know.' Mimi curls her nose. 'When they left, apparently they had to unblock the bath and clean all the sofa covers, the place was so full of crap. Apparently they started out ordering egg-white omelettes but soon resorted to bacon sandwiches and full-fat milk because they'd taken so many drugs. And the place was full of rent boys.' She smiles. 'Who would have thought it? I always thought they designed such shagging dull clothes.'

'Is that the same designer who takes nude photos of his celebrity guests after dinner?' asks Alexander.

'No,' says Mimi. 'Or at least I don't think so.'

We are laughing when I see this other designer we know come over to the table. She has a bit of a reputation as a drinker and coker, and judging by the way she is tottering towards us, she has been at both. Well, it is Christmas.

'Wotcha,' she says, holding onto the table for support. 'Merry Christmas!'

We once had the misfortune of sharing a stitcher with her, so we have to sort of make polite conversation.

'Hi.' I smile tightly. 'Having fun?'

'Just left my own Christmas party, and then someone said that you lot were up here having yours. So I thought I'd crash.'

'Great,' I say, thinking anything but.

'You got any drugs?' she asks.

'Sorry, no,' I say.

'Oh,' she says, and flops down next to Alexander.

He's in the sort of mood where he could talk to soft furnishings, so I decide to leave him to it and go down the other end of the table to talk to my pattern cutters and Dorota and her mates. Fifteen minutes later I come back to find the sloshed designer straddling my business partner, mumbling something like 'I want to fuck you' in his ear. They sort of sit and ride each other for a while. She is getting increasingly fruity, and Alexander is getting more and more reticent. She suddenly gets up off his lap and announces that she needs the loo.

'You two seem to be getting on,' I say, as she turns the corner towards the toilets.

'Get her off me,' hisses Alexander. 'Her breath stinks of puke.'

Fortunately, the sloshed designer finds someone else to straddle or someone else to score from and leaves us to it.

We all drink some more and smoke some more, and three glasses get broken. Dorota and the pattern cutters are the first to leave, and they zig-zag their way through the chairs. Some of them have drunk their weight in champagne. Mimi and Lydia are slumped in one corner discussing male models and underwear. Mini is asleep on the banquette. I see Alexander has Trish backed up against the pillar. She is looking a little bit afraid.

'Drugs are endemic in this industry because it is all about make-believe.' He is clearly on a roll. 'You can't really talk seriously about fashion – there is nothing to talk about. You can't just say I have done this great skirt this season. It's all about dressing this bitch because she's cool and she's going to help my brand. If she goes out in this dress she is going to give me some kudos, so I have to get up her arse, and then I have to be nice and suck cock with some journalist, and then I have to be nice to this buyer to help my brand. It is all so soul-destroying.' He pauses for breath. 'You don't make friends in this industry. There is no camaraderie. There is no-one trying to make real connections. People are parasites. They do the fashion rubbish talk. That's why people are high all the time, to help them escape it all. They'd rather not confront the reality. We all live on fresh air, so it has to be high-octane and fun otherwise we would all sit here and say, "I'm not making any money. What the fuck am I doing?" '

'Alexander,' I say.

'Yes?' He looks up. His eyes are glassy and his face appears to have melted off his cheekbones.

'Do you want me to take you home?'

'Oh, yes please.'

10

I come back from a five-day break with my parents in Exeter to some amazing news: Vanessa Tate has been nominated for a Golden Globe for the role of Natasha in *War and Peace* and she wants me to make the dress. Kathy calls me the day before New Year's Eve at the studio. She sounds all whisky and cigarettes down the telephone – she's clearly had quite a heavy night of it. She'd found out before Christmas about the nomination but Vanessa has been on holiday in the Maldives, so they've only just managed to celebrate. She says that she is sorry it's such short notice but would I be interested in designing the dress? I do think about it for a second. It is a big responsibility. Can I afford the time? I have a collection to deliver in just over a month and it's not even half finished. But then, the exposure and the kudos and the credibility of it all – it is so tempting. And just for one second, say that she wins?

Alexander can't believe it when I tell him. He is lying

in bed watching morning television when I call. He is nursing a hangover, tucked up with some barman he picked up on the street on his way home from a club. He is supposed to be coming into work today. Unlike the rest of the civilian world who hibernate between Christmas and New Year, fashion people have to work. It is one of our busiest periods, with the Fall collections looming around the corner.

'Well, I'm not surprised,' he yawns down the telephone. 'You did make her famous.'

'I don't think I did,' I say.

'Don't be ridiculous,' he says. 'That dress has been on the front cover of every low-rent glossy magazine in the country, from *Heat* to *Hello!*. We haven't been able to move for purple chiffon with a glitter bodice. You even had someone from the *Mirror* asking if they could wear one around the office for a "what's it like to wear an It dress" feature. It's just a shame we haven't got any to sell. Trish's waiting list must have at least seventy people on it by now.'

'Yeah.' I laugh nervously. 'The sooner we get that dress into production the better.'

'Can't you give her something that we've got ready to go?' he mumbles.

'What, this season?'

'Yeah.'

'I don't know,' I say.

'Well, see what you can do.'

I am sitting at my desk gazing into space, trying to

think of something that says 'sexy successful ingénue'. I've been upstairs to the sewing room to see what material they have lying around in an effort to get some inspiration. I have a swatch of black silk satin in my hand when Alexander bursts through the door downstairs.

'Hey, hey, hey,' he says as he bounds up the stairs. 'I've had the most amazing idea.' He grins. 'And before you say anything I want you to hear me out.'

'OK,' I say, looking up from the desk and smiling at him standing in the doorway. He looks remarkably energized for someone who was on a podium until two in the morning.

'I think you should show in New York – there,' he says, taking a step back.

'There what?'

'There's my great idea.' He smiles.

'That's not an idea,' I say, 'it's a statement.'

'OK, my statement then.'

'Why do you think that?'

'Well, you've outgrown London. If you show here again they will only slag you off again. You'll have the *Sunday Times* saying you're boring. Style.com will say you're under-performing. *The Times* will say something caustic and we'll be sunk. The label will be tarnished and you'll go down the pan like every other British designer. I think we should strike while the iron is hot, so to speak. You will have a dress on the back of a nominated actress for the Golden Globes. The dress will be beamed around the States. In every magazine and newspaper. It could help launch us in the US. We need more buyers. We need a more reliable supply chain, with better manufacturing.' He pauses, as if trying to decide something. 'I didn't tell you this because I thought you would be shit scared, but back in October we nearly got a £75,000 order from Joseph.'

'No,' I say. 'That's amazing.'

'Well, it is,' he says. 'But it would have fucked us because I would have had to take it and it would have ruined the supply chain. We just can't do big orders like that, and that's terrible.'

'That's true. It's also kind of pathetic, isn't it?'

'I know. I'd like to expand into the US and the Far East, expand our buyer base, get some good manufacturers onside.'

'We need a production manager,' I say.

'We need a production manager,' he repeats. 'I can't do it all on my own.'

'I know,' I say.

'They can travel all over the world. They can sort out the Far East, they can keep their eye on our stuff in Hungary. I just can't keep my finger in all those pies. And in the meantime we can get some better manufacturers, get the supply line working properly, and we can conquer New York.'

'What made you think of all this?'

'Oh, I was lying in bed this morning with this bloke and I mentioned you and where I worked and he said that he'd only vaguely heard of you and I thought that was wrong.' He smiles. 'I told him about the dress that you did for Vanessa Tate and he said his sister had loved it. But she didn't know where to buy your clothes.'

'Did you tell him Harrods?' I smile.

'Of course I did.' He smiles back. 'But what do you think of New York?'

'I don't know,' I say. 'It sounds a bit daunting.'

'Don't worry, I'm going to sort it all out. Come the first week of February you'll be showing in the tents. Seventh on Sixth.'

'If you don't think that it's too late?' I ask.

'I'm sure they'll have a slot somewhere. If you're not fussy about the time.'

'Like I can afford to be. Talking of which, how much is it?'

'About twice the price of London and half the price of Paris,' he says. 'I think it's about $40,000 for an hour in the tents. Or something like that. For all the lighting, the catwalk, the technicians and the music as well as the backstage. It's not bad.'

'It's not cheap either.'

'We can afford it.'

'Don't tell Trish,' I say, 'or she'll want paying.'

'Get on with your work,' he says, walking next door.

The idea of New York Fashion Week, or Olympus Fashion Week as it is now called, suddenly fills me with inspiration. There is something about not being in

London that is extremely liberating. I remember how depressing London Fashion Week was back in September. I have this dreadful abiding memory of someone looking for a designer at the Jonathan Saunders party only for the two of us to suddenly hear him puking his guts up behind a curtain. It just about summed up the week for me. I have got to concentrate. Find my muse. And get something down on paper. It is about time I embraced my commercial child and made some money. Vanessa Tate could be my golden ticket.

I can't believe she has asked me to make her dress. It is quite unusual for a nominated actress to call the designer and ask for clothes. Normally it's the other way around. As soon as the nominations come out they are usually inundated by requests from designers to wear their clothes. I suppose it's because Vanessa is new to this game that she hasn't got the requisite stylist on hand to help her make these decisions.

Not that stylists are lovely, selfless people who have only their client's welfare at heart. Hollywood stylists are universally disliked by most of the fashion industry and they make a lot of money putting people in other people's clothes. They can charge up to $20,000 a day for advice, and the kickbacks and sweeteners they get for suggesting Chanel over Givenchy or Dior over Galliano are amazing. I know of two stylists who were given BMWs by one fashion house because they got their client to wear their dresses to the Oscars. The actress gets sweet FA; the stylist is the one getting all the money. They know how to work the system for everything they want. A stylist never pays for any clothes. If they want a handbag, they simply call up and ask for it. Fashion PRs bend over backwards to accommodate them. One extraordinary story concerns the woman who put an actress in a tumbling diamond necklace and got very well compensated for her excellent idea. And if their actress wins, they are in clover. One stylist received full body lipo as her reward for getting an actress in a frock when she won. I know of someone else who got a $20,000 diamond necklace. The free advertising and global reach of the winner shots is supposedly priceless, so you can understand quite how grateful the designers are.

But if you're a designer, it costs you a fortune. I remember hearing one designer made four dresses for an actress for the Oscars at a cost of some $120,000. In the end she wore someone else down the red carpet. A little caprice like that is enough to bankrupt some brands, which is why not everyone can afford to play the Oscar game. You make a one-off dress for someone to wear once. She goes up and down the red carpet, keeps it, and doesn't give it back. You can't archive it, and then three years later it turns up in some AIDS charity auction and you have to sit back and smile at her fabulous generosity. It's a nightmare.

They can also hold dresses and ensure that they never go into production. An actress will be trawling the net and will come across something she just loves in your catwalk show. She'll call up her stylist, get the dress called in, and sit on it until her première in March. She wants to be the only person to wear the dress. She doesn't want Nicole to get her thin white hands on it first. It's hers, and hers alone. And then begins this awful chain of hope. Is she going to change her mind on the day? Will she be inundated with dresses? Is her film any good? Can she act? Or have you backed a stinker? The film bombs. The actress doesn't wear the dress, and one of your key pieces never makes it into production. It never gets photographed in any magazine. It never sees the light of day. It is a depressing and dangerous game.

Amazingly, there are some actresses who are not up for grabs. They are loyal fans of the designer and have some sort of relationship with them. Renee Zellweger will always wear Carolina Herrera, and Kate Winslet can almost be guaranteed to wear Ben De Lisi. And Liz Hurley is never out of Versace. But for the most part they are as mercenary as their stylists and flit from one designer to another. Sometimes the actress doesn't even need to see her stylist at all. L'Wren Scott is Mick Jagger's girlfriend and one of Hollywood's biggest stylists. She apparently hasn't seen her client Nicole Kidman in months. She doesn't need to. She has a dummy made to Nicole's exact measurements in her office and does all her styling from there.

Image is all in this business, and I suppose they are all trying to protect themselves. They are just trying to guard against a Lara Flynn Boyle moment – she arrived at the Oscars in a tutu and ballet shoes. It is fashion death to be Bjork in the swan dress or Celine Dion in the back-to-front cream gentlemen's jacket and jaunty hat. Get it wrong and the stylist is unlikely to work again. Get it wrong and you will find it difficult to get a dress the following year. Get it horribly wrong and your picture is beamed worldwide for everyone else's entertainment.

I can't afford to get it wrong. I have one shot at this, and I can feel the pressure. Kathy calls again and suggests that she and Vanessa come in for a chat this afternoon. I can't really say no. That I don't have any ideas. So I close my office door, turn the radio off, and get my head down. There is nothing like fear to get the juices flowing.

By the time they turn up at three p.m. I have six sketches to show them. Five of them are original designs; one of them is the same shape as the white and silver *Some Like It Hot* dress I sent down the catwalk back in September. I'm thinking I'm not going to make the same mistake as I did last time, sending her down the red carpet in the purple dress we didn't already have stocked. It makes me wince to think of the length of our waiting list for a dress that we have yet to show and make. I'm thinking I could make the white and silver Monroe dress in black, and keep the sequins silver. It could easily hold its own. In fact, I think it might be rather beautiful, especially as she has the figure to carry it off. And if it works we already have the white version in the shops. It is a win-win scenario. Just so long as she can be persuaded to wear it. Maybe if I promise that the black version will be exclusive to her?

Kathy steams into the room, mobile glued to her cheek, fag hanging off her maroon bottom lip as she tries to write something down on a piece of paper. Vanessa walks in behind her. She has changed since I last saw her. There's a gentle dusting of tan, her hair is not so cropped, and she looks rich. I don't know if it's the understated, severe Martin Margiela dress she is wearing or the Prada flats, but suddenly she looks successful. There is more than a whiff of money. I remember sitting next to Jude Law in a restaurant once when he was riding the *Talented Mr Ripley* wave. He'd just come back from holiday and he looked so blond and tanned. It was almost like he was made of gold. It is amazing what a nomination does for someone. How sweet success does smell, and how a bit of cash and a good dress can change you from a sexy, cool actress into a star.

'Happy Christmas,' she says as she walks in. 'Did you have a lovely holiday?'

'I think it should be me asking you that question,' I say, kissing both her earlobes. 'You look amazing.'

'Thanks,' she says, raising her shoulders, smiling sweetly, pretending to be coy.

This is definitely the one and only shot I have at

dressing her, I think. Give it two months and she will not want to know. Valentino will be on the phone suggesting she wears one of his beautiful pieces for the Oscars. This girl is going all the way.

'Nice to see you've put some backs on your dresses,' says Kathy, who has snapped shut her mobile and is stubbing her fag out in my half-drunk cup of Starbucks. 'I was beginning to worry that the girls were riding bareback down your catwalk.'

'No.' I laugh. 'I have managed to finish off a few frocks. The collection has to be ready in six weeks.'

'Looks good,' she says, walking up and down the line of designs stuck to the wall. 'More forties than it was before.'

'Yeah.' I smile. 'That's what we are all feeling right now.'

'Hmm.' She walks over to my rail of 'inspiring' garments. 'What do you think of doing vintage?' she asks Vanessa.

'What?' she says. 'Just getting something from the archives and wearing that?'

My heart starts to beat a little faster. I can feel my Golden Globes opportunity slipping away. If Vanessa wears vintage then I can kiss goodbye to the press, the exposure and New York.

'Why not?' suggests Kathy. 'It would make life a lot easier. We could get some forties dress?'

'I don't know,' she says. 'What do you think?' she asks me.

'Well,' I say, 'I'm not sure . . .' I am trying to look cool and not desperate. There is nothing more unattractive than someone who looks too keen. You can see it in their eyes and smell it on their breath. It's enough to make someone sprint in the opposite direction.

'The only thing about vintage is . . .' says Alexander, suddenly standing in the doorway, listening in to our conversation. 'Is . . .' He pauses. I can tell he is about to lie because he has half a smile on his lips. 'Well, it's quite hard to get it to fit properly. Once you have sourced the thing there are hours of tweaking and fitting and it does still look like you've stolen it from your grandmother's wardrobe. It has to be a truly remarkable dress from the Dior collection, say, for it to work. Otherwise you look like you've gone down the Portobello Road and picked up a bargain.' He spits the word 'bargain' like it's some foul fly he has just made the great mistake of swallowing.

'A bargain,' repeats Kathy, mulling it over. 'No, you're right,' she says. 'I agree. The only time it has really worked was with Julia Roberts at the Oscars in that black and white dress. Valentino?'

'Valentino,' I confirm.

'You have to be so careful,' says Alexander. 'You have to remember that vintage only really means old, or second-hand. It has to be pretty fabulous to get something smelling of old BO and mothballs down the red carpet. Sometimes these dresses aren't even that old.

You could find something that was worn by someone else to the same event, say three years previously, shove it on and say it's vintage, and then suddenly you realize that just means it's last season or a few seasons ago. It's just already worn old tat.'

'Has that happened before?' asks Vanessa.

'I'm not sure,' says Alexander. 'But it is surely only a matter of time.'

'So we are all agreed that it is no to vintage,' I say breezily, like my whole future did not depend on it.

'I don't like the idea of someone having worn it to a red-carpet event before,' says Vanessa. 'That would just be too much.'

'Particularly if they looked better in it.' As usual, Alexander manages to say what we are all thinking. And his final comment swings it.

'That would be too awful,' says Vanessa, walking over to the mood wall and looking at the photos torn from the eighties *Cosmo*s. 'Let's have a look at your ideas.'

The next two weeks are possibly the busiest I have ever been in my life. Vanessa comes back and forth to the studio every other day, initially to discuss ideas and then for fittings, and more fittings, and then tweaking and final fittings. Through the gentle art of persuasion Vanessa is pointed in the direction of a black version of the white satin dress with sequins. She's whippet thin, with thin arms, a tiny waist and a perky bosom. She is about the right age and shape to wear such an iconic silhouette. But she is one of the few women I've met who could really carry it off. I tell her my suggestion and I show her the look book of the dress coming down the catwalk on the flatulent supermodel in my show. And she immediately agrees to my plan. We do have a brief debate about the colour. We discuss red again. I say that it's a possibility. She, on the other hand, doesn't want to be the only actress dressed in colour. Nude or white seems to be the award ceremony shade of choice at the moment. It is a rare actress who dares a red or a yellow or a green. And, as Vanessa keeps saying, she won't win, so she doesn't want to stand out too firmly from the crowd. So she agrees with me to play it safe and go for black. I tell her that although the design has been seen before and is currently stocked in the shops it will still be exclusive to her as she will be the only one who has it in black. The idea seems to appeal to her.

By day I am designing the Fall collection. The tartan has finally arrived in all its 150-metre glory and Dorota is upstairs swearing away and sighing like the Slav she is. The only woman I have ever met who manages to exude tension and depression at the same time, she is heading up a team of six seamstresses who are hard at work making toiles. A mixture of Portuguese and Polish, with a Japanese pattern cutter, they all seem to gossip and get on using a mixture of sign language, grunts and giggles. Buoyed by endless cups of tea, cigarettes and the vast bowl of dolly mixtures and wine gums that sits in the middle of the sewing table, their days are long and their patience is endless. Although I tend not to spend that much time with them, I have been party to their endless superstitious banter.

I suppose it is inevitable in a profession entirely dominated by women that everything that happens in the sewing room should have some significance. You drop your scissors and it means that someone will die. A box of pins hits the deck and there will be some sort of argument. Prick the index finger of your right hand and someone loves you; the middle finger means that you will get flowers; the index finger on your left hand signifies jealousy. If you sew a hair into a wedding dress the stitcher will get married or find love. And so it goes on.

I have given Dorota sole charge of making Vanessa's dress, and by the end of the first week she has made a toile. It looks nothing special, hanging like a lethargic ghost off the hanger. Vanessa looks more than dubious when she turns up to try it on. She stands stiffly as I pin her into it. I jab her twice in the behind as she stands there. She sighs and twitches irritably in her heels. I mutter some pleasantries about how it will look better in the flesh. How toiles always look rubbish. Last time it turned out OK. But she doesn't seem convinced.

She must have called Kathy on her way out because twenty minutes after the fitting Kathy rings me.

'All right there?' she coughs down the telephone.

'Fine,' I say.

'Just to let you know you're on speaker phone,' she

says. 'With Vanessa's agent Chris. We're on our way to some restaurant awards to meet Gordon Ramsay.'

'Great,' I say.

'Anyway, how's the dress?'

'It's going well. She is going to look great in it.'

'Really,' says Kathy, sounding very unconvinced. 'If it's not going to be ready you need to tell me. I have had loads of phone calls. Valentino's people have been on the line saying that Mr Valentino would be happy to dress her. So, you know . . .'

'Have they really?' Chris's voice comes down the line. The mobile goes dead for a second.

'It will be fine,' I say. 'Hello? Are you still there?'

'Because if you can't,' Kathy says, 'I can always . . .'

'Do you want Valentino?' I ask.

'No.'

'Are you sure?' I hear Chris trying to whisper in the car. 'He's very good.'

'I know he is,' replies Kathy, not bothering to temper her voice. 'But we want something fresh and young-looking, as she is fresh and young. Is it fresh and young?' she shouts.

'Very,' I shout back.

'Great. And on time?'

'Don't worry.'

'I trust you.'

'Trust me.'

'Good.' The line bleeps. 'Well, there's nothing more that I can do,' I hear her say. I suddenly realize that she thinks she has turned her phone off. 'I mean, I'm slightly fucked now. We could go with Valentino but that would mean flying her out to Milan, and we just don't have the time. Vanessa's got back-to-back press. If she fucks the dress, I will make her life hell. I'll ruin her. Simple as that.'

'Can you?' asks Chris.

'It wouldn't take much,' she says.

I hang up. I don't want to hear any more. There is something very uncomfortable about eavesdropping on your own potential downfall. I light up a cigarette, down my cup of cold latte and get back to the dress.

Ten minutes later Alexander comes bouncing into my office. He is grinning from ear to ear, looking incredibly pleased with himself. He stands in the middle of the room and declares that he has managed to secure us a runway slot in New York. I don't know how he has done it at such short notice. He must have been right up the backside of someone at Seventh on Sixth – the organizer of New York Fashion Week. But apparently someone has pulled out at the last minute. Some poor designer's collection must have gone tits up. Otherwise how can he explain the sudden availability of a ten a.m. slot on the Wednesday morning?

'It's not a bad slot,' he says. 'The Americans drink a lot less. They don't have to have flutes for fashion.'

'That's amazing news,' I say. 'You're a genius.'

'Yes, I know. Bryant Park here we come!'

'There is so much to do,' I say, a feeling of panic

rising so fast in my throat that I retch slightly over the desk.

'You OK?'

'I'm shit scared actually. The collection is nowhere near ready. I've got this bloody dress to do. We've got to cast the show. Get hair and make-up. We have no contacts in New York. We have to invite the right buyers. The right press. Get a front row. Ask Anna Wintour.'

At the mere mention of her name we both stop still and stare at each other. I smirk. Alexander lets out a squeak. And we both start to laugh.

'Do you think she'll come?'

'She has to,' he says.

'Why?'

'She usually comes to the first show that everyone does in New York. Just in case you are brilliant. She went to Luella's first, Matthew's first, Roland's. She did Alice Temperley.'

'Really?'

'Yeah. It's the second show you have to worry about.'

We stare at each other again.

'What have we done?' I ask.

'I have no idea,' he replies with a smile.

'Shit.'

11

She won! No-one can believe it. I can't believe it. Vanessa can't believe it. Alexander was so excited he went on a two-day drinking binge to celebrate. Kathy rang me in the middle of the night to tell me. I'd thought about staying up to watch the show but I couldn't find it on my Sky package and I was so tired from changing my mainly seventies silhouettes into a much more appropriate forties that I couldn't summon the energy to stay awake.

The next day Vanessa and the dress were everywhere. She was on the front page of every newspaper, clutching her Golden Globe, smiling elegantly, looking bowled over yet serene. The fashion press went to town on the dress. She looked 'elegant'. It showed off her 'young curves'. It was 'young and fresh'. It ticked 'all the right boxes'. The 'perfect red carpet dress for someone so young'. I couldn't believe it. It was in all the round-ups as a 'winner' dress. She was pictured next to

Gwyneth Paltrow in Balenciaga, Scarlett Johansson in Valentino, Renee Zellweger in Carolina Herrera, Keira Knightley in Valentino, and Kate Beckinsale in Christian Dior. The 'loser' dresses were very interesting. Drew Barrymore looked a little hefty in a high-necked Gucci dress – never a good look for a girl with a bust. And, as Alexander had predicted, Reese Witherspoon wore a 1950s-style baby doll dress by Chanel, which turned out to have been worn by Kirsten Duntz to the same ceremony three years earlier. So, not so old and vintage after all. Opinion was divided as to who'd looked best in it.

Back in our office, Trish could hardly contain herself. Never had working for nothing seemed so appealing. She found herself at the cutting edge of fashion with the phone ringing off the hook, as everyone who is anyone in the business called up for the dress. In the four days that followed Vanessa's victory, the white version of the dress appeared on *LK Today*, *This Morning* and *Richard and Judy*. Lorraine Kelly's stylist told the viewers how to recreate the look at home and they trawled the high street looking for something similar.

I have to say I am finding the whole thing rather amusing. I now know slightly what it feels like to be Roland Mouret after he'd designed the Galaxy dress. What was already a hit dress has now become an It dress. My only gripe is that I wish I'd manufactured it in black as well as the white but there is nothing that

I can really do about that now. Alexander, on the other hand, is finding the whole thing incredibly frustrating. He calls a meeting with Trish in my office.

'Right,' he says, sitting on the edge of my desk, looking at Trish, then turning to face me. 'I think we should have a conversation about image control.'

'OK,' I say. 'Is this really necessary? I have a lot to do.'

'Yes,' he says, sounding tense. 'Last night I only just managed to stop a bike going out to Kate Thornton on *The X Factor*.'

'Who authorized that?' I ask, suddenly paying attention.

'Um, I did,' says Trish.

'You did?' I ask.

'I love the show.' She smiles weakly.

'Yeah,' I say, 'but Kate Thornton is not the sort of person we lend to.'

'Oh?' says Trish.

'Not all publicity is good publicity. You can kill a dress if you get it on the wrong person,' explains Alexander.

He is, of course, right. Fashion circles are becoming increasingly small these days. It used to take about six months for an iconic dress to filter down from the high-end trend makers to the also-ran celebrity, but now it goes from A list to Z list in a matter of days. Stella McCartney's over-the-knee non-leather boots are a case in point. They were worn by Madonna on Monday,

Posh on Wednesday and a footballer's wife on the Friday. In fashion terms they were dead and buried within a week.

Half the reason why companies like Balenciaga are always churning out new versions of the same bag is because they are constantly being killed off by the wrong sort of celebrity. You can imagine how much Roland must have wanted to slash his wrists when he saw *Countdown*'s Carol Vorderman wearing his dress. It went from Scarlett Johansson via Cameron Diaz and Rachel Weisz to Carol in three months. As a result, Scarlett is now running miles from the Galaxy dress. In the end, I suppose that is the price of having a hit collection.

The other downer of hitting the big time is that every high-street store in the land copies your look. No sooner has it gone down the catwalk than it is in the high street. They are ruthless about it, and because someone like Top Shop has ten clothes deliveries a year compared to our two, they are much better at getting the clothes into the shops. I have lost count of the number of times a jaunty top or a skirt of mine has appeared in Karen Millen or Miss Selfridges or Hennes before I have managed to get it into production and onto a hanger in Harrods. You can't really do anything about it. There are some designers who have tried, or thought about, suing. But there really is no point. It's not as if there is that much of a crossover. The woman who spends £20 on something on Oxford Street is not the same woman who spends £800 down Sloane Street. The material is of poorer quality, the finish is not as clean and the look of luxury is not there. You have to think of it as a form of flattery. Last year the whole of the high street was looking like Chloé, and I have to say it didn't harm Chloé at all. Although I did a triangle top this summer and it was ripped off so much it eventually drove me mad. All I had to do was walk down the road and nearly every single heavy-breasted girl was wearing something similar underneath a jacket or a cardigan, over some jeans. Then I switched on *Top of the Pops* and saw Girls Aloud in one of my tops. I almost gave up designing for ever.

'Right,' says Alexander, tapping his hands together like he is about to deliver a lecture. 'From now on we have a no-slags-or-sluts rule.'

'Slags or sluts,' mutters Trish, taking notes on a small pad.

'What constitutes a slag or a slut?' I ask.

'Anyone who presents a reality TV show or would go on *Celebrity Love Island*, and/or who sleeps with a footballer,' says Alexander.

'So no Colleen Rooney, or whatever her name is,' I say.

'McLoughlin,' says Trish.

'Is that what she's called?' asks Alexander.

'Yeah,' says Trish.

'Not Rooney?'

'No.'

'Oh, anyway, no to her,' he says. 'She's bloody fashion road-kill. Do you know, a mate of mine was styling her the other day and a couple of PRs said no to lending clothes, or that they would have to get back to them?'

'Really?' says Trish. 'I'm not that surprised. She does do that footballer's wife uniform, teaming Juicy Couture with a tangerine tan and fake nails. Why do they think that looks good?'

'No fucking idea,' says Alexander. 'Talking of tangerine, you know Kenny Lowe, Posh's stylist?'

'She has one?' I ask.

'I know,' says Alexander, curling up his nose. 'Apparently he doesn't have much luck calling McQueen.'

'That doesn't surprise me,' I say. 'He is quite particular who he lends to.'

Lee McQueen is one of the more discerning lenders of frocks. He won't have his stuff in any magazine that he deems homophobic. He won't lend to anyone who doesn't fit his cool criteria. Although Mimi has told me many times how stylists get around these barriers. She was doing Charlotte Church a while back and was finding it a little difficult to get stuff. So she called up Selfridges. The best way to get past the PRs is to go directly to the department stores. Harrods, Harvey Nicks and Selfridges are only too happy to lend you anything, and there is fuck all the designer can do about it. She popped Charlotte into a couple of jackets (interestingly, she is smaller than you would think – a size 8/10 with a 34DD bosom), she appeared in *Grazia* or *Glamour* or wherever it was, and the jackets sold out within a week. Most of us designers spend our lives wanting to dress Nicole or Uma, but put something on a curvy, more female-friendly girl like Charlotte and things fly out of the shops.

Celebrity selling power also comes in useful when you are trying to shift some dodgy stock. So, much like the wrong celebrity can ruin your sales of a good dress, the right celebrity in a crap dress can send it flying out of the shops. As a result stylists are always being offered little bribes and sweeteners by PRs to help them get rid of something that is not selling. A shop is weighed down with sixty skirts that are going nowhere. A stylist puts the skirt on someone who is PR friendly, they jazz it up with a nice belt, and everyone is pleased. The shop makes money, and the stylist gets preferential treatment – first dibs at the new stock, an invitation to the staff sale, a nice new winter coat. Sadly, the celebrity only gets a nice picture in a magazine.

'OK,' continues Alexander. 'Other slags and sluts are anyone who has been on *Big Brother*, *Pop Idol* or *The X Factor*.'

'Including the winners?' asks Trish.

'Especially the winners,' says Alexander. 'Anyone who has been in *Hollyoaks*. And obviously anyone who shows their tits for a living, or who appears in any one of those men's magazines with their legs mysteriously wide apart. So no to Jordan, the Titmuss, Jodie Marsh . . . or someone who used to be a kids' TV presenter and has now reinvented themselves by wearing a bikini for *FHM*. Fearne Cotton . . .'

'Doesn't she do morning TV?' I say.

'No, that's Fern Britton,' he says.

'There are two of them?' I say. 'What's the difference?'

'About twenty clothes sizes,' says Alexander.

'So, what do we say when they phone up?' asks Trish.

'Ahhh,' says Alexander. He leans back on my desk and picks up one of my pencils.

'We could just say no thanks?' I suggest.

'You can't do that,' he says. 'We may need them one day. If they become acceptably famous.'

'Who's done that? Ever?'

'Kylie,' he says. 'From bouclé perm to pop princess via Michael Hutchence.'

'OK,' I concede.

'And that other *Neighbours* girl. Natalie Imbruglia. From Mike's girlfriend to "Torn" in about two years.'

'Oh yes,' I say.

'Hell, even Russell Crowe was in *Neighbours* – or Russ Le Roq, as he was known then, when he used to run school discos in New Zealand.'

'You know too much,' I say. 'Sometimes I worry what actually goes on in your brain. Bearing in mind you are supposed to be running this business.'

'Gay men and teenage girls have the same tastes.' He smiles. 'Why do you think I know all the words to "Don't Stop Movin'" by S Club?'

'You do?'

He nods.

'I try not to think about it,' I say.

'So, what do we say then?' asks Trish, pen poised.

'That the clothes are in Japan,' Alexander replies.

'Japan,' she notes.

'And we don't expect them back for a while,' he adds.

'OK,' she says. 'And if they call again?'

'They are still in Japan. They are always in Japan. They will never come back from Japan. A designer mate of mine uses this excuse every time, and it works a treat. Most of the people who call up are so thick-skinned they won't notice the brush-off, and if they do, we have not been rude. Just in case they ever become useful.'

'We could just say "all of the looks you have requested are unavailable", which is what most people say,' I suggest.

'I think that is bland. I like the Japan thing.'

'OK, Japan it is.'

'Japan,' says Trish again, just to make sure. I look at her with her tongue poking out from between her teeth as she concentrates and think to myself again that I really must get myself another assistant.

The next few days are total chaos. Trish tells at least twenty undesirable celebrities that the white Monroe dress is in Japan, and we manage to get it on the back of a few more acceptable lovelies. Jodie Kidd teams it with a pretty jacket out to dinner at the Cipriani. Cat Deeley wears it to some *Elle* magazine thing. Joss Stone sings in it on *Parky*, and *Heat* gives it a double-page spread at the front. *Grazia* does a feature. *Glamour* calls it in for a shoot. And *Tatler* asks if there is a purple or a pink version for a Jade Jagger cover.

Alexander makes a call to Hungary to tell them to get a move on with the silver sequinning, and two days later the stock finally arrives. We get it into the shops, and the white dresses sell out within forty-eight hours. Alexander has Pandora's Box on the telephone three times in one morning wanting to reorder. He delights in keeping her on hold for fifteen minutes each time. He is punishing her for her piss-poor order in the first place. Net-a-porter get their stock in on the Wednesday morning and sell out by Thursday afternoon. We have Harrods and Harvey Nichols on the phone asking if we have any in black. Selfridges want more. Matches want more. Everyone wants more.

Two weeks after the delivery of your stock, you can normally tell if your collection is a goer or not. It dress notwithstanding, 40 per cent of fashion sales are made in the first month of the collection hitting the shops. The high-fashion customer is so aware of what is going on, and of what they want, that they are actively waiting for the collection to arrive. They have followed its progress on the net and in the magazines, and they know exactly when the new stuff is arriving. While the rest of us are half asleep in the first two weeks of January, thinking about joining a gym and shedding those brandy butter pounds, the high-fashion customer is planning their spring/summer wardrobe. These are the sort of women who are very happy to buy fur in July/August and think about shoestring straps and little summer dresses when it's minus three outside.

Some of them, like Jimmy Choo boss Tamara Mellon and handbag designer Anya Hindmarch, are what are known as key piece buyers. They know what the hit pieces are in each collection and will go from designer to designer picking off the cream of the crop. They will get the best Missoni knitted dress, the perfect tailored trouser from Balenciaga, the quintessential McQueen jacket or Prada dress. They will end up with a jigsaw of high-quality pieces that are the hits of the season. Others, like Jemima Khan, are loyal to certain designers and will buy the best of what they have to offer in each collection. The Russians, on the other hand, just tip up and buy the lot. They'll walk in and stock up on most of the collection, only to wear it all once. Much like that fantastic photograph of Daniella Westbrook and her child dressed head to foot in Burberry check, I have lost count of the number of times I've seen Irena, Luba or Valentina sporting £5,000 worth of my clobber when they turn up for a private view.

There aren't many clients I would bother to give a private view to. But I have about five Russian clients who always get a peek at the collection before it goes down the catwalk, or just afterwards. They put in an order and get it all before it goes into the shops. It is a pain in the arse to do and involves a lot of stiff smiling and hilarious laughing at their incomprehensible jokes, but it is usually worth my while. As I don't have a shop, it is the closest I can get to selling on without the shops making their commission. Ironically, for women who have more cash than they know what to do with, they get their clothes at discount. I sell at about 80 per cent of the retail price in the shops. It does seem a little unjust that the one group of people who really don't need a discount get one, while the rest of us have to save up. But, you know, life is unfair. The rich and famous get most of their stuff for free. Madonna gets a box of tracksuits every month from Adidas: then again, she is about the only A list star who actually wears them. And she does like a freebie. But then, she is a woman well known for going through her telephone bill with a fine-tooth comb, so it can't have come as that much of a surprise.

In the end, we are catering for a very small group of women who are so highly fashion aware that once a collection has been on the rails for more than four weeks it has lost its allure. Most designers are running to keep up. In an attempt to keep piquing the interest of these fickle women they are coming out with pre-Fall and pre-spring/summer collections in the middle of the season to keep their sales figures on a more even keel. If you can keep people buying throughout the year instead of in great bursts in January, when spring/summer hits the shops, and July, when the winter stock arrives, your cash flow situation is much improved.

Alexander and I are always discussing the merits of doing a cruise, or a pre-spring/summer collection, and a pre-Fall, but then you are entering a whole new world of different demands, plus the creative exhaustion of doing another two collections a year. Some designers who head up their own brand, and others like Karl Lagerfeld for Chanel, Galliano for Dior and Williamson for Pucci, have to design eight collections a year. I know I couldn't do it. It's no wonder, then, that fashion looks like it is running out of ideas. Some designs have become so watered-down and derivative. If you are working that hard to keep up with the consumer whose appetite is increasingly insatiable, you have to ask yourself, where will it all stop?

Some people are saying that fashion shows will become unnecessary. Pre-Fall and pre-spring/summer collections traditionally go into the shops without being shown on the catwalks – although some Americans broke that mould last summer and showed their pre-Fall. But usually they don't get shown, which brings into question the reason for showing in the first place. Firstly, your clothes get ripped off and go straight onto the high street before you have managed to contact your stitchers in Hungary. Secondly, the internet, Style.com and the weekly fashion mags deliver their verdict on your show and display the images way before *Vogue* and *Harpers*, so your collection feels old hat before it even hits the shops. Quite how the monthly glossies can compete with the weeklies and the internet I don't know. What is the point of their discussing a show we all saw and read about three months earlier? I know they will argue that they do it better and definitively, but frankly, who cares? And thirdly, why bother to show a dress when all you really need to do is put it on the back of someone famous? You shove it down a red carpet. Create a hot garment, get it photographed, and make some cash. It is no longer about creating a look, challenging what people think, crossing boundaries and coming up with ideas. It's, will Nicole wear this? Can I get Paris Hilton to open a shop in my clothes? Who cares what Style.com thinks? No-one can be bothered to wait for *Vogue*. In the end we'll be making a dress a week, shoving it on a celeb, and getting it into the shops. How depressing is that?

I am slumped at my desk trying to come up with a new skirt design while contemplating the end of the fashion business as we know it when Trish walks in.

'Morning,' she says. 'I've got some actress downstairs who wants to borrow something for her theatre opening.'

'Theatre?' I say.

'I know,' says Trish, curling up her short nose and snapping her chewing gum. 'Who goes to the theatre? Gay men and grey men.'

'And my mum,' I add.

'Well, it's her first night or something.'

'Oh.'

'Kathy sent her.'

Kathy has been doing this quite a lot recently. Since Vanessa's win and the launch of the white sequinned It dress, she now thinks I owe her a favour and she keeps sending all her clients to me, no matter how unfamous they are. And theatre actresses, I'm afraid, fall into this category. They may well be brilliant at their job, they may well entrance audiences worldwide, but they don't get magazine covers or 'my style' pages in magazines. While they won't give a dress bad press, they won't get it any press either. And this is the third stage actress she has sent me in a week. Don't get me wrong, I don't mind dressing the woman; it's just that more often than not they aren't the right size. Some of Kathy's clients are, to put it bluntly, too fat for fashion, and that's when it becomes a pain. If the woman is model size and can slip into a sample dress, then that's fine, but if she is a 12 or a 14 then it costs me money. Kathy thinks I can take a dress from stock and lend it for the evening, but I can't. Once it has been worn I can't sell it. No-one will buy something that is not entirely fresh and new. Even if they say they will look after it, the dress always comes back smelling of perfume and cigarettes, and there is nothing I can do.

'What size is she?' I ask.

'I'm not sure,' says Trish. 'Ten?'

'Sure?'

'As sure as I can be,' says Trish. 'She's wearing a big fat coat.'

The actress comes up the stairs and is utterly charming. In her mid thirties and starring in some Tom Stoppard play in the West End, she is clearly a woman at the top of her game. It is just unfortunate that no-one has ever heard of her, and that she is not the perfect 10 Trish predicted. Kathy has put me in an awful situation. After an initial introductory chat we both go downstairs and I stand around in the back room as she leafs through a selection of clothes we both know she can't fit into. She tells me how much she loves the clothes and how much she loves Vanessa Tate's dresses. I stand and smile and wait for her to ask if she can borrow something from stock. Out of embarrassment she doesn't ask, and out of sympathy I suggest that she borrow the loose-fitting black dress that I wore to the Fashion Awards.

'It has done the rounds a bit,' I say, having sent Trish off to find it among the old rack of samples that stands in Alexander's office. 'It is last season.'

'That's OK,' she replies, circles of embarrassment pinking her cheeks.

I really do feel sorry for her. There is nothing worse

than being confronted with a whole load of clothes you know you can't fit into. It has to be every woman's nightmare, to be hot and sweaty and embarrassed, trying to squeeze into something you are obviously too fat for.

After five minutes of huffing and puffing next door, she comes into my office in the black crossover dress, and I have to say she looks rather good in it.

'You up there?' Alexander shouts from the bottom of the stairs.

'Ye-es.'

'You won't believe the amount of editorial you've got. Vanessa's première dress is in all the must-have sections of the glossies ... Oh, hello,' he says as he walks in the door. 'My God, are you Michelle Adams?'

'Yes,' the actress replies with a smile.

'Oh, love your stuff,' he says. 'D'you know, Michelle's won two Olivier Awards,' he says to me. 'And an *Evening Standard* Theatre Award. You're in the new Tom Stoppard?'

'That's right,' she says.

'It's the hottest ticket in town,' he says.

'It is?' I ask.

'Oh, yes,' he says. 'Are you wearing us?'

'Yes.'

'Cool,' he says. 'Good call.' He winks at me. 'It's opening tonight, isn't it? You'll be in all the papers tomorrow. It's a great ensemble cast. You, Jude Law and someone from *Friends*.'

'That's right,' she says.

'It's so exciting,' he says. 'Just as well everything is back from Japan.'

12

Alexander is extraordinarily pleased with himself. Not only did he predict the good coverage that we got from Michelle Adams and her star-studded opening night, which included half the cast of *Friends*, but he thinks he has something to do with the huge amount of editorial we have been getting. 'Honestly,' he keeps saying, 'you couldn't buy that sort of coverage.'

Well, that's not actually true. One of the best kept secrets in the world of glossy magazines is that advertising does buy you editorial. One of the many jobs of the executive fashion director on a glossy is to make sure that the advertisers get enough mentions in the editorial. If they don't, not only do the advertisers ring up and complain, they have also been known to threaten to pull the plug on their £500,000 perfume campaign. A friend of mine who used to edit a girls' glossy said that during her first week in the job she had phone calls from the assistants of a couple of couture's big hitters. They both said something along the lines that Mr X is not very happy, he hasn't seen his clothes in the magazine for a while. She said that she was awfully sorry but she didn't quite understand the significance of the conversation . . . until she spoke to her executive fashion director.

Some designers employ companies whose sole job it is to count the number of column inches and picture credits they get in a magazine, and pressure is applied accordingly. So, just as an editor is about to go out on a shoot she'll find her rail of clothes called back in and the white Viktor and Rolf shirt will be exchanged for a MaxMara, or a Versace, or an Armani. The black trousers they'd called in from Vivienne Westwood will be exchanged for a pair from an advertiser. It won't be the fantastic silk dress that they change, but something that no-one would really notice. After all, black trousers are black trousers, particularly when they are in a photograph. Some magazines have started handing out perfume credits to keep their wage payers happy. So next time you see clothes by Dries Van Noten, and perfume by Chanel, you'll know why. US *Vogue* only ever has advertisers on the cover, and there are plenty of magazines that do the same. Independent designers are doing battle on an uneven playing field where your financial backing is more important than the cut of your clothes.

So you can understand quite how annoying it is to sit reading the *Evening Standard* and see that Ted bloody

Nicholls might well be being bought by the Gucci Group. The idea of seeing one of his piss-poor dresses on the cover of *Vogue*, with the rehabilitated Kate Moss pouting forth, is enough to make anyone reconsider their day job.

'Have you seen this?' I ask Alexander as he walks into the office.

'Yeah, I know,' he says, not sounding particularly perturbed. 'Best of luck to him.'

'Best of luck? I thought we wished him nothing short of congenital herpes on a daily basis?'

'Yeah well, spots and pox on his first born.' He shrugs. 'He doesn't have a possible perfume contract on the horizon.'

'What?' I say, shoving the newspaper to one side.

'Oh yes.' He grins.

'It has come through?'

'Well, it might come through. And all the publicity is certainly helping.'

Alexander has been working on a perfume deal for the last six months and neither of us had ever expected him to get anywhere. He has been writing to companies in the US, informing them of our success and offering up our services, and apparently he now has a reply. This is so exciting it could be the making of us, the launching of us as a global brand. The perfume market is worth billions of dollars a year.

Although the business is run by about five or six companies, including Estée Lauder, L'Oréal and Juniper,

Alexander has been concentrating all his energies on Coty. It has annual sales of over $2.1 billion, 72 per cent of which is in fragrance and toiletries. They produce Marc Jacobs, Jil Sander, Calvin Klein, Vera Wang, Davidoff, Jennifer Lopez and Sarah Jessica Parker, all under licence.

In terms of global sales, perfume is the most valuable asset a fashion house can buy. If you were to carve up the luxury goods pie, 10 per cent is ready-to-wear, 25 per cent is accessories, and a whopping 28 per cent is perfume and cosmetics. Get it right and it is a licence to print money; get it wrong and you can lose a fortune. It is a high-risk industry where seven out of eight new perfume launches fail each year. There is a magic alchemy to perfume for which no-one quite knows the formula. However, in order to appeal to Marbella Jane on her way through Gatwick for a cut-price week in the sun, a certain amount of celebrity helps. In perfume, the name does 70 per cent of the work, unlike in the ready-to-wear market, where it's more like 50 per cent. This goes a long way towards explaining the number of celebrity-based scents, such as Britney's Fantasy, Sarah Jessica Parker's Lovely, Shania Twain's Shania and, um, Alan Cumming's Cumming, that are currently gracing department store shelves.

Over and above the name, it is all about to whom you are licensed. The bigger your backer, the more money they throw at advertising and the better your position on the department store shelves. Walk through the ground floor of Selfridges, Harrods or Harvey Nichols and there is nothing haphazard or accidental about the Ralph Lauren display, or the wall of Chanel. It is all about eye-level placement, and if you are made under a large licensor, like Coty, you get the best shelves in the shop. All the perfumes are also packaged up together, so in order to get their hands on the big-hitting scents the stores will also have to purchase new or flagging brands as part of the deal. So the bankrollers support the underachievers and keep all the shelves stocked.

'What have they said?' I ask. 'Have Coty got back to us? Are we about to be rolling in cash?'

Alexander explains that it is not Coty who have finally returned our call, but a smaller, less well-known group called West, who might be willing to have a meeting. He says that normally they would offer between 8 and 12 per cent royalty agreement for the use of our name, which sounds very little when it is our necks that are on the line.

'Well, actually it's not,' says Alexander, sitting down in the chair in the office to explain. 'They take all the risks, developing the perfume, packaging it, selling it to the shops, advertising the arse off it. All you have to do is turn up, sniff a few smells, say what you like and be there at the launch.'

'Now you put it that way,' I say, 'it sounds like a bargain.'

This is our first proper foray into the world of

perfume. Last year there were vague mumblings about our being approached by a small independent, to sell soaps out of the boutiques. You know the sort of stuff that you have hanging around at the till that you pop into your bag when you've run out of gift ideas for your girlfriend's birthday. But the idea went nowhere. They said that we weren't big enough. That our brand wasn't strong enough. I kind of think they had a point. But a whole twelve months later, it might be different. The Vanessa Tate stuff must have helped.

West say they aren't promising anything, that they're thinking of expanding into the UK market a bit more, and that they're looking at a lot of junior, or young brands, to see if they might sign them up now, and develop them at a later date.

I know that we're clutching at straws, and that technically we're nowhere near ready, well-known or glamorous enough to get a deal, but these are serious people with serious money, and if they are prepared to meet us then I'm prepared to drop everything and get on the Eurostar even on the off-chance.

So two days later I find myself sitting next to Veronique in a blacked-out Mercedes on my way to an industrial park outside Paris. Neat and petite, Veronique sits in the front seat with her left arm hooked over the seat, chatting. Her dark brown hair is blown straight and glossy and cut into a sharp bob. She has finely plucked eyebrows and a bright red mouth.

'Oh, we are so, so lucky,' she says. 'Today you will be

meeting Xavier. He is such a brilliant nose. He comes from a long line of brilliant noses. His father is the man who invented Poison.'

'No, really?' I say. 'I spent my whole teenage years wearing Poison. I sprayed it on all the boys' pillows. I thought it was so sophisticated.'

'That goes a long way towards explaining why you are single,' says Alexander. 'I think it smells like bog cleaner.'

'But it is so, so exciting,' says Veronique, ignoring or failing to understand Alexander. 'He is so, so important. It is like his father was a Beatle.' She smiles.

'Great,' mutters Alexander as he stares out of the window at the thousands of rose beds waiting to come into bloom. 'We've got a meeting with Stella McCartney.'

Alexander is in a right old grump. The problem is he hasn't had enough sleep. Alexander needs a full eight hours in order to function along something resembling human lines. And since we had to take the 6.30 a.m. Eurostar to get here in time for our meeting, he is going to be in a foul mood all day. This is one of the reasons, he says, why he won't father children.

'Stella McCartney?' says Veronique. 'Oh, she has a perfume.'

'Yes, I know,' says Alexander.

'It does quite well,' says Veronique.

'Yes, I know,' says Alexander.

'We have many of you English out here,' she says. 'A

colleague I know looked after Vivienne Westwood when she came.'

'Really?' says Alexander. He is now actually sounding rather rude.

'Was she nice?' I chip in, trying to keep the show on the road.

'Oh yes,' says Veronique. 'She wanted her perfume to smell like a freshly washed fanny.'

'What?' says Alexander. That got his attention.

'Fanny?' says Veronique. 'That is right?' she asks, her eyes glancing towards her crotch. 'My English is not so good . . . cunt?'

'Your English is spot on,' grins Alexander.

'There was a problem of course,' she continues. 'Most of the noses are homosexual so they have never smelt fresh fanny in their lives.'

'I can imagine,' says Alexander. 'Did she get her wish?'

'Oh, I don't know, I have not smelt it. Have you?'

'Yes, I have,' says Alexander. 'But being gay I am afraid I am also none the wiser.'

'Oh,' she says, turning to look at the road ahead. 'Pity.'

We continue on in silence, driving through this strange suburban landscape of low white buildings that look like laboratories, surrounded by banks and banks of flowerbeds. The place must look and smell beautiful in June and July.

'Not long now,' says Veronique. 'Another three minutes or so.'

The car pulls up outside a long, low white building and we are met by four men in white lab coats. They each introduce themselves. There is Philippe the MD, Jean François his assistant, Alain who works in business affairs, and Xavier. Tall and handsome with dark hair and a fairly substantial nose, he is immaculately turned out with buffed nails, shining shoes and a fastidiously clean-looking shave. Alexander fancies him on sight, but Xavier looks right through him. Philippe, who is short and florid and who obviously enjoys a good lunch, whisks us through the building to a stark and clean-looking office with a large white round table, hard modern pine chairs and a large plate-glass window. We all sit around the table. Alexander and I stupidly sit opposite the window, as the cloud suddenly breaks and the sun pours in through the glass.

'So,' says Philippe, rubbing his fat hands together, 'you have some ideas?'

I sit squinting into the light as Alexander pulls out a black portfolio that contains photographs, tears from magazines, a press pack, a look book, some fashion spreads of my clothes from magazines, plus laminated front pages of Vanessa Tate and shots from Michelle Adams's première. We lay them all out on the table, and all the men plus Veronique lean in to take a look. They leaf through the pages, flick through the look book, and start muttering and mumbling in French. They don't look very impressed. It all looks quite amateur. I knew this was a long shot. A wasted day. We are so out of our depth it's actually quite funny. Alexander and I stare at each other like a couple of morons.

'Very intéressant,' says Philippe. 'What sort of woman are you appealing to?'

'Oh,' I say, 'I kind of hoped that it was obvious.'

'Ah non,' he says.

'Oh,' I say again. 'Um, a woman who is feminine.' He nods. 'Strong?' He nods again. 'And knows where she is going?'

'She is not afraid to say who she is,' chips in Alexander. 'She is in control. Powerful. Runs her own company . . . ?'

'Oh, right,' Philippe says, and clicks his fingers. Jean François leaps out of his seat and presses a switch. The electric blinds draw over the window and an overhead projector comes up from the middle of the table. 'This is the sort of thing that we are interested in.'

Graph after graph appear on the wall, followed by a selection of attractively coloured pie charts. Philippe goes on to explain that they are thinking of a more 16–24 market, youthful women in summer dresses planning holidays with friends to Greece or Spain. Alexander and I sit there. Any illusion I had of heading up a sophisticated brand is slowly being eroded. They have no idea who we are. But then again why should they? We are small and new and quite clearly not what they are looking for. Alexander starts to scribble on his note pad. The perfume market is difficult to crack, Philippe informs us. It is down between 17 per cent and 20 per cent on last year and their inclination is to play safe. We could go for a heavy incense-based product that would appeal to a mature woman, but market research says that the florals are where it is at. Heavy scents are not popular. Occasionally there will be a breakthrough scent that is heavy, but it is more likely to be something light and airy that captures the youth market.

'What is interesting,' he continues, 'is how the taste differs from country to country. In France we like the heavy perfume, and in the UK you like flowers. So something like Calvin Klein does very well worldwide but is not even top thirty here in France. So for a brand like yours we would be thinking flowers, flowers, flowers.'

And with Philippe's ideas ringing in our ears we are ushered next door to do some sniffing. This is where Xavier comes into his own. Down one side of the room there is a long table that contains racks of phials and bottles of essential oils. A vast array of colours from translucent to dark purple and gold, and they range in intensity, strength and volume. Some are obviously rarer than others. Some are clearly incredibly expensive, whereas others are simply there to make up the numbers. Xavier walks back and forth between the racks of scents and a small table on the other side of the room. On the table are sticks of white tapered paper, each with a small dimple on the end.

'So,' says Xavier, 'roses, with a base note of violets.'

He walks across the room and comes back with a selection of paper sticks and a bottle of essential oil. 'We spray,' he says, spraying. 'And then we wait five seconds.' We all wait five seconds. 'And then we smell.'

Alexander and I both inhale and then violently cough. There is no mistaking the scent of violets. It goes straight up my nose and hits the back of my throat, making me want to gag. It reminds me of those horrible purple sweets that even I couldn't manage to eat as a child, mixed with the large gussets in my granny's knicker drawer.

'God,' I say. 'That is actually unpleasant.'

'Really?' says Philippe. 'But it goes down very well in your country.'

'With who?' asks Alexander.

'The young women,' he replies.

'Are young woman really that basic?' asks Alexander.

'Research indicates that this is the case,' confirms Philippe. 'We could stray into the oriental area if you want, and make it a little warmer? Florientals also go down well in the UK.'

Xavier disappears again and returns with something that smells hot and heavy and rather fantastic – it's amber. Alexander and I are suddenly rather excited. This is all rather fabulous and quite fun. It is obvious that the deal is going to go nowhere so we may as well start to enjoy ourselves. He and I start asking to smell different oils. This is a process Xavier clearly enjoys. He sprays and sniffs and pronounces smells to be sublime and subtle and sexy. We say we like amber, jasmine and lotus, all of which are deemed too rich and sophisticated for our sort of market. They say they are a little like a Comme des Garçons perfume. Slightly too churchy and full of incense.

'You are going to have to trust us,' says Philippe. 'You know, Xavier comes from a long line of hit makers. His father came up with Poison.'

'Really?' says Alexander, pretending not to have heard the story before. 'That must be like being the son of one of the Beatles.'

Xavier looks unimpressed. 'Not exactly,' he says.

'But listen,' says Philippe. 'Let us not decide now. We shall call you, as they say.' He smiles. 'Perfume is a long process. Should we decide to go ahead, we shall have more meetings. Then we shall come up with something together, and it has to be stability tested and cooked for three months. Once we are all happy, that is.'

'Right,' I say, sniffing my jasmine paper strip. 'So there is more collaboration?'

'Well, you know,' replies Philippe with a smile. 'It was lovely to meet you both.'

'Absolutely,' says Jean François. 'It is lovely that we all agree. Summer florals are what we are looking for.'

'Very good,' says Xavier.

I am afraid to say that Alexander and I just stand there and smile. We are a small brand with a crack at the big time in terms of perfume sales and this is clearly not it. We are too small, it is too soon and they know it. Some small companies do have perfumes that do well but they are more developed and with a greater brand awareness than we have. Anna Sui and Carolina Herrera both do well. I am sure Viktor and Rolf can make a success of Flowerbomb with L'Oréal – 'an antidote to the reality against which we have only one weapon: dreams'. Our turn will come.

Back in the car on the way to Gare du Nord and Alexander is in a bit of a mood. Not only has our perfume foray clearly proved to be a waste of time, but Xavier didn't give him his telephone number. Alexander tried to organize a card exchange at the end of the meeting to which Xavier was not only non-committal, he positively looked the other way. And Alexander was slightly wrong-footed. He always scores when he puts his mind to it.

'So anyway,' says Veronique, 'I thought that was rather good.' The woman is taking public relations to an extreme. Surely she must have noticed the brush-off? 'The next step would be the box,' she says. Maybe she wasn't paying attention? 'We'll develop the box and bottle idea, with you of course, and then come up with something.'

'Right,' I say, slightly puzzled.

'What we don't want to do is come up with something that doesn't work all over the world,' she continues. 'I remember another designer insisted that he wanted his perfume in a pyramid. It was a very bad idea. They didn't want to buy it in the Middle East.

Unfortunately for the designer, it is one of the biggest fragrance markets.'

'Yes,' I say. 'Not a good idea.'

'It will cost us something along the lines of £80,000 to develop,' she says.

'Eighty grand?' I ask, suddenly waking up. 'That is a lot.'

'I know, but once it is organized it doesn't cost much at all.' She smiles. 'You know, perfume in general is only 35p a bottle.'

'I heard Chanel No. 5 is about 55p, and that is including the box. They retail it for £75,' I say.

'Jesus Christ,' says Alexander, joining in. 'No wonder they can afford Nicole in that dreadful advert.'

'Oh, I know,' says Veronique. 'It was £10 million. Who directed it?'

'It's so dreadful. Baz Luhrmann,' says Alexander, leaning forward.

'She has a three-year usage contract,' she says.

'I love dancing!' says Alexander, doing a woeful Nicole impression.

'We will meet again!' mimics Veronique.

'And the cross-eyed guy!' squeals Alexander.

'And she can barely wrinkle that nose,' she adds.

'And Karl Lagerfeld,' says Alexander. 'Is he cool any more?'

'He's lost so much weight.'

'Do you think?'

'Oh yeah.'

'What about Donatella?'

'What about her?'

'I reckon she only wears full-length gowns because she has lost her ankles.'

'She has ankles like an elephant.'

'It has all gone south, baby. And when she looks down she says, "Oh my God, I'm wearing puppy slippers."'

They both burst out laughing. Alexander gives Veronique a little tap on the shoulder. It is one of his signature moves that means he likes someone.

'God,' says Veronique. 'Did you hear the story about the designer who had someone make up a perfume to smell like bread?'

'No!' says Alexander. 'Like the smell they pump into a supermarket to make people hungry?'

'Yes!'

'Can you imagine the idea of being one of those women who never lunches and you go around smelling of bread all day? It's enough to make you crazy. Or eat your own arm off.'

'I know,' she says. 'It didn't go on the market.'

'Thank God,' I say. 'What is the sort of new stuff that is going on the market?'

'Oh, right,' says Veronique, looking for her professional face. 'Well . . .'

She goes on to explain that the smart money at the moment is backing a sort of fragrance diffusion line. Called flankers, they are a twist on a brand classic. So you get new perfumes coming along called Marc Jacobs Light, YSL Summer or Fahrenheit Blue.

'Tom Ford is making over Youth Dew for Estée Lauder,' she says.

'Really?' says Alexander. 'I thought he was making movies.'

'Apparently not,' says Veronique. 'I have some gold thing here.'

She looks through her pile of papers on the front seat and pulls out a stiff bit of gold card covered in gold writing.

' "Now your skin and your senses are under the influence of Tom Ford",' she reads.

'Thank God for that,' says Alexander.

'What has he done?' I ask.

'I'm not sure,' says Veronique. 'He has made over Youth Dew and has now called it Youth Dew Amber Nude.'

'Oh, OK,' I say.

'Here,' she says. 'He says this: "I drew my inspiration from the brand. My goal was to take the glamour, the history, the quality and the spirit of Estée Lauder, and work within that to create a collection for today. It also marks a turn away from disposable beauty and a return to the ritual of making yourself beautiful. The ritual of opening a slightly heavy compact and applying a high-quality product with a beautiful applicator. This reflects the intimate side of a woman, at her most glamorous." '

'Do you have any idea what that means?' I ask Alexander.

'Not really,' he says. 'But I bet he was paid a small fortune.'

'Probably,' I say.

Alexander and I leave the delightful Veronique behind and take our seats on the Eurostar. We are travelling first class for a change.

'So, what do you think?' he asks as we sit back with a large glass of wine each.

'It was not what I expected,' I say. 'I was rather hoping they'd be all over us like cheap suits.'

'I know what you mean,' he says. 'It's quite obvious they didn't want us. That we're too small.' He sighs. 'Fuck 'em, the stuff they made us smell was rank.'

'I know,' I say. 'It all smelt like teenagers' bedrooms.'

'Or the toilets at a Take That concert.'

'Yuk.'

'Take it from me, they were foul.' He smiles. 'No wonder people like you and I only buy bespoke perfumes. We don't like smelling like a toilet or indeed the rest of the nation. When was the last time you bought a lead brand fragrance?'

'I can't think,' I say.

'When you were seventeen or something, I bet. Perfume is all about mass market. And we, let's face it, we know nothing about that.'

'You're right,' I agree.

'It's such a shame because the deal would be so good.

We'd give them the licence for three years and they'd have to make certain targets and certain sales figures and, if they didn't, the licence would revert back to us.'

'I see.'

'So we'd be in a win-win situation. We couldn't lose money. We could only make money, and if they fucked it up we could look the other way, rebrand the product. Hell, we could even get Tom Ford in to write some marketing copy.'

'Oh well.'

'Maybe next year?'

'Or the year after?'

'Or the year after that?'

We chink our glasses.

13

Alexander and I return from our trip ever more determined. After three small bottles of wine we both decided that it was only a matter of time before we would be flicking perfume offers away like flies. And that when the time came we would be perfectly happy to sell out, just so long as we got a say in the packaging and advertising. After all, we concluded, when it came to a smell test neither of us could pick Chanel No. 5 from Stella or Marc Jacobs Light. Anyway, who cares if our fragrance smells like the changing rooms in Top Shop just so long as it flies off the shelves.

Trish is a little shocked when we share the idea with her. Her Hoxton sensibility re-emerges.

'What?' she asks. 'You'd be prepared to put your name to something you don't like?'

'If it comes to that, then yes,' I say.

'I could never do that,' she says. 'I've got too many morals.'

'Some of us can't afford morals,' says Alexander.

'Some of us never had them in the first place,' I say, looking at him.

'Ouch!' he says.

'Well, I don't know how you could,' says Trish, shaking her head. 'I mean, it should be illegal.'

'Right.' I smile. 'When you have a label of your own, Trish, then you can cast the first stone.'

'I'm never going to sell out,' she says. 'I'm never going to make money. I'm never being commercial.'

'I like those trousers,' I say, looking down at the knee-length flared trousers she is wearing. 'Where did you get them?'

'A mate,' she says. 'He's a designer's intern.'

'Really? How much?'

'I paid £75.'

'I see.'

'Well, if they don't get a Christmas party . . .'

Upstairs on the top floor, Dorota and the rest of the girls are hard at work. The collection is three weeks away and we are beginning to feel the pressure. Lydia is coming in this afternoon along with Mimi so that we can think of styling and fitting the clothes. Meanwhile, it is all hands to the machines.

The sewing room smells of fags, coffee and stale biscuits. Capital Radio is belting out the charts and no-one is talking. The closer we get to the show, the less conversation you hear tumbling down the stairs. Dorota is bent over a midnight blue silk shirt with frills all the way down the front. Inspired by Balenciaga's last spring/summer collection, it embraces the prim Edwardian look I am going for. There are three plaid jackets hanging on the rail with a bright pink silk lining that picks out the stripe in the check. I am very pleased with them. They look much better than I thought they would. It is often quite interesting to see the limits of one's own imagination.

'This is looking great,' I say to Dorota.

'Yes, it is OK,' she replies. 'But you know, it is a bastard to get all the checks to line up and match.' She sighs. 'I make that jacket twice already before it look OK.'

There is a murmur of agreement through the sewing room. This collection has been the most difficult so far. But then every collection is always the most difficult so far. And we have yet to reach panic stations and I have yet to get the girls over from Poland who work eighteen hours a day for £18 an hour in the last moments before the show. Although this year it will be a bit different as we are going to New York.

I wonder if anyone will lend us their atelier, or will we be doing all the last-minute changes in the hotel room or in some draughty warehouse somewhere? I remember hearing a lovely story about how Azzedine Alaia lent Vivienne Westwood his atelier when she first came to show in Paris. It was incredibly kind of him as there is nothing worse than trying to make your last-minute tweaks on the hoof. And it sounds as if he really looked after her. He had his chef prepare a fabulous Moroccan lunch, and they were joined by Kylie, who happened to be there for a fitting. And when the show was over both the designers called their teams together for an ideas and skills swap. Vivienne and Alaia talked each of their groups through how they designed from scratch, how they tailored and the way they worked. It all sounds so very civilized. Vivienne even asked Azzedine to come onto the catwalk with her at the end of her show. Alaia apparently refused. He doesn't do catwalks, possibly because he is so tiny – about four foot eleven. But he did lend Vivienne his prize dog Patapoof instead. Vivienne went down the runway with Patapoof and all of Paris knew that Alaia approved of her collection. Somehow I don't think that Michael Kors or Marc Jacobs will be doing me the same favour in New York.

I am starting to worry about this now. I must sort both this and the collection out. I can't travel to New York with the usual half-done collection, hoping that it will all come together at the last minute. I have also just realized that I won't be able to check up on Marc Jacobs or Roland to see if I am on track for this season. I am feeling a little sick as the amount of work I have to do in the next few weeks finally dawns on me. I am going to have to pull a few all-nighters in order to get it all finished. We've got buttons to cover, dresses to make, shirts to re-shape and at least three coats to line. My heart races just thinking about it.

I leave Dorota to her sewing and Toni, my Japanese pattern cutter, to work out exactly how to get the sharp shape into the tartan skirt. Coming down the stairs I can hear laughter coming from Alexander's office.

'Hello there,' he says as I walk in.

He has a cigarette in one hand, a latte in the other, and his feet are up on his glass desk. Sitting across the room from him in the two leather armchairs that he picked up from Les Couilles de Chien (aka The Dog's Bollocks) on the Golborne Road are his 'A Gay' pals Nick and Patrick.

'Morning,' says Nick, giving me a quick wink.

Dressed in a flowered shirt and a deconstructed jacket from Dries Van Noten, with his head shaved and his cheeks well moisturized, Nick is looking so next season I almost want to laugh. I heard on the grapevine that his department was given an invoice from Prada a few months ago because they had half-inched so much stuff. It doesn't look like he has learnt his lesson.

'Hi there,' says Patrick. 'Have you lost weight?'

Whenever I see Patrick he asks me the same question and the reply is always the same.

'No.'

Perhaps I am fatter in his mind's eye? Or maybe someone told him once that in order to be ingratiating you should always ask a woman if she is thinner? She is bound to like you after that.

'Have you heard the gossip?' asks Alexander.

'What gossip?'

'Anna Wintour is coming to London Fashion Week,' Nick announces with a grin, his buttocks perched on the edge of the chair.

'Fuck,' I say. 'Just as we plan to show in New York.'

'You're going to show in New York?' asks Nick, his voice rising an octave in surprise.

'No-o-o,' says Patrick, tugging at his ginger hair and then moving on to one of the fifteen silver rings he has in his right ear. 'You're not?'

'We are,' I say.

'You should alert the media,' says Nick.

'You are the media,' I say.

'I know.' He rolls his eyes. 'But you should do something.'

'Like what?' I ask.

'Have a dinner,' he suggests. 'You know, to tell them and to keep them onside. If you just tip up there and expect them to be nice to you, you'll have another think coming. Moving to New York is kind of like saying you hate London Fashion Week.'

'But we do,' I say.

'I know.' He rolls his eyes again. 'So do they, but there is nothing so patriotic as a Brit abroad. What you need to do is make them feel part of your gang. Bring them along with you. Make them feel part of the adventure.'

'That's a great idea,' says Alexander.

'Everyone's doing PR dinners these days. It's very now. Makes us all one lovely fashion family.'

'How ghastly,' says Patrick with a shiver. 'I barely speak to my own family. I've no desire to become part of another.'

'So, where are you showing?' asks Nick.

'The tents,' I say.

'Fuck me, that's exciting,' he says. 'Are you having an after-show?'

'No,' I say.

'Yes,' says Alexander. I turn and look at him. 'Only if we can get it sponsored,' he adds with a shrug.

'I'm sure I can help you with that,' says Nick, crossing his legs. 'Champagne houses are always throwing money at fashion. Did you hear about that big party Moët gave Matthew Williamson?'

'Yeah,' says Patrick. 'Like he deserves a retrospective. He's only been in the business for like eight years. I mean, who's next? Ted bloody Nicholls?'

'Talking of Ted bloody Nicholls,' says Nick.

'We weren't,' says Alexander. 'His name is banned here.'

'Oh right, of course,' says Nick, pointing a buffed fingernail in my direction and pulling a pseudo sad face. 'Well, you know he's sold to Gucci?'

'No,' says Alexander.

'Shit, no!' says Patrick.

I'm afraid I am too angry to speak.

'Since when?' asks Alexander.

'Since last night,' replies Nick. 'A mate of mine bumped into him in the George and Dragon and they were all plastered. They'd been drinking since lunchtime.'

'Oh God,' I say, slumping on Alexander's desk. 'It couldn't have happened to a nastier bloke. What do Gucci want with him? They've already got enough bloody British designers.'

'I know,' says Nick. 'Word on the street is that he'll only last a few collections and then they'll kick him out.'

'Bit like Julien Macdonald at Givenchy?' asks Patrick.

'Not really,' says Alexander. 'They didn't buy his company, and anyway, some people say that he walked from that job.'

'Is Ted Nicholls moving to Milan?' I ask.

'He'll be coming back and forth, I think,' says Nick. 'To be quite honest my mate didn't get all the details. Ted was too jazzed to talk that much and my mate thinks he's a tit so he didn't want to be seen hanging out with him.'

'Too right,' I say. I put my head into my hands and inhale. 'Is it wrong to want a drink at this time of day?'

'Did someone say drink?' The unmistakable flat tones of Lydia's voice drift up the stairs. 'Cos that would make a change from coke. Oh, hello boys,' she says as she walks into the room. 'You wouldn't believe it,' she continues, addressing me. 'Well, yesterday on this thirty grand shoot in New York – for a very good make-up company I might add – all this charlie gets

delivered at eleven a.m. Eleven in the bloody morning –
can you believe it? And it was the photographer's
assistant who ordered it in. What a cheek. I mean, you
can always rely on the hairdresser to have some dope in
his bag. In there, among the curlers and the grips, there
is always a big bag of weed. But coke? At eleven in the
morning? I thought it was very eighties.'

'But the eighties are back,' says Nick.

'Are they?' sighs Lydia. 'Does that mean we're going
to have to go through all that heroin chic thing again
too?'

'There are a few people who are still on it from the
last time round,' says Nick.

'Really?' asks Lydia. 'I am so fucking naive. I work in
this industry and I know nothing.'

'Very expensive heroin preserves you and gives you
that waxy glassy skin,' he continues. 'So if you are very
rich and front a couple of make-up company campaigns you can have it delivered to your door without
it being cut with rubbish and shit from the street. A
mate of mine who was producing a show quite recently
had a run-in with a model who was refusing to go
down the catwalk arm in arm with a male model, doing
the bride and groom thing. She said that she was the
star and that she didn't want anyone to detract from
that. After much consultation with the designer they all
agreed that she could go it alone. Anyway, come the
end of the show the model stands there, in the wedding
dress, arm out, waiting for the groom to turn up. She

comes off stage and shouts at the producer, asking where the bloody male model was. Turns out she'd shot up between the rehearsal and the show and couldn't remember the change of plan.'

'So no-one would mind if I had a drink?' I ask. 'I kind of need one. I just don't think I can even pretend to be happy about Ted Nicholls and his Gucci deal without a vodka.'

'Vodka?' asks Alexander. 'Is that what you want?'

'Definitely.'

'Hang on,' he says, rooting around in the cherry-wood drawer underneath his glass desk and pulling out a half bottle of Red Smirnoff. It's about a third empty. 'Here you go.'

'I can't believe that,' I say, taking the warm bottle.

'What?' he says, looking at me like I'm stupid. 'Hair of the dog.' He shrugs, and looks around the room. Everyone else nods in agreement, like it's the most normal thing in the world. 'A few shots plus three Nurofen and you're ready for any meeting.'

I pick up the bottle, unscrew the cap and knock back two big swigs in succession. The warm alcohol burns slightly as it goes down. My eyes water and I cough. I can feel a warm sensation creeping down my throat and chest, hitting my stomach.

'Better?' asks Alexander.

'Much,' I say, clearing my throat. 'I'm going to leave you guys to it. I've got work to do.'

'Don't think about it too much,' says Patrick. 'Karma

will out, you know. Ted Nicholls might well be on his way up at the moment but it won't be long before he comes right back down.'

'D'you think?'

'I know so,' he says.

'Are we talking about Ted Nicholls's Gucci deal?' asks Lydia, following me out of the room.

'Not any more we're not,' I say.

'I've heard he won't last long. Everyone says so.'

'Who's everyone?'

'Everyone on my shoot yesterday.'

'How do they know?'

'Something to do with an advertising job. You know there are no secrets in fashion.'

'How was the shoot?'

'Oh, you know,' she replies, walking over to the rail of clothes we are going to fit this afternoon. 'There was so much bloody food in the room. I couldn't believe it. Breakfast, brunch, lunch, afternoon tea, and then some pizza came. No-one ate anything. The coke came at eleven and the wine was opened at one. And all I could think was, I wish all the money that was being spent on food and entertainment was going into my bank account.'

'Yeah.'

'But the great thing was when we went out after the shoot for cocktails, which I can never be arsed to do because you have to get pissed and the photographer always hits on you because that's the law. Except this time it was great because they were all too wired to speak. They all had drug-induced lockjaw, so they sat in a row drinking their champagne, not saying a word. Have to say, I downed my glass, went back to the hotel and had room service.'

'Thought you had a flat in New York?' I ask.

'I did,' she replies, 'but I sold it. I'm thinking of buying in Paris.'

'Oh right?'

'Don't ask me why, I just fancy a change. One of the advantages of having no boyfriend. This is fabulous.' She has pulled out the tight-fitting tartan jacket with the pink silk lining. 'I love it.'

'You do?'

'Oh, I think it's very forties.'

'Great.'

'It's one of the best things you've done,' she says. 'Can I have one?'

'Of course,' I say. 'Shall we start the fitting? I don't think I can wait much longer for Mimi.'

'Sure,' she says.

Lydia has slipped off her tight black trousers and black V-neck sweater before I've even managed to get the jacket and skirt off the hanger. She is standing there naked but for a white thong and some deeply un-attractive flesh-coloured pop socks.

'Sorry about the socks,' she says, following my eye-line down to her calves. 'I've run out of proper socks. One of the hazards of never being at home. You always

248

come back to dirty washing and an empty fridge.' She pulls the skirt up over her hips and zips it up. 'Although, fucking hell, guess what I got for free last week? Only a bloody vacuum cleaner.'

'Really?'

'Yeah,' she says, buttoning up the jacket. 'I don't know what I'm supposed to do with it. Be photographed hoovering at home? Or say, when I do one of those I-drink-fifteen-litres-of-water lifestyle things, that I like hoovering in my Manolos? Honestly. I had a mate who was given a motorbike. She sent it back. She didn't want to be photographed doing her bike test.'

'She could have given it to her boyfriend.'

'Don't be stupid, she's a model, she doesn't have a boyfriend.'

The front door slams and I can hear Mimi coming up the stairs. Her dog is yapping at her heels and she is yapping on the phone. Together they make quite a noise.

'I told you where the trousers are,' she says. 'I put them in a cab and they are on their way to you . . . a cab . . . of course they're reliable. It's Addison Lee . . . yes . . . good . . . goodbye.' She hangs up and lets out the most enormous sigh. 'Honestly,' she says. 'You would think we were reinventing the fucking wheel. I have lost count of the number of times I have been called by Joss Stone's people to check up on a flared high-waisted trouser, and I now find out that it's not even for her, it's for one of her backing dancers. I mean,

Jesus.' She drops all four of her bags in the middle of the room. 'Picture me giving a shit. So . . .' She pauses, and looks Lydia up and down. 'I'm feeling that outfit.'

'You are?' I say.

'Oh yes,' she says. 'It's very Miss Marple.'

'I'm feeling it too,' says Lydia, stroking the tight-fitting skirt.

'How about if the skirt came up a bit?' suggests Mimi.

'D'you think?' I ask.

'Mmm. What are you saying this season?'

'Well,' I inhale, 'I'm thinking Scottish sort of house party in the forties?'

'Oh yeah.' She nods, picking up a short, sharp jacket. 'I remember.'

'It's opulent and decadent and sexy, but just a bit stiff and stifled. You know, hence the buttons and the tight-fitting skirts and cropped jackets.'

'Repressed sex?' she suggests.

'That's right.'

'That would figure,' she says, smiling.

'Yeah, well, thanks.' I smile right back.

Mimi, Lydia and I spend the next three hours going through the collection. Some of the clothes are made up, the others are in toiles. Every time Lydia puts a skirt or shirt on Mimi and I sit back and check to see if the ensemble is working. This is when Mimi's input – and, I have to say, Lydia's in her capacity of designer's muse – is invaluable. I am too close to the collection and perhaps a little too emotionally involved, so a couple of fresh pairs of eyes really do help. Mimi thinks that all my skirts are just a bit too long. She says that they look too repressed with not enough sex. She says if you stop in the middle of the calf all you get is the full width of the calf and then the ankle; if you stop a little higher up you get more shape. And she is totally right. It's the difference between looking like a 1940s Wren and a noughties sex kitten.

While I crawl around on all fours with a mouth full of pins, Mimi bobs in and out of her chair, scrutinizing the seams, the sleeve lengths, the lines and the shapes of the collection. And Lydia just stands there, staring at herself in the full-length mirror, getting jabbed by pins and being pulled left and right.

'D'you think I should have a boob job?' she asks, looking down at her cleavage and pressing together what little she has. 'I know they are a no-no over here, and they strap your tits down in Paris. But I could make a fortune doing Victoria's Secret. They like tits in the US.'

'How much would you make doing Victoria's Secret?' I mumble, lying on the floor, looking up her skirt.

'I don't know.' She shrugs. 'But it's got to be more than *Vogue*.' She laughs.

'Most things are more than *Vogue*,' says Mimi, sitting back in the chair with one eye closed, looking at Lydia.

'I know,' Lydia says. 'But it is tragic. I got £250 the other day, cash in hand, and they asked me to do a cover try.'

'Really?' I say.

'I always think it's a bit cheeky that they pay you by the day and not the page, and they always ask you to try for the cover to get your hopes up.'

'But you've done a cover before,' I say.

'Yeah, one.'

'That's not bad,' says Mimi.

'But it's not Kate, is it?' she says. 'She's done more *Vogue* covers than anyone else.'

'Don't you get overtime?' I ask. 'On a shoot?'

'Only when it's an advert,' she says. 'After six p.m. you get time and a half. That's why models always start to faff around at about three, to get their money up. When you get forty grand a day it is kind of worth adding a bit extra on at the end. Then they turn it on about seven thirty so they can get home in time for *EastEnders* or *Lost*. It's that obvious.'

'You get forty grand a day?' asks Mimi, suddenly becoming interested. For a posh girl she is uncommonly keen on cash. 'Is that the best you can get these days, what with all those actresses taking the best jobs?'

'Oh no,' replies Lydia. 'You can get quarter of a mil for a catalogue. We pretend that we want to do *Vogue*, *Vogue Italia*, *Pop* and all that shit, but what us girls really love is a catalogue. Freeman's, Saks Fifth Avenue, that sort of thing.'

'Harrods?' I add.

'No, Harrods and Harvey Nicks always play at being poor, which is very dull,' she says. 'So it's a good catalogue or a perfume or jewellery ad. Less trendy the better. The older and more prestigious the brand the less they change their advert. So you don't want something too cool. The tackier the jewellery house, the more they pay.'

'What, with your bloody great trucker's hands?' asks Mimi.

'They aren't that bad,' says Lydia.

'They're not great either.'

'Yeah, well. They use hand and arm models. I am always standing there all dolled up in my dress with an arm behind my back, and there's a girl behind me with a fag in one hand and a whole load of diamonds on the other, posing away.'

'Poor girl,' I say. 'That can't be fun.'

'I don't know,' says Lydia. 'She makes a fortune and doesn't have to have her face in the magazine and spend hours in bloody make-up. I think it's more difficult if you are stunt legs.'

'I can imagine,' says Mimi. 'I knew a girl who was a stunt bum. She made a lot of money in films. But it must be more difficult if you've got to be someone's legs in a photo shoot.'

'They spend hours with them stuck in the air,' says Lydia.

'I know a man not very far from here who would

be very suited to that job,' I say, glancing towards Alexander's office.

'He wouldn't earn much,' says Mimi. 'It's about the only industry on the planet where girls do better than boys.'

'Porn?' I say.

'Except for porn,' she concedes.

'I do feel sorry for them,' says Lydia, striking a stunning pose in the mirror by way of relieving her boredom. 'Would I bother to do this if I got a third of what I am earning now? Probably not. Also, their shelf life is so short. It is amazing how quickly those queeny designers tire of a pretty face. Most of the male models are straight so they don't realize the game that is being played.'

'There's always another Russian or Pole to take their place,' says Mimi, on the verge of French-kissing her dog.

'Actually, weirdly, they are mainly skinny boys from the north of the UK or sun-kissed hunks from the Deep South. Wherever they are from they are destined to be miserable.'

'And starving,' I add.

'You have to feel sorry for the girls who starve,' says Lydia. 'I mean, don't do the job if it's that hard. You can always tell who they are. They get these blue/red Nicole Kidman hands because they have starved so much that their circulation is so poor. They then get this thin layer of hair all over them, like a gerbil, because their body has gone into shock and it's trying to keep warm. Then they get covered in bruises because their nutrition is bad. It is always the downy anorexics who are being touched up by make-up before they go onto the catwalk. It does make me feel ill sometimes. But if you are seventeen and you've got £300 in your back pocket for the first time in your life, what does it matter if you don't get your periods any more and you haven't eaten for days? It does make me angry though. At least in the States they like their models a bit bigger. You can be healthy there. But in Milan they expect you to be as thin as a bloody toothpick. In Paris they are less money-orientated so they are more likely to alter their clothes for you because it's more about art than cash. I remember a designer going up to a mate of mine and saying to her that she looked so much better since she'd lost her puppy fat. The girl had been in hospital with dysentery. He turned around and said, "Doesn't matter. Whatever it takes, that's what I say." I nearly punched him.'

'No-one makes the big bucks these days,' says Mimi.

'Not really,' agrees Lydia. 'The supermodel is dead and the actress is queen. The big contracts aren't going to models any more. The only time you know that someone has been paid a small fortune is when they have been asked to endorse something. Like when you see their signature at the bottom of the ad for some watch. Omega by Cindy Crawford, or someone like that. That's when you know they have the GDP of a small country.'

'Jesus Christ,' I say suddenly, my mouth still full of pins. 'What is that disgusting smell?'

'Is it this new perfume I'm wearing?' asks Mimi.

'No,' I say, looking around the room. 'It's your bloody dog.'

We all turn to look under my desk. There is a small trail of piss and a tiny pile of dog shit. Next to it we spot the hunched haunches of Mini Me, shivering with constipation.

14

There are two weeks to go before the collection and I can really feel the pressure. What am I thinking, going to New York? I keep having nightmares about it. I keep dreaming that I am walking down the catwalk on my own, with no clothes on, and all I can hear is the sound of one man clapping. I know it's a classic anxiety dream, but that doesn't make it any less scary.

After clearing up Mini Me's pile of crap, Lydia, Mimi and I worked until midnight, going through all the clothes and trying to work out what works with what, and what, if anything, needs dramatically reshaping. Weirdly, we all agreed that the Vanessa Tate purple première dress needed updating. Perhaps it was because we'd all seen it so many times in *Grazia* and *Now* and all those other mags that we were fed up with it. Or maybe it just never really worked outside a red carpet situation. But as soon as Lydia put on the pink version,

Mimi yawned so long and loudly that we had to take note.

'I'm just not feeling it,' she said about eight times by way of explanation. She added finally, 'It doesn't fit in with the rest of the collection. There's nothing sexually repressed or Scottish about it at all. It looks tired, and anyway, Top Shop is ripping off Ossie Clark something rotten at the moment. You shouldn't join that bandwagon.'

So we sat back and decided to take the skirt off. We kept the top as a blouse, to be worn with skinny jeans or a large pair of high-waisted wide-leg tartan trousers I'm working on. We are not sure which. But it is much improved. I have decided to make the top a feature of the collection. Without the skirt, it looks sexy forties. I've also decided to put covered buttons down the front to tie it in with everything else. Dorota and half the seamstresses in Poland are upstairs making it in black and white as well as the pink silk satin as I sit here and panic.

'All right?' asks Alexander as he wanders through on his way to his office.

'No. I've got diarrhoea, insomnia and an enormous spot on my face,' I say.

'Sounds like you should lay off the jazz.'

'Don't be annoying. You know what I'm like before every collection.'

'Yeah,' he says, popping a teaspoon in his mouth, 'a total nightmare.'

'Anyway,' I say, slightly annoyed by his lack of support, 'what the fuck are you eating?'

'Oh this,' he says, looking down at the small pot in his hand. 'It's baby food.'

'Baby food?'

'Hedi Slimane, the most influential menswear designer in the world, swears by it.'

'He does?'

'It helps him keep thin.'

'What? Eating baby food?'

'He doesn't like to do too much digesting, apparently.'

'I don't know what to do with that information,' I say.

'I'm giving it a go,' he says.

'Can't fit into your skinny jeans any more?'

'Funny you should say that.' He turns and smiles at me.

'What have you done to your face?' I ask. 'You look different.'

'Can you tell?' he says, tripping into my office and shoving his face in mine.

'You look weird.'

'Brighter? More alert? Awake?' he asks, turning his face left and right so that I can view it.

'Have you had a face lift?'

'I think I love you!' he exclaims. 'No, I've put Anusol under my eyes.'

'What? Bum cream?'

259

'You can call it that if you want. It works miracles. Lydia told me about it.'

'She was taking the piss.'

'No she wasn't,' he replies indignantly. 'You can use any pile cream. Preparation H, anything. It makes all the capillaries around the arsehole contract, and it does the same for the eyes. Models use it all the time after a heavy night out on the tiles. It does the trick. Why do you think top models always look so good?'

'That's down to genetics, not arse cream,' I say.

'Whatever,' he says. 'You noticed a difference.'

'It can't be good for you.'

'Who cares?'

'For a man who only eats organically you seem quite profligate with the rest of your health.'

'God you're boring,' he says, and walks out of the office.

Two minutes later he is back.

'Oh, by the way,' he says, thrusting a piece of paper towards me. 'I think Mark One might want to meet us.'

'Wonderful,' I sigh. 'Ted Nicholls gets bought out by Gucci and we get to talk to Mark One.'

'Don't knock it,' says Alexander. 'Anyone who is anyone in the fashion industry has a mass-market diffusion line.'

Much as it pains me to say it, he is right again. Betty Jackson, John Rocha, Gharani Strok, Pearce Fionda, Jasper Conran, Matthew Williamson, Ben De Lisi and

Julien Macdonald all have ranges at Debenhams. Luella is at New Look. Stella is at H&M. In fact, the high street is what really keeps British fashion afloat. There isn't a British designer who doesn't have a high-street store behind them, except McQueen, but then he is backed by Gucci so he can afford not to. But for the rest of us, high-street backing buys us freedom. It pays the bills and gives you a more constant cash flow than if you had only two collections and two drops a year. All you need to do is walk past the designer stores in the West End on a Saturday afternoon to see how much ready-to-wear needs the high street. The big designer stores are empty. There are just not that many people in the world who can pay £1,500 for an unstructured cotton jacket.

Alexander and I have been trying to get a meeting with Mark One for a while and since all the Vanessa Tate publicity that we've been getting they've finally decided to return our calls. They're offering us the standard 5 per cent of sales deal that everyone else gets. But Alexander is worried about the publicity and PR aspect of it all. Our problem is that as we are a small brand that is just beginning to take off, we can't afford to be swamped by them. Jasper, John Rocha and Julien Macdonald's diffusion lines are very heavily advertised, but they have been around long enough for it not to matter. We could launch headlong into the deal and allow ourselves to be promoted everywhere, we could make a lot of money very quickly, but the long-term damage to the label would be enormous. There are a couple of Debenhams designers who don't really have a mainline business any more. But they make so much at Debenhams that they don't really seem to care.

'So,' I say, 'do they want a meeting?'

'Yeah,' he says. 'And they want a sort of strategy document from you to say where you think the brand is going, and where you think fashion is going for the next couple of seasons.'

'Christ. Who knows where fashion is going in the next couple of seasons? Who knows where fashion is going at all? Some people say that the high street is going to take over and others say things are going to become more and more exclusive. Everyone's loving bespoke. Burberry made a loss last year, and now they are £1.2 million in profit. Dior is up 30 per cent. So are Chloé and Cavalli.'

'Cavalli?' spits Alexander. 'Who the fuck is buying that?'

'Posh?' I suggest. 'And all her mates?'

'You really know how to make a man depressed.'

'What do they want then?'

'You know, a bit about how no-one wants to look boho any more, and about where you think it is headed.'

'Now *I* feel depressed,' I say.

'Keep thinking about the 5 per cent,' he says. 'And you don't even have to put pen to paper.'

The best bit about a diffusion line deal is that they're

not allowed to copy any of the designer's clothes. So they can't take a £700 dress and make the same thing for £70 but in different material, like everyone else does on the high street. Also the designer doesn't actually have to do any of the drawing. They tell them what they are feeling and the chain's own designers come up with sketches and ideas for their client's approval. It's the closest I am ever going to get to knowing what it is like to be Tom Ford.

'When do they want it?' I ask.

'By the end of the day?' He smiles, wandering back into his room.

'That's not possible.'

'Just think of them as an annoying chihuahua yapping at your heels. You have to feed it, nurture it and occasionally clear up its crap.'

'God,' I say, as my head falls into my hands.

I don't really need this right now. I am so behind. Every designer is always behind with their collection, but I am really behind. And the New York thing is not helping. The other side of the Pond I won't have my usual support system of friends, relatives and slave labour to do the final tweaks and radical last-minute changes the night before the show. I am going to have to travel to New York with the whole thing more or less finished. Obviously I'll have to find some stitchers over there to help fit the models, but I won't be able to demand silver anoraks or a total change of look at the last minute like I did last season. I also won't be able to rely on Marks and Spencer to get me out of any tight spots.

'Just a few paragraphs,' shouts Alexander from next door. 'Of your carefully chosen ideas about the future of fashion.'

'Can't you do it? I've got so much to do!'

'What do you think I'm doing?'

'I have no idea, actually.'

'Well, I've got people to talk to, deals to make, and I am sorting out all the shit for New York.'

'Good for you.'

'But if you want me to write about the world of fashion as well as run a multi-million-pound company . . .'

'Please?'

'Well . . .'

'Pretty please?' I can hear him crumbling. 'I'll buy you the martini of your choice at the Light Bar.'

'OK then.'

I knew I'd clinch it with the Light Bar in the St Martin's Lane Hotel. Alexander is a sucker for a Martini, and a total sucker for a hotel bar. Such is his penchant for overpriced alcohol and expensive cheese straws that he once announced to me that he was going to give up hotel bars for Lent. It was apparently a huge sacrifice. So huge, in fact, that it only lasted a week before he found himself in the lobby of the Soho Hotel. His excuse was that it was new and it had to be tried out. He ended up paying both Trish and me £20 each for the lost bet.

Alexander walks back into my room and slumps down on the chair. He has a pen and pad in his hand.

'So, if I say something along the lines of fashion is moving very fast. The high-street slut is moving just as fast as the Sloane Street bitch. In order to make this collection, sorry, diffusion collection work, it has got to be fashion forward enough to appeal to the *Grazia* reader, who eats, breathes and craps brands for breakfast. The direct effect of our obsession with celebrity is that what slebs are wearing is now filtering down more quickly. Do you remember that chart they had about ten years ago? Where what was high fashion would be medium fashion in six months? And Marks and Spencer a year later? Now it's catwalk to Marks in about three months.'

'Which is quicker than we can get it into the shops,' I say.

'Almost,' he agrees. 'So do you think that is OK?'

'Yeah,' I sigh. 'Perhaps with a little less bile.'

'Oh, I think the bile is what makes it interesting.' He grins, gets out of the chair and walks next door.

I am just about to concentrate on skirt lengths when the telephone goes.

'Hiya,' says Trish. 'I've got *Tatler* on the line. D'you want me to put them through?'

'*Tatler*?'

'Yeah, I know,' says Trish.

'OK.'

'Hi there,' comes a voice so posh that it's actually hard to make out exactly what she is saying. 'It's Fluff Cee Jay here from *Tatler*.'

'Hi, Fluff.'

'Yah, anyway right, we're rally rally keen on getting you into the mag, right? So was just wondering if you could do a shoot for us?'

'Right?' I am more than a little dubious.

'It's for all the most fantabulous designers around at the moment, and you are one of them, so I was wondering, are you free next week for a shoot? With you and your muse, right?'

'Sorry?'

'It's for all the best designers around, right? It's for a pull-out thing for London Fashion Week. It sticks on the front of the mag, right?'

'Oh, I'm not showing at London Fashion Week.'

'Oh, right,' she says, sounding confused and disorientated, although that could be her natural state. 'Shit. Hang on.' I hear her hand and a set of bangles try to cover the telephone as she relays the information to someone else more senior in the office. There is some mumbling that I can't quite make out before she comes back on the line. 'Can you do it anyway?'

'Um,' I say, getting a whiff of desperation and the sense that someone must have pulled out.

'With your muse . . . whassername . . .'

'Um . . .'

'Lydia Sharp.'

'Well . . .'

'If we can secure Lydia, you'll do it, right, yah?'

'When did you say it was?'

'Next week.'

'Um . . .'

'Great!' she says. 'I'm so pleased. We'll send a car, and sort it all out with your PR person, whasser-name . . .'

'Well, Trish deals with that sort of stuff.'

'Fantabulous. I'll talk to Trish.'

'OK then,' I find myself saying.

'Cool,' she says, and hangs up.

'Alexander?' I say.

'What?' he barks.

'I've just found myself agreeing to do a shoot for *Tatler*.'

'What the fuck did you do that for?'

'I've no idea.'

'Oh well,' he says, 'it might sell a few frocks.'

Alexander is clearly too busy to dwell on the *Tatler* shoot, as indeed am I. Normally, we would have both searched our souls for at least a couple of days, trying to work out if it was the right thing to do and what everyone else might think. But these days we are both trying to make some money, move forward and get out of the parochial rut of caring about Katie Grand, or worrying if Ted Nicholls is laughing at us behind our backs. We knew a long time ago that *Pop* magazine was never going to let us grace its pages. That we would never be invited to the alternative fashion party in the East End. It's just recently that I have begun to care less. If our Mark One deal happens and New York goes well, I won't ever have to think about Hoxton and Ted again.

The phone goes.

'Hiya,' says Trish. 'I've Emma Price to see you.'

'Oh great,' I say. 'Send her up.'

Emma Price is one of the fashion industry's more eccentric characters. A close friend of Mimi's, she is so fashion forward and on the button that she is actually ahead of the herd. She doesn't really have a job other than being cool. In another, more logical business like advertising, she would be a trend spotter, but in fashion she is a sort of stylist and accessories designer. Basically she comes to the studio every couple of months or so and tells me what she is into. It could be plastic flowers, charm bracelets, thick hairbands, diamanté badges or Russian dolls. Emma is among this elite group of people, along with Marc Jacobs's accessory designer Katie Hillier, who can really create a flash-in-the-pan trend. Last season Katie was accredited with coming up with robots. Made of silver and gold, they hung from every It girl's handbag. They were the sort of things that are so hot they are almost out of fashion as soon as they leave the shop.

'Hello there,' says Emma as she comes in through the door. She is dressed in yellow check drainpipes and a tight black jumper. She has dark scraped-back hair and a clean, stunning face with a slash of red lipstick.

'How are you?'

'I'm exhausted,' she says, sitting down in the chair and putting her lemon yellow handbag on the floor. It is covered in small trinkets and dangling things. 'I've just come back from ten days in China.'

'Really?' I say.

'Yeah,' she says. 'I was sniffing around to see if there is any kitsch Olympic stuff I can shove on some knickers.'

'Right.'

'Like a reworked Hello Kitty thing,' she says. 'You know, that everyone liked last year?'

'Did you find anything?'

'A few bits and pieces that I think will work next year.'

'Right,' I say. 'Sounds great.'

'It should be,' she says. 'Anyway, let's have a look at the collection.'

Emma goes through the rail in my office in complete silence. Unlike Mimi, who feels the need to re-enact Meg Ryan's famous restaurant scene from *When Harry Met Sally* every time she looks at clothes, Emma is not that willing to please. I take her upstairs to look at the toiles and the other half-finished clothes that are hanging on the rails. She picks up the pink satin version of the Ossie Clark top and strokes it between her fingers.

'This is nice,' she says.

'Do you think?' I ask. Somehow her one low-key comment is worth all of Mimi's gushes and groans.

'Yeah. I like the puffs and the plunge. Very madonna/whore.' She smiles. 'That should do well.'

'I hope so,' I say.

We walk back downstairs to my office. She sits down in the chair, gets out a bag of trinkets and must-have accessories, and shows me hairbands, badges and a range of necklaces that don't really do that much for me. Then she produces a bag of diamanté skull and crossbones. Attached to a small silver clip keyring, they are instantly desirable, cool and kitsch, and my heart beats a little faster.

'They're great,' I say.

'Aren't they?' She grins. 'They hang off handbags or tops or jackets.'

'Where did you get them from?'

'A mate is knocking them up in a studio in this village outside Gloucester.'

'Gloucester?'

'I know.' She smiles. 'Not exactly the hotbed of the fashion industry, but she makes lots of cool stuff.'

She opens up another bag, which contains broaches and necklaces made out of cracked mirrors with diamanté and coloured glass.

'They look a little bit like Andrew Logan's stuff, don't you think?' she asks.

'That the guy who used to do Alternative Miss World?'

'That's him.'

'I remember going to a party at his house, years ago,' I say. 'He has this giant Pegasus in his sitting room made out of mirror mosaic. I mounted it and split my leather trousers all the way up the arse. I had to leave the party immediately.'

Emma laughs. 'Were you drunk?'

'Of course.'

'Thank God for that!'

She sits and talks me through the skull and cross-bones options. Her mate is churning them out at £2 a pop. I should sell them on wholesale at about £25, and then they could retail at about £75 each. She would take a 10 per cent cut on all the ones I sold. She stands up and clips one onto the buttonhole of the pink Black Watch tartan jacket. It looks great.

'It's a little bit punk,' she says. 'Gives it a bit of an edge. You could put them on handbags as well.'

'Sadly, I don't do those,' I say. 'Although I really like the one you've got there.'

'Oh, this?' she says. 'My mate Peter is importing them from Milan. He's got about fifty of them in his flat in Primrose Hill. He is looking to sell them. You could put a few of them down the catwalk if you want.'

'Really?'

'Yeah, why not?' She smiles. 'They're cool, aren't they? Soft and reconstructed. Not like the other stiff stuff that is on the catwalk.'

'No, they're great,' I say. 'What sort of colours are they coming in?'

'Black, yellow and white.'

'Right.'

'Why don't you take six?' she asks. 'You can cover them in skull and crossbones and see how you go.'

'Sounds brilliant,' I say.

Alexander is a little dubious. A few minutes after Emma leaves, he wanders into my room and picks up the skull and crossbones keyring sample she has left on my desk.

'What's this tat?' he asks, turning up his already short nose.

'Tat for the collection.'

'It's horrible.'

'No it's not.'

'It is,' he sneers. 'It's really horrible.'

'You hate anything like that.'

'I know, and with good reason. Because it's shit.'

'It's gorgeous and desirable and I'm putting it down the catwalk.'

'Fuck off you are.'

'I am.'

'You're not.'

'Emma is never wrong.'

'But she really is the shit side of fashion,' he insists. 'She is all about rubbish that people put in newspapers, that brings our profession into disrepute, like ankle socks with shoes, crappy arm tat bangles and bows.'

'You wouldn't understand.'

'No?'

'It's because you are not a girl.'

'No.' He grins. 'I'm a gay man, which means I have much better taste.'

'Hi,' says Trish, walking into the office. 'Just thought you might want to see this.' She flashes a double-page spread in *Grazia*. 'Kim Cattrall is wearing the Vanessa Tate Golden Globes dress to her theatre première.'

'Great,' I say. 'That looks fabulous.'

'Oh look,' she continues, picking up the skull and crossbones keyring and turning it in the light. 'This is great. I'm loving that. Where's it from?'

'See?' I say.

'That means nothing,' Alexander says, picking up the Kim Cattrall shots and leafing through the pages. 'Oh look – "Jennifer Aniston looking sad in Balenciaga". Don't you just love *Grazia* magazine?'

'Why don't you go and finish off your pitch? I'm extremely busy.'

'I can see that,' he says.

I spend the rest of the afternoon upstairs in the sewing room turning up trousers and taking in jackets. After my session with Lydia and Mimi the whole collection has become a little sharper, shorter and neater.

The atmosphere upstairs is becoming increasingly fraught. You can almost hear a collective sigh of annoyance every time I put in an appearance. Each time I come into the room, it means they have to change something. And every change, of course, means more work.

'I'm thinking of adding these little keyrings to the collection,' I say to Dorota, who is making a mini kilt out of the remains of the tartan. It was Mimi's idea. I am not actually very sure about it, and I have a feeling that it won't even make it onto the plane to New York. 'What do you think?'

Dorota looks up from her stitching. Her face is puce, her pores are open. She looks like she's in the throes of a menopausal hot flush. 'What?' she asks. Her mouth hangs open slightly, giving me a flash of her golden molars.

'What do you think?'

'That from that girl?'

'Emma? Yes.'

'What for?'

Fortunately, I am used to Dorota's general lack of enthusiasm. She fails to see the point to most things, especially at this late stage of the collection.

'I thought I might have them hanging off the jackets and handbags.'

'Why?' she asks.

'Because they are pretty and fun?'

'I don't think so.'

'Oh.' I'm suddenly losing confidence in my decision. 'What does everyone else think?'

A nonchalant murmur goes around the room as

about ten women look up from what they are doing, and curl their collective, somewhat hirsute top lips.

'No-one likes them,' declares Dorota. 'They are vulgar.'

'Oh,' I say. 'Thanks for that.'

Walking back downstairs feeling rather frivolous and a little stupid, I resolve to have a word with Mimi about the keyrings before I ditch the idea entirely. I wouldn't normally take the opinion of the sewing room above my own instinct, but after Alexander has been so negative as well, it's hard to feel totally confident.

'Done it!' shouts Alexander from the other room. 'The pitch is ready. Shall I come and read it to you?'

Before I have the chance to tell him that I'd rather read it later, he's in my office, computer printout in hand.

' "Dear Mark One," ' he starts. ' "I am very much looking forward to meeting you all but in the meantime blah blah blah. Having thought how our young brand might work as a diffusion line, here are a few suggestions: We are a sharp, well-cut, tailored brand and would like this to be reflected in the diffusion line. We appreciate that this may well be difficult to achieve, but bearing in mind costs and constraints we still think that it should form the essence of the label. While other brands are still looking for the feminine, we are after simple lines and clean cuts for our size 12 and over 25-year-old customer, with an eye to such young fashion icons as Chloé Sevigny and Tess Daly . . ." '

'Tess Daly? What has she got to do with fashion?'

'I couldn't think of anyone else off the telly.' He smiles. 'Anyway, I love *Strictly*.'

'Go on . . .'

'Tess Daly, and we should keep it as fashion forward as possible. As she is clearly moving faster than she was before.'

'What?'

'Oh, I don't know,' he says. 'It sounds good.'

'OK.'

'Anyway . . . "Irrespective of what other people are doing for the next few seasons, we are keeping things simple. Shapes should be unfussy, although fabrics are more forgiving – blues and pinks, rather than blacks and whites. We see our future with you as a young yet grown-up brand. Something that is worn out and about but more formally than the 'boho' look that everyone has had before – as seen in Roland Mouret's new show and the slim-fitting Balenciaga suits in their current spring/summer collection. We are very excited about the potential of this relationship, and look forward to hearing from you. I hope this makes sense, blah blah blah. Best regards etc. . . ."' He looks up. 'What do you think?'

'Well, I'm not sure what any of it means.'

'But it sounds good?'

'It sounds, um . . .'

'Like I know what I'm talking about?'

'Yes.' I am trying to be supportive.

'Great, then. I'll send it.'

'Excellent. Well done.'

'Light Bar?' suggests Alexander.

'Light Bar,' I reply. 'Because you're worth it.'

15

Two days later I find myself sitting at my desk writing out placements using my best calligraphy pen, and trying to work out if we have enough tat for a goodie bag.

'Alexander?' I shout from my room. 'We're giving them skull and crossbones keyrings, some soap, and what else?'

'One of those chiffon T-shirts,' he replies.

'But that's last season's stuff,' I say. 'And all the guests will know.'

'You can either be generous and out of date or not generous and fashionable,' he says. 'And I suggest that we err on the side of generous, seeing as we have the whole of British fashion coming.'

'What are we going to give the blokes?'

'Ah,' he says. 'Patrick has managed to five-finger-discount some Versace ties that don't look too Versace, so I thought that if we re-label them they could be re-gifted.'

'You can't re-gift something that has been stolen.'

'Liberated,' he corrects.

'Liberated, then.'

'What else do you suggest?'

I sit and stare at the mood wall for a second. The collection is less than two weeks away. I really don't have time to worry about exactly what the blokes from *Dazed and Confused* and *Another Magazine* are going to get in their goodie bags. They will only leave them behind anyway. I wasted much of yesterday with a hangover after our two a.m. session drinking raspberry martinis in the Light Bar. I have only got tonight's PR dinner and my *Tatler* photo shoot to get through before we travel to New York, but every time I think I'm nearly there, Mimi, Alexander or Dorota comes up with something that doesn't quite work. Yesterday, the frills that we put on one of the silk shirts were so dreadful they even made the mannequin look like a seventies stand-up. They had to be unpicked and remade in a thinner, more forgiving chiffon that Trish had to go and score down the market. I really don't need to ponder the whys or wherefores of Patrick's dodgy ties.

'They sound fine,' I say. 'Just so long as they don't look too Versace.'

'They don't,' he replies. 'Even with my finely tuned eye, I can't tell.'

There is an hour to go before the party, and the sublimely glamorous Notting Hill restaurant, E&O, has done us proud. Mimi is an old friend of Will Ricker, the owner, and Alexander knows Russell, one of the maître d's, from his days of living in West London; together they have managed to sort out the dinner for almost next to nothing. We are paying cost price for the alcohol and food, and in return they get to give dinner to twenty of the most powerful players in the British fashion industry. Rather than clutter up the main restaurant, they have given us the use of the private dining room downstairs. Trish and Mimi have been there all afternoon, sorting out the table decorations and dressing the room for the event. And I have to say, as I walk in the place looks fabulous. They've taken their theme from Vanessa Tate's Golden Globes dress, and the whole room is draped in black and silver. There are black and silver place mats (with a silver goodie bag at every setting), black tumblers and silver goblets, black linen napkins, and a black tablecloth with silver stars sprinkled all the way down the middle. Hundreds of silver balloons filled with helium float on the ceiling.

'Well done you two,' I say, standing in the doorway, taking it all in. 'I think it looks great.'

'It looks ma-jor,' says Trish, leaning against the wall and running her hands through her short hair. 'Absolutely ma-jor.'

'I agree,' says Mimi. 'I haven't seen a room look this lovely since Freddie Windsor's twenty-first. Happy going to New York party.'

'Well, it's not exactly a "going to New York" party,'

I point out, 'seeing as everyone knows that now. This is a "please be our friends in New York" party.'

'Or, more realistically, "don't slag us off in New York" party,' says Alexander.

'Do you think they will?' I ask. 'We could be crucified.'

'I think they might well give us one season, a stay of execution, before they dive in for the jugular,' he replies.

'Let's get them really drunk,' suggests Mimi. 'I always find if someone's let themselves down a bit, they are more vulnerable and less likely to stitch you up at a later date.'

'Talking of alcohol,' I say, 'any chance of a drink before all these people arrive?'

'I've got to do the seating plan,' says Alexander.

'I've got to go home and change,' says Mimi.

'Me too,' says Trish.

'But I've done the seating,' I say. 'It was worse than trying to do a front row.'

'And I am giving it a few tweaks,' says Alexander. 'I am more up to date with the gossip than you. Anyway, Nick is on his way to help.'

'OK, then,' I say. 'Well, I can't stand around here waiting. I'm feeling too nervous as it is.'

'Go for a walk,' suggests Alexander.

I can't be bothered to argue with him about the seating plan that I sat up last night until one a.m. doing while plying myself with Nurofen and ginger tea, or about the fact that women don't go for walks in four-inch heels. There are walking shoes, there are cocktail party/standing around shoes, and then there are dining shoes. Dining shoes get you out of your cab, take you into the restaurant, escort you to the lavatory and get you back to the table and home again. I am wearing dinner shoes and a tight black dress, so I don't much feel like walking the streets of West London.

I step outside onto the pavement and the blast of cold air makes me feel a bit better. I am so nervous and tense about this dinner that I can actually feel my heart beating in my chest and sweat breaking out on my palms. I light a cigarette and inhale. It makes me feel even more sick. But I persevere. What am I doing having all these people to dinner? What am I trying to prove? That I am a player? That I'm so big and swinging that I'm showing in New York? It is going to take a bit more than a few flutes of Bolly and some tasty canapés to convince these guys that I am worth supporting.

After about ten minutes of walking I find myself in McDonald's on Notting Hill Gate. I don't really remember how I got here, but I am sitting with my face squashed against the large plate-glass window. I'm playing with two plastic straws, looking as if I'm waiting for table service. And I'm crying. It is stress and nerves and worry and the terrible idea that I don't know what I am doing. Do I have enough ideas for New York? Are they going to crucify me? Is my career in a terrible state? Why can't I be bought out like Ted Nicholls?

Alexander calls me on my mobile and demands to know where I am. The girl from the *Sunday Times* Style section and someone from *Wonderland* are already there. 'Get a fucking move on,' he barks. 'Oh, hello Claire,' I hear him say as he greets one of the buyers from Matches.

I try to get myself together. I spend five minutes in the downstairs toilets in McDonald's. I stare at my greasy, puffed face in the mirror. Every spot and blemish shines in the strip lighting. Christ, I think as I clear the eyeliner from under my eyes, even Kate would have a problem looking good in here. I wander back down the road and stand outside my own party for a second. I watch the girl from the *Standard* and another from *You* magazine walk in. A black cab pulls up and out get the elegant ankles of some assistant at *Vogue*. I take a deep breath, run my hand through my hair, and walk across the road.

Inside, and the room is humming with chat and gossip. I smile at a buyer from Harrods, say hello to the girl from Matches, spot the assistant from *Vogue* plus the blokes from *Dazed and Confused* and *Another Magazine*. I pick up a glass of champagne and head over to the comparative safety of Mimi and Nick.

'So Gwyneth, right, is pregnant on this shoot and we are all pretending that we don't know. She is trying to squeeze into these clothes and everyone is saying that she looks lovely to her face, and then as soon as she leaves the room the photographer turns round and says: "Bloody hell, I know she's pregnant and everything, but fuck me she's got fat." I couldn't believe it!' Mimi's eyes are round with shock as she takes another large swig of champagne. 'I mean, what is the woman supposed to do? She is having a baby for Chrissake. Get off her back.'

'Hi,' I say. 'Having fun?'

'Yeah,' says Nick, giving me a smile. 'Anyway, perhaps she shouldn't be doing a shoot. I mean, time and place and all that. I did a shoot in Ibiza last year and the model was still lactating. It was disgusting. Made her tits look quite big though.'

'You can't have it both ways,' says Mimi, lighting up a cigarette. 'I mean, I want to have a baby quite soon.'

'You do?' I say, trying to join in.

'But you don't have a boyfriend,' says Nick.

'Why is that a problem?' asks Mimi. 'Haven't you heard of having it all?'

I decide to leave Nick and Mimi to their conversation about post-feminist single motherhood and do a tour of the party. The girl from the *Standard* seems to be having a good time talking to the assistant at *Vogue*. I'm afraid I don't feel brave enough to interrupt.

'Seems to be going OK,' whispers Alexander in my ear. 'I have changed the table plan slightly.'

'Oh yes?' I say, smiling at the buyer from Matches.

'Well, it was just becoming too political who was going to sit next to you.'

'Right . . .'

'Well if the *Standard* sat on your right and *Vogue* on your left then *You* magazine might be put out or the *Sunday Times*, *Dazed* or *Wonderland* might be pissed off. So I have given you Mimi and Nick as they are mates and no-one can be annoyed about that.'

'OK,' I say. I am actually rather relieved. Last thing I want to do is sit and network anyone. I'm too tired and too tense to make small talk, so sitting next to the two chattiest Cathys in the UK suits me down to the ground. Alexander can do all the networking. That's what he is good at. 'Who have you got?'

'*Dazed* and *Vogue*,' he says, his voice sinking along with his heart.

'*Vogue* is fun,' I say optimistically.

'Oh, we're going to have a ball.' He smiles. 'Can you stand at the door and meet and greet a bit? Some of your private clients are on their way.'

'Sure.'

'You'll recognize them.' He winks. 'They'll be in ten grand of your clobber.'

I stand around the door with a fixed grin on my face like some first-class flight attendant. I smoke a cigarette and make quick work of my second glass of champagne. It is a good way to look busy and eavesdrop on other people's conversation.

'Did you read that piece about Marc Jacobs in the *Telegraph* magazine?' says a voice behind me.

'Oh yah,' replies another. 'I didn't know he used to have such a drug problem.'

'Oh, I know,' says the first. 'He used to binge coke and booze like it was going out of style – which of course it never is.'

'Extraordinary.'

'I know. Apparently, when he was creative director of Louis Vuitton he used to go out all night on a bender and then come back to the office and crash out on the sofa to sleep it off.'

'Really?'

'Yeah. And when Monsieur Arnault turned up for a meeting they'd cover him in coats and pretend he wasn't there.'

'How sweet.'

'I know, I thought it was rather touching. But he was such a party animal. I bumped into him at some party the other day with a very well-known Hollywood actress who used to do coke with him, and he introduced himself extremely politely like they had never met before. She was a little put out, I have to say.'

'I am amazed he is so successful. Last year Marc Jacobs International made something like £400 million in sales.'

'He's been clean for six years. If you don't count the coffee and the fags.'

'Who does?'

It is nine p.m. and the champagne is beginning to dry up. My two Russian private clients are either late or not coming. Alexander decides it is time to sit down to dinner. Not that anyone is really going to eat. This being a fashion dinner, the food must look amazing, be incredibly expensive, and arrive in the smallest of portions. That's why, I always think, caviar is so popular with the couture crowd. And when the food does arrive there is really only one way to eat it. You make a great noise about how lovely and fabulous it looks. You announce to anyone around you that you're quite hungry, that you haven't eaten since yesterday because you are so busy and your hectic life is so important. Then you take one mouthful, proclaim that it's delicious, squash the rest under your knife and fork, and light up a cigarette. Then, just to prove that you are not anorexic and don't have an eating disorder, you talk about chips and memorable meals you have eaten for the next few minutes, and then move on to handbags/shoes/Brad Pitt.

As I sit and watch everyone make a great fuss of their chilli salt squid and prawn dim sum, I wish that Lydia were here. She'd have had three prawn balls and two bowls of edamame to everyone else's forkful.

'Did you just say Heidi Klum?' asks Mimi, already on the cigarette section of her starter.

'Yeah,' says Nick.

'Don't you just think she is the most overrated model in the world?'

'Well . . .'

'Honestly, she is worth ten times more than half the other models who are, in my opinion, so much prettier than her. Talk about working it. She must sit back and think, what am I famous for? Oh, I know, I'm German, I'll bring out a range of diamanté Birkenstocks. Or, I know, I've got quite nice tits, let's do some bras. God, she's annoying. Why is it the British girls never really do any of that endorsement stuff? Kate could have made a fortune if she did Kate knickers or something. She could have done Kate World like Elle. But she doesn't.'

'Perhaps there aren't that many people who could cope with the pace of her world.' Nick laughs. 'I mean, it probably wouldn't sell that well in Middle America.'

'I don't know. I think she can sell snow to the Eskimos.'

'Was it you who told me the other day how Kate lost her baby weight?' asks Nick.

'No,' says Mimi. 'But I don't really believe that story. There are so many Kate Moss stories in the fashion world. She's not a C-section and tummy tuck type. She isn't one of those let's-take-your-baby-out-early-so-that-you-don't-put-on-weight women. Your baby's a bit thin but you look great. Can you imagine? I'd never do that.'

'But loads of models have had surgery,' I say. 'They are always having a nip here, a tuck there.'

'I don't know why anyone cares,' says Nick. 'It's all about image anyway. Like, who cares if they behave badly? They used to be so much worse behaved, even a few years ago. I remember a mate of mine who was a model on a fifty grand advert for some Japanese campaign. She had Bailey shooting her, and the best make-up artist. She went to the loo just before they started shooting and twenty minutes later she still wasn't back. Eventually someone went into the cubicles and broke down the door. She'd climbed out of the window and taken a cab home.'

'I agree,' says Mimi, puffing away with one hand and flicking her prawns with a fork. 'What about that fabulous story of the model who shot the Italian prince in the hotel room? Not because she found him in bed with her best mate but because they had finished her coke.'

'Although things aren't entirely well behaved these days,' I add. 'Don't you remember the story about the birthday party in a hotel suite where one of the girls got down on all fours in the middle of the room and announced, "Who wants to fuck me first?" '

'Yeah, but she's really sad,' says Mimi. 'And no-one really takes her seriously.'

'That's true,' I say.

'Hi,' says Mimi, turning to the woman to her right. 'How are you?'

'Oh, very tired,' she replies.

'IVF?' asks Mimi.

'Nearly,' says the woman.

Nick turns and talks to the buyer from Matches on his left, and I sit and stare up the table, wondering how you can nearly be doing IVF. Alexander is at the other end and catches my eye.

'OK?' he mouths.

'OK,' I mouth back.

We are about to enter into a lip-reading conversation when Irena Antonova walks into the room dressed head to foot in this season's collection. As she stands by the table, pausing for effect, I mentally tot up how much clobber she's got on. She is wearing the tight grey pencil skirt that I wore down the runway at the end of my last show, but she has teamed it with the looser white shirt that was originally from Marks and Spencer and has now been remade in top-quality cotton with mother-of-pearl buttons. Over the top she has one of my tight grey jackets with the pale pink lining that did rather well at Harrods. All in all, it's about £1,600 worth of outfit. She's also sporting an extensive amount of Chanel jewellery and about £10,000 worth of Fendi Crocodile handbag. God, I wish I did accessories.

'Irena,' I say, getting out of my chair. This woman is important to me and worth making a fuss of. 'How lovely to see you. Do please sit down.'

She apologizes for being late – something about a Red Cross Ball committee meeting. Irena loves a charity. Well, she has an awful lot of money and time to give. Sometimes I think I might be one of her lost causes.

'Don't those Russian girls adapt to money quickly?' whispers Mimi as I sit back down. 'Honestly, I remember the wedding of Natalia Voladianova and Justin Portman. She must have been straight off Aeroflot when she met him and she still had Tom Ford do her wedding dress. Do you remember? And all her bridesmaids wore head scarves, which I thought was a very patronizing take on rural Russia.'

'I know those two,' says Nick. 'He is always coming up and snogging her on the runway or backstage in a very public, look-at-us manner. I always find that sort of behaviour a bit weird.'

'The Russians always have weird relationships,' says Mimi. 'There's that one model whose husband/manager follows her everywhere with a video camera. He's about forty years older than her and films her backstage getting dressed and undressed, and coming down the catwalk on the monitor. I think he's a bit scary.'

'There are lots of those young girls who arrive in the West and think they've made it because they have some old bloke looking after them. But you know, they're only model/whores. There's a whole load of them who are run by gangs in Paris. They do the runways during fashion week and then they are farmed out to rich businessmen on yachts in the Riviera.'

'It's only the really clever models who survive,' I say. 'Lydia's always telling me that you can tell the ones who will only do a season. The ones who will be eaten up by the business. Who will end up in the wrong nightclub with the wrong sort of man. They are the ones who need fashion more than fashion needs them. It's the smart ones who survive. She tells a lovely story about Stella Tennant backstage at Dior. Some annoying bloke was shouting, "Come on, girls, get into a line." Treating them like cattle. She apparently turned round and said, "Why don't you go and do one?" With those piercing eyes of hers. He just shut up.'

Down the other end of the table, Alexander starts tapping his glass with his knife, calling for silence. The conversation grinds to a halt, and he stands up. With the self-confidence of a private education behind him, Alexander is an accomplished public speaker. He judges moods well and is good at telling jokes. Firstly, he thanks everyone for coming, informing them that they are the cream of the British, and possibly the world's, fashion industry. Everyone smiles modestly at one another. He then goes on to thank them for their support, without which we would both be on a stall on the Portobello Road. He says that we are all part of one family and that, as our best friends, he would like them to share in the news of our new successes. So he tells them about the talks with Mark One, and that we are moving onwards and upwards and forwards. Everyone puts on their pleased and excited faces.

'We are also,' he continues, 'taking very tentative

baby steps into New York. We are both a little nervous and a little tense.' He smiles.

'Ahh,' says someone.

'You may laugh, but you should come and see the number of cigarettes that are being smoked off Berwick Street. Anyway, we are hoping that we can take you with us. And, as great friends, allies and mentors, you will still be our friends across the Pond. So if this evening is about anything, it is about you guys. It is about thanking you for your support and thanking you for coming this far and hoping that you will stay with us on this incredible journey. To you!' He raises his glass. 'And all who sail in you!'

There is a gentle ripple of laughter and applause.

'I think I'm going to be sick,' whispers Mimi.

'Yeah.' I smile. 'He should really get a job in PR.'

The whole table stands and clinks glasses.

'Cheers,' I say to Nick. 'Very good idea of yours.'

'I know.' He smiles. 'I'm a genius.'

Everyone sits back down again as the chocolate mousse is served.

Giving chocolate to a fashionista is like leaving vodka out for a recovering alcoholic. Some will snap it up immediately, others will wait until coffee before they sneak a cheeky teaspoon. Some will pretend to ignore it, unable to concentrate until they devour three spoonfuls in quick succession. And others will eat one mouthful and then stub their cigarette out in it to prevent them from eating any more. Mimi is the spoonful-and-fag variety of chocolate eater. She is already on her cigarette chaser before the tired woman nearly doing IVF has decided which route to take.

'No, no, I swear they did have an affair,' says Nick. 'And no, he is not gay. He does both sets of the ballroom.'

'Who?' asks Mimi, desperate not to miss out on anything.

'This mate of mine who did a friend of Coco's wedding dress.'

'Oh,' she says. 'Why don't designers do wedding dresses any more?' She turns to me.

'I don't know,' I say. 'They have become a little old hat, I suppose. They do the occasional ironic one in couture.'

'The last wedding dress I saw on the catwalk was a little problematic,' says Mimi. 'The model had two other models either side to lift it as she walked along because the catwalk was too narrow. Only they lifted it too high and the pantless model flashed her trimmed minge all the way down.'

'I wish I had seen that,' says Nick. He is beginning to slur his words as he leans on his elbow and slides slowly towards the table. 'You don't see enough minge on the catwalks these days.'

'You used to be able to rely on Vivienne Westwood for minge,' says the potential IVF candidate. 'She always wore a transparent dress with no knickers.'

'Those were the days,' says Nick.

The dinner is beginning to thin out now. *You* magazine has gone, as has the *Vogue* assistant. The *Standard* girl is still here, having a gossip with the girl from the *Sunday Times*. The Harrods buyer is chatting to Alexander. But the boys from *Dazed* and *Another Magazine* have both headed home, leaving behind the hot Versace ties. In fact, most of the goodie bags are still hanging off the backs of chairs or have been kicked into touch on the floor. I walk up and down the table, asking everyone if they have had a nice evening and if they are coming to the show in New York. The mood seems optimistic and well lubricated. Everyone seems to have enjoyed themselves. A couple of pairs of eyes are glazed by booze, some cheeks are merely pinked, but on the whole the mood is jovial and conducive to banter.

'She's a right little chipmunk-faced bitch,' I overhear. 'I don't care if she is doing her A levels and thinks she's going to Cambridge, she refused to wear fur in London Fashion Week and then complained when she couldn't open the show. Eventually she had to get the third outfit and shove it on her skinny back so that she could come out first. Where does she get off? She's only twelve.'

I make my way back to my seat to find Mimi and Nick practically curled up together.

'Sadly, no,' says Nick.

'What's this?' I say.

'He's never been to Thierry's shower,' replies Mimi.

295

'Thierry's what?'

'Thierry Mugler has an atelier where there is a glass shower by the gym so anyone who is in the gym can work out while watching someone hosing themselves down.'

'I need one of those,' I say, getting back out of my seat to see the Harrods buyer to the door.

We stand and discuss sales, and how well the new collection is doing, particularly since Vanessa Tate won at the Golden Globes. They say they can't get enough of the white and silver dress and I tell them that the next collection will be bigger and better as we are in the process of hiring a production manager.

I see them off, smile at a few more guests, then come back to the table to find Mimi with her arms around the shoulders of the IVF woman. She appears to be crying.

'What happened?' I ask Nick.

'Fuck knows,' he says with a shrug. 'One minute they were talking about Lily Cole versus Lily Donaldson, and then she suddenly burst into tears. It's the champagne. She must have had at least a bottle.'

I watch Mimi making all the right noises as she leads the woman out of the room, her arm over her shoulder. Five minutes later she comes back having put her in a cab.

'Thank God for that,' she sighs as she slumps back down into a chair and lights a cigarette. 'Well, that's at least one good review.'

'What?' I say.

'She drinks too much and makes a tit of herself at your party. She is hardly going to slag you off in New York, now is she?'

'She's right,' says Nick. 'What a hugely successful evening. Did anyone get which magazine she was from?'

16

It is 9.30 a.m., and Madonna's on full volume. It's cold, dank and dark outside, but Lydia is sitting in a chair in a pair of white hot pants with her legs in the air having them oiled by some girl who introduced herself as Daz. I am sitting in the corner smoking my seventh cigarette of the morning, waiting to have my make-up done.

We have all been here since eight, during which time I have managed to eat three croissants and half a pain au chocolat. Meanwhile, Max Davies has called me babe six times, dude five times, shot me twice with his imaginary finger pistol, and once rubbed his leather-clad crotch against Lydia's shoulders.

I have always hated photo shoots, and sitting here now, full of pastries, coffee and nicotine, I remember why. There is so much bloody waiting around. Having waited to have my make-up done, I shall wait to have a twenty-something trustafarian style me. She'll persuade me to wear something inappropriate and I shall feel fat, foolish and a bit of a pantomime pony. I shall wait for Max to set up his lights. I shall wait some more for his assistant to load the camera. We shall all stand around a bit longer. Then we shall be 'roided – have a photo taken with a Polaroid. Some tit will rub it on their thigh for three minutes to warm it up and speed up the developing process. Then they'll frame the 'roid with a piece of white card. Everyone will gather around. And eventually either Lydia or I will have to have our clothes/hair/shoes changed because it is 'just not working'.

I'm annoyed, bored and, let's be honest, a little hung over. Thanks to the huge efforts of Alexander, Mimi and Trish, last night was a bit of a success. My mobile has been going for over an hour now with messages and texts from all the guests saying how much fun they had. Alexander has called me from the office – apparently we are drowning in Wild at Heart bouquets and Jo Malone grapefruit candles. He has suggested that we send Nick a little something, and I am inclined to agree. His idea was inspired, and it may well turn out to be one of the things that makes all the difference in the US. If the majority of the UK press are onside, it won't matter so much when we are sent to fashion hell on Style.com, or when Anna Wintour fails to come to the show. I think a magnum of Moët and Chandon should do the trick.

'You all right over there?' asks Lydia as she extends her long left leg for creaming. 'I feel just like Naomi.'

She giggles. 'She's always standing there stark naked with her full Brazilian being oiled up like a salad before she goes out on the catwalk.'

'That's why she always glistens like a panther,' growls Max across the studio, making a claw with his right hand. 'She's one sexy dude.'

Fuck me, he's an annoying man. I have been on three shoots with him and he has always irritated the crap out of me. I'm not sure whether it's that mid-Atlantic drawl – the one some fashion people affect because their lives are 'just so international' they don't know where they are half the time. Maybe it's his constant name-dropping and talking about who he's done lines with. Perhaps he tries so hard because we all know he comes from Solihull. He certainly tries, and he is trying in return.

Confessions on a Dance Floor begins its third play of the morning and everyone is dancing and mumbling along to 'Hung Up' when the stylist and the fashion editor come over.

'Tho Fluff and I have been talking,' says the super-skinny pubescent-looking stylist who has one of those speech impediments where the 's' comes out as a 'th'. 'And we've dethided that you would look great in your thignature thilver and white dreth.'

'Right,' I say, putting down *Now* magazine and stubbing out my cigarette in my third cup of tepid coffee. I'm beginning to get a migraine behind my right eye. 'Um, the thing is, I'm not really the right shape for the silver and white dress.'

'Yah, but the thing is, it's what you are known for,' says Fluff, who turns out to be anything but. In fact she has thighs like a point-to-point hunter and a backside like a tractor.

'Can't Lydia wear it?' I ask, feeling my sense of humour ebbing and my anger rising.

'She's in the hot panth,' says the stylist.

'I'm afraid I am not wearing the white dress,' I say.

'But, right, the dress would look so good on you,' says Fluff.

'No,' I say. 'I'm too old and too fat to be bullied into anything that does not suit me. And if you think I will change my mind, I won't, and I'll walk.'

'Dudes, dudes, dudes,' says Max, running his hands through his long dark hair as he strides over. 'What's the aggro about?'

'I'm not wearing the white and silver dress,' I say. 'It is very unforgiving and I will look like a fat slag in it. I'm the sort of person who needs tailoring and some good seams.'

'Fine,' he says. 'Wear what you like, man. This is your shoot. It's about you. I want you to feel it and enjoy it. I want you to be comfortable and happy. With the vibe.'

I smile at him. Suddenly all his surfer-chat philosophy is not that bad, and the leather trousers are a witty signature.

'Lydia can wear the dress and you can wear whatever you want.'

He smiles, bows, clicks his heels and shoots me for the third time that day with his index finger. He goes over to tell Lydia the change of plan, kissing the back of her hand as he does so.

'D'you mean I've got greased up for nothing?' shouts Lydia from across the room.

'Sorry,' I say.

'Oh, I don't mind,' she says. 'I love that white dress. Come over and talk to me while I have my eyes done.'

I wander over and sit next to Lydia while Daz gets to work on her face. Sitting there with her mouth slightly ajar and her eyes closed, she looks stunning. Her nose is short and perfectly straight, her brows are finely arched, her lips delightfully plump, and her blonde hair is smoothly scraped back into a ponytail. She can definitely carry off the white dress. I would look like a pig in knickers.

'So, are you well?' I ask. 'Haven't seen you for a bit.'

'It's not that long,' she says.

Successful models all have this self-sufficiency thing. They are always travelling, mostly on their own, and rarely have a base. They tend to make friends easily but find it more difficult to keep them. That's why everyone is darling because no-one can remember anyone's name.

'Have you found a place in Paris yet?'

'Oh,' she says, 'I'm not sure about that now. I've just done the haute couture shows and it was a bit of a nightmare.'

'Really?'

'Oh, it was so depressing. Firstly, I couldn't fit into any of Mr Armani's stuff despite virtually starving myself for a few days beforehand.' She pats her flat and toned stomach. 'His couture sixes are really and truly sixes. I couldn't get any of them on. And then there were, you know, all the same old characters. There was that old bloke I told you about once before.'

'Who's that?'

'Oh, this wrinkly old bloke who comes every year. He looks like Freddie Kruger and is always desperately trying to say hi to all the models in his leather shirt, leather trousers, mink scarf and cowboy hat. There he was, sitting in the Hotel Costes, drinking on his own, trying to coerce some young model into sitting with him, and I just wanted to go home.'

'I always thought you liked couture, much more than ready-to-wear.'

'I just felt strangely irrelevant in my £60,000 dress. It just all seemed so pointless. I'm in this work of art. It was so impossible to walk in I had to rip it up the back just to get it down the catwalk.'

'You didn't?'

'Well, I could hardly just stand there in it.' She smiles. 'And I saw all these rich Gulf State women who buy the dresses and take them home, where they are never worn.'

'You what?' asks Daz, her mouth full of brushes.

'Oh, it's this weird thing,' says Lydia. Her eyes are

closed and her face is steady. She is used to talking without moving a muscle. 'All these women sit in the front row of couture and they buy these dresses they can't wear. Or actually sometimes they don't even see the show; they send someone in their place. Anyway, they buy these dresses, which they can't wear in public because their religion forbids it, and they take them back to their palaces and exhibit them to their girl-friends. Like Devil's dresses, they are put on display in glass cases to be admired like works of art. Which I suppose some of them are. Their mates come, drink tea and take a peek at what a £60,000 Dior dress looks like.'

'So they're never worn?' asks Daz, taking a step back to look at Lydia's face.

'No,' she says. 'Most of the time they buy the sample size so no-one can fit into it. Least of all me.' She laughs. 'If it's a Mr Bloody Armani frock.'

'How weird,' says Daz.

'You know, I used to love being turned into Boudica, or Joan of Arc, or covered in cobalt blue paint by Pat McGrath.'

'I love her work,' says Daz. 'She is the best make-up artist in the world. Her work is pure fantasy. She changes faces.'

'I know,' says Lydia. 'And that's the thing. You can understand why Kate doesn't do couture because she is too much of a character in her own right. They just want girls who are chameleons, and I have to say I am a little bored at being unrecognizable going down the catwalk. I want one of those adverts where I get to sign the bottom of the page, like Cindy.'

'I love Cindy,' says Daz. 'She was the original super-model for me. Don't you love the way her mole used to be always appearing and then disappearing depending on how "Cindy" they wanted her to be? If the advertiser wants the full Cindy, you get the mole; if they just want a well-known beautiful face, they Photoshop it out.'

'I've never noticed that,' I say.

'Really?' says Lydia. 'You surprise me. I hope they are going to give us some airbrushing and some Photoshop on this shoot.' She opens her eyes and leans in towards the mirror surrounded by glaring light bulbs. 'My skin looks terrible and I'm tired.'

'Oh, don't look there,' says Daz. 'I hate that mirror. Actually, I hate this studio. No-one looks good in these lights, and the catering sucks. In the place I usually shoot in Islington they do this great chicken chow mein, and sometimes they have this great Thai green curry. Here, they only ever give us poached bloody salmon. And I hate salmon. Well, I don't hate it. I'm just really bored of it. I said to my agent, "Don't book me to go to these studios over the river. I don't do over the river and I don't do salmon." But she never listens. She always says, "Daz, a job is a job." But, you know, I care about my food.'

'Yeah,' says Lydia, clearly not listening.

Thin and attractive with short black hair and tanned Anglo-Indian skin, it is difficult to see quite how Daz manages to eat that much. She has a stud in her tongue, two metal rings around her lips, and another stud coming out of the top right-hand corner of her mouth like some post-modern beauty spot. It's a wonder she can down anything other than soup.

Over the other side of the studio, Max is struggling with a huge white roll of paper that he's pulled down from the ceiling to create the background for the shoot. He's attaching it to the floor with large black weights, but appears worried by some dark scuff marks on the floor and is in deep discussion with Fluff and the stylist.

'How much longer?' he asks, shouting over to us.

'Not long!' Daz shouts back. 'Lydia's got to have her hair done next. Where's Dennis?'

'Over here,' says a handsome black guy who is lying back on the sofa near the pastry tray reading *Vogue*. Dressed for a skateboarding park, with small dreadlocks and black-rimmed spectacles with clear glass, he is horizontal with cool. 'Any time you want,' he adds. 'The rollers are hot and I'm ready.'

'Two minutes,' says Daz.

'Whatever,' says Dennis.

Fifteen minutes later and I am finally in the make-up chair staring at my plain, tired, pink face. Lydia is sitting next to me, her long legs up on the shelf in front of the mirror, shouting over the noise of the hairdryer. Dennis is smoothing out her hair with a large brush.

A strong smell of marijuana emanates from his clothes.

'So, have you seen the new Mario Testino exhibition?' yells Lydia.

'I went with a mate,' replies Dennis. 'I thought it was OK.'

'Yeah,' says Lydia. 'I think it should have been called Access more than anything else. There were so many famous people. I went to see if there were any shots of me. But I am obviously not super enough for him. He isn't that brilliant a photographer, it's just that he is such a nice man everyone wants to be shot by him. The last shoot I did with him he was so sweet. He just kept on saying, "Girls, zis is not a holiday." And laughing at his own jokes. He gets everywhere on charm, that man. He just famously makes girls look beautiful. He's good mates with Kate. The last time I saw them she arrived with fresh flowers from the garden for him.'

'That's very her,' shouts Dennis.

'I know,' says Lydia. 'Did you hear that story about some young girls bumping into her on Oxford Street and asking her what it's like to be a style icon?'

'No?'

'She was sweet about it, signed some autographs, and asked them if they liked fashion. They said yes, and she took them into H&M and bought them all some clothes.'

'That's nice,' says Dennis. 'Strange how you never seem to hear stories like that about Naomi.'

'Yes,' agrees Lydia.

'You're done,' says Dennis, running his hands through Lydia's long blonde hair and fanning it out over her shoulders. 'You are so done.'

Lydia leans into the mirror and turns her face left and right, inspecting the makeover.

'That looks great. Thanks, guys.'

She does indeed look great. All glossy and shiny, like she has walked fresh from a shower. Her make-up is light, her hair is like gold. I look at my own face, puffy from last night's drinking and stressed from months of work. I seem to be going through a second adolescence. The only woman on the planet to combine bad skin with lines.

'We'll just see if we can cover some of those blemishes,' says Daz, squeezing an industrial amount of foundation onto the back of her hand. 'And maybe get some Touche Éclat on those bags.'

Max walks out of the studio to go and feed the meter on his sports car, and Lydia walks over to the clothes rack. She slips off the shorts over her greased legs and pulls off her T-shirt. I watch in the mirror as she takes off her underwear and stands stark naked in her heels, leafing through the clothes.

'It's a no-knickers dress, don't you think?' she shouts to me across the room, seemingly blissfully unaware that her Velcro strip of golden pubic hair is on show for all to see.

'I would have thought so,' I say.

'OK then.' She strides over to the seating area in her

heels. 'I'm starving,' she announces. She tucks into a croissant, and flicks the buttered flakes off her stomach.

I look around the studio. I appear to be the only person watching her. I remember a friend of mine telling me about a photo shoot where Nadja Auermann, who famously had the longest legs in the world, walked around naked for an hour in a pair of heels with a landing strip of pubic hair on display. She told me she was the only person to pay her any attention as every man on the shoot was gay and they were only interested in flirting with each other. It is only now that I believe her.

Unfortunately for Max, whom I presume to be straight, Lydia already has the white dress on by the time he gets back from feeding his meter.

'Wow, baby,' he says as he walks in. 'You look fantastico.'

'I do hope you are airbrushing and Photoshopping,' she says, her arms in the air as the stylist pins her into the dress.

'Baby, don't you worry about that.' He winks. 'You'll be brushed and tweaked and stretched and made to look glowing and lovely.'

'Mert and Marcus did this shoot with me the other day where they made my skin so flawless I didn't have a single pore.'

'They are 80 per cent computer,' he replies. 'They pull out your eyes, pump up your lips and make your skin whiter than white.'

'I didn't like them very much,' says Lydia. 'They dressed up and took the piss out of the models. Apparently, according to the other girl I was with, they did this "ma-jor impression of me on the catwalk". It was "ma-jor, really ma-jor". I'm afraid I didn't find it very funny.'

Daz announces that she has done all she can to make me presentable, and Dennis sets to work with his hot rollers and hairspray. It takes him about another twenty minutes of spraying and backcombing before he turns me into an alcoholic Shirley Temple. I have tight curls all over my head. I look like I've had a fight with a cheap demi wave. But I don't say anything. What's the point? I just want to get this over and done with.

I walk over to the rack of clothes from the current collection and realize they are all sample sizes. My heart sinks. This is turning into a nightmare. After another five minutes of toing and froing, I find myself standing next to all six feet plus of Lydia in a white waist-cinching dress while I am pinned into a skirt with the zip undone at the back and sweating in a tight jacket of my own creation.

Max and his lights start popping away. Madonna gets her fourth airing, and everyone gathers around the 'roid to see just how badly the shoot is going. Max's assistant rubs the photo on his thigh, peels off the back, and everyone leans in.

'Yeah, yeah, dude, yeah,' says Max, nodding away as Fluff puts her considerable all in. 'Good idea. Um, ladies?' he says. 'Could you' – he points to me – 'step back somewhat, and then Lydia, you can come forward. I think it's important that we have the signature dress at the front. This is a photo about muses after all.'

We take a few more shots, with me fading ever more into the background. Lydia, meanwhile, is striking pose after pose, her hips twisted, which makes her look narrow, and her hand on her hip to give her waist and attitude. She knows all the tricks. But then she has been in the business for over ten years. I stand at the back of shot with my arms folded, making my already square shape even more boxy, but I am hoping that no-one is really going to be looking at me. Why would you when you have a long-legged blonde front of shot?

'OK, let's go for it,' announces Max bravely, like he is about to attempt open-heart surgery. His assistant hands him the canister loaded with film. He clips it to the back of the camera. Everyone falls silent.

Everyone, that is, except Dennis and Daz, who are sitting on the corner sofa chomping away on the houmous and carrot sticks that catering have brought in just in case we are peckish. Dennis appears to be rolling a joint, while Daz sits there clutching her powder puff. No wonder the fashion industry is fuelled by gossip and rumour, I think as I try to stop my eyes from closing with every flash. Those two on the sofa have effectively finished work. They have made up the model and blown her hair, but they have to spend the rest of the day puff and brush in hand in case of touch-ups. They are bored. They can't go anywhere. What else have they got to do except gossip?

'Baby, baby, give it to me. Sexy, sexy, yeah,' says Max, straddling his bag of film and thrusting his leather-clad pelvis towards Lydia. 'Oh baby. Baby.' He walks towards her and rubs himself up against her satin backside. 'I want you looser around here,' he says, running his hands over her buttocks.

'Powder!' says Daz, running over from the sofa, fag in hand.

'Are you offering?' says Max with a laugh.

'What, before lunch?' asks Daz. 'Really Max, that's so rock and roll.'

'No, dude, even I've got standards. Never before four on my shoots.'

'I was about to say,' says Daz, covering the non-existent greasy patch on Lydia's forehead. 'I'm done.'

'Oh, hang on, hair,' says Dennis. I can see that his eyes are a little bloodshot as he ambles over, pulling a large brush out of his back pocket. 'There,' he says, running his hands through Lydia's hair and brushing the front.

I think everyone has forgotten that I am actually here.

We have been posing for about twenty minutes when Max decides to break for lunch. The salmon, salad and potatoes arrive along with a couple of bottles of white wine. Fluff cracks them open and fills some glasses.

Lydia, I notice, takes one sip and puts her glass down, never to pick it up again, whereas the sibilant stylist drinks hers down in about three large glugs and immediately develops bright pink cheeks. Max is still all over Lydia, rubbing his hands up and down her creamed legs and telling her she is the prettiest model he has ever photographed. I know that fashion shoot protocol dictates that the photographer gets to shag the model, or at least to try; perhaps I should tell him that Lydia is not interested. Then again, maybe she is? Models always have rubbish boyfriends who scrounge off them or treat them badly. He could be just her sort.

She gets up to go to the toilet, so I follow her.

'Everything OK?' I ask eventually, washing my hands at the basin.

'Fine.'

'He is being a bit difficult,' I suggest. 'You know, rubbing your legs and stuff.'

'Oh please.' She grins. 'Some guys are so much worse than that. I was on one shoot once when I got my period so I took my knickers off and put them in my handbag and went to the loo. The photographer took my pants out of my bag, put them on his head with the crotch over his nose, and stuck his tongue into the gusset. He took a Polaroid of his face and popped the photo and the pants back into the bag. I didn't discover what had gone on until I got home. So I think I can cope with a little groping.'

'I suppose.'

'Most photographers are charming,' she says. 'Avedon was fabulous. He was full of stories about Marilyn and Audrey Hepburn. Testino is lovely. But there are some who are really creepy and pervy. You just try not to get booked with them. I won't do jobs if the knicker sniffer is booked.'

'Not even a catalogue?'

'Oh, I don't know.' She smiles. 'Don't worry. I'm quite a big girl. I can look after myself.'

Lydia and I spend the rest of the afternoon in various posed positions trying not to laugh at Max's ham-fisted advances. He rubs his leather package against her thighs and keeps getting himself rather obviously excited. The wine starts to flow, the gossip hots up, and despite protestations from both Lydia and me Madonna continues to thump out of the speakers.

Come four p.m. and Max is as good as his word. A delivery of drugs arrives in a jiffy bag and both he and his assistant disappear off to the toilet. I don't know why he doesn't do it in front of us all, as he has already told us about it. But no-one else wanted any, so perhaps he felt embarrassed. He comes back from the lavatory with verbal diarrhoea and a runny nose. He cranks up the music and starts to dance around like he's at his own private party. Lydia looks bored. Daz and Dennis are too busy sharing other people's secrets to bother that much, and Fluff and the stylist are laughing tensely, trying to look cool and relaxed about the whole thing.

An hour later and a plate of sandwiches arrives, just

in case anyone is going starving. Max is talking about changing his film, boshing out a few black and whites for good measure. I walk over to the sofa to stuff myself with some tuna and sweetcorn bap, and overhear gossip in full swing.

'Do you know, *he* is perfectly capable of speaking English but he won't, and all his staff run around after him like they are terrified,' says Daz.

'Well, I heard that *she* used to have amazing cocaine parties with goblets of the stuff on the tables,' adds Dennis.

'Hi there,' I say. 'How much longer do you think we are going to be here?'

'I don't know,' says Daz.

'Not much longer I should think,' a smiling Dennis replies. 'I'm not sure he's shooting straight any more anyway.'

'Have you booked a car?' asks Daz.

'No.'

'Oh. I was at this shoot the other day and the model was dropped off by Craig from *Big Brother*,' says Dennis.

'Really?' asks Daz.

'That's what she said.'

'The one that won?'

'Apparently.'

'I always preferred Nasty Nick.'

'Mmm,' says Dennis. 'Wasn't there some nun on that show? Oh, Lydia, your hair needs a brush.' He gets off his chair and wanders over to run his hands through Lydia's hair for the tenth time that day.

I pour myself a glass of wine. I am really quite fed up now. I have smiled and strained and held my stomach in all afternoon. I am a designer, not a model, and I have reached the end of the road. I am about to dismiss myself when Max suddenly announces that he's got the shot and we can all relax. This appears to be the cue for the music to be cranked up even louder and for everyone to start smoking, cracking into the wine and sitting on the sofa, while watching Max's assistant clear up. Dennis and Daz packed their air-hostess cases before lunch so they enjoy putting their feet up. Fluff and the stylist suck up to Lydia.

The suggestion is aired that we all retire to the wine bar around the corner. Fortunately, just as Max is forcing everyone to join him, my mobile goes. It is Alexander.

'Guess what?' he says.

'What?'

'You'll never guess.'

'What!'

'Vanessa Tate has been nominated for an Oscar. Kathy's just called. They want you to do the dress.'

17

It's two days before the show and Alexander and I are really feeling the pressure. We arrived in New York two days ago and we are still both suffering from jetlag. I keep waking up at four in the morning and wanting to pass out again in the early afternoon.

I have been to New York on numerous occasions but I always forget how packed and hectic it is. The streets are full of people busy going somewhere, the roads are gridlocked with cars slowly going nowhere, and everywhere there is energy, edge and excitement. The last couple of days the weather has been glorious, extremely cold and crisp with a bright blue sky. The air chills your lungs when you breathe.

Alexander and I are ensconced in the Soho House in the Meat Packing District. A fabulous building in a groovy area, the place is the worst-kept secret in town. Ever since Sarah Jessica Parker and the rest of the *Sex and the City* crew were filmed lounging by the swimming pool on the roof of the club, the place has been packed. Half of happening New York and the majority of swinging London hang out in the restaurant and games room, where, unusually for this city, you can actually smoke! And this being one of the hippest weeks in the year in one of the hippest establishments, we've had to pull a lot of strings to get our room. Or, more precisely, Alexander pulled some string somewhere through a friend of a friend and as a result we've got one of the largest suites in the place. It doesn't come cheap, but with the logic of someone who borrows from Egg to pay Barclays, Alexander has justified our $1,000-a-night Playground Suite room rate by our sharing the bed and using the rest of the 950 square feet for fittings and meetings and anything else we can cram in here. Like the collection itself.

Not that it was at all easy to get the clothes here. We had to fill out a carnet from the Chamber of Commerce declaring that the clothes have no intrinsic value whatsoever. We had to list each of the thirty-five looks we were taking, including all the accessories. We had to have everything stamped out of the UK and stamped into the US. Then, once we'd finally cleared customs, Alexander and I had to work out how we were going to get the huge suitcases to the hotel. Fortunately we found some limo service that would fill one car with clothes while Alexander and I followed along very closely behind, making sure that no-one drove off with them.

For the first twenty-four hours neither of us left the hotel. I was too busy having Knackered Cow treatments in the Cowshed Spa, eating my bodyweight in chips and looking at views of the Hudson River to be bothered to go out. We made one trip to the nearby Jerry's store to see how our rack of clothes were selling, but as soon as I saw a row of unsold white shirts I had to leave. I returned to a leather armchair at the bar to sink two Bloody Marys in quick succession, then curled up in the corner with the newspapers.

Meanwhile, fashionable London swanned around us. Hiding behind my *Telegraph*, I spotted Jefferson Hack lunching with some thin girl and a man with tattoos on both his forearms. They looked like Hoxtonites. Over the other side of the dining room I saw one of the Sykes sisters lunching with someone who was just as thin, with the same blow dry. Over in the corner hip New York was keeping its end up: *Sex and the City* author Candace Bushnell was lunching with Jay McInerney and Salman Rushdie. I just gently downed my cocktail, ate a bowl of peanuts and sneaked back to the room.

Room service has just cleared away our breakfast and we are trying to smarten up the room before Aiden arrives. Aiden is one of the best casting agents in town. A Brit living over in New York, he has only really agreed to do our show as a favour to Alexander, who he has known for years. I suspect they might once have had a bit of a thing, but they remain firm friends. Alexander has been in email contact with him for the past few weeks. A flurry of messages has gone back and forth across the Pond. How many girls we need. When we are showing. How much we can pay.

Sadly, we are not what you would refer to as a prestige show, so there would not normally be a long line of models tripping over themselves to get down our catwalk, but Aiden is going to call in some favours and indulge in some very basic blackmail. As a top casting agent he is doing numerous shows, and in order to be in his team, as it were, models have to do the rubbish shows like ours as well. And that doesn't just apply to New York. Fashion is obviously international, and Aiden casts shows in Milan and Paris. So in order to do Gucci and McQueen, the models have to do our poxy show for $500 each. In London the pay is so bad that even with all the arm-twisting in the world the agents find it hard to cast some of the shows. If supermodels famously never get out of bed for less than £10,000 a day, can you imagine how difficult it is to get someone to go down the catwalk for as little as £100 a show? In order to help the struggling designers, models' wages in London work on a sliding scale, starting out at £100 for your first show, working up to £140 for the next, then £280, and finally £320, all including the agency fee of 20 per cent of course. Sadly, things are a little different in New York, and quite honestly, if we didn't have the support of Aiden I'm not sure we would be able to show here at all. That said, we are paying him $7,000 for all his hard work.

Aiden knocks on the door and Alexander answers it. Alexander is effusive and cheerful, neither of which comes naturally to him. Aiden is dark and handsome and dressed in jeans, a black polo neck and a long leather coat to the floor. He stands in the doorway stamping his biker boots on the wooden floor and makes a lot of noise about being cold. He pushes his expensive shades to the top of his head and heaves a large black portfolio case through the door.

'How are you guys?' he asks, slapping Alexander's back and kissing each of my earlobes. 'Nice to see you in the Big Apple. Hey, like your room.' He walks around, running his hand over the yellow four-poster bed and taking a look at the freestanding egg-shaped bath. 'This is great. I've never actually stayed here before. Although I tell you, it is impossible to get a bed by the pool in the summer.'

Aiden has one of those mid-Atlantic fashion voices that seems to change accent depending on who he is talking to. With us he sounds quite English, but as soon as he engages anyone from this side of the Pond he comes over all New York.

Alexander orders up a pot of coffee and some more pastries while Aiden tells us how New York Fashion Week is shaping up.

'Paris Hilton is in town, Nicole Richie is also about,' he says. 'And I think Scarlett Johansson is opening for the Imitation of Christ.'

'Cool,' says Alexander. 'I like their stuff. Is she taking

over from Chloé Sevigny as their muse?'

'Don't know,' says Aiden, unzipping his portfolio. 'I think they are both kinda cool.'

'So, who have you got for us?' I ask, rubbing my hands together, pretending to be enthusiastic.

I have always hated this part of the show. Models are annoying, difficult and problematic. They are also expensive. Much as I love Lydia, I always think it's a bit of a cheek getting paid so much money just for being thin and being able to walk in a straight line. Then again, you'd be amazed how many of them can't actually walk. Last season I had one girl I was planning to put in three outfits, but as soon as I saw her walk I decided she could only get down the runway once. She lifted her knees too high and wobbled so much from side to side she looked like an arthritic donkey on Blackpool Pleasure Beach.

'So,' says Aiden, bringing out his first headshot, 'bland is back. Bland is the new beauty.'

'What? I thought beauty was the new beauty,' says Alexander. 'Or at least that's what Damiano is saying.'

'No, I'm afraid not.' Aiden smiles. 'It's all about bland. As simple and as clear and as flawless and as unremarkable as you can.'

'Oh,' I say. 'I can't help but think that is a little sad.'

'Yeah, well.' He shrugs. 'So, this is Yulia from Kiev.'

Since the death of the supermodel and the demise of those real beauties like Helena Christensen and Amber Valletta, there are really only two ways to become hot in modelling terms nowadays. The first is to be truffled out by Anna Wintour and shot for the editorial pages of US *Vogue*. If Anna puts you in her pages you're a happy bunny and on your way to a fleeting sniff of stardom. The second way is if a powerful designer like YSL, Prada, Louis Vuitton or Gucci puts you in their campaign. These advertisers thrive on new talent. They don't want an old household name, they want some sixteen-year-old Nikita fresh from the taiga. And the way the bookings work for the catwalk shows is simple. If Prada have signed the skinny girl from Yalta for their campaign, you can guarantee she'll be booked by every designer in town. Even if no-one has seen the campaign yet and the girl is totally unknown. Everyone will have her in the show just to prove how fashion forward and on the pulse they are.

And it is Aiden's job to know who these hot girls are. Who has the new, as yet unpublished, Prada campaign. And who is so hot and happening even she doesn't know it yet. Sometimes I suspect that some of this is lost on the fashion editors who watch the show. We think we are showing off how switched on we are by having these new girls come down the catwalk. All they see are a load of unknowns, and when Yulia finally hits the big time they will have forgotten that she opened for us in New York.

'I have to say that she doesn't look that exciting,' I say.

'She is bland,' says Aiden enthusiastically.

'You can say that again,' says Alexander.

'She has a perfume contract.'

'Let's have her then,' says Alexander.

'OK.' Aiden pulls another mugshot from the pile on the table. 'Natasha. She's seventeen, from Vladivostok.'

'Oh Jesus Christ, she's a moose,' says Alexander.

'A pig scarer,' I add.

'She's got a campaign,' says Aiden.

'Oh God no,' I say.

'Over my dead body,' adds Alexander.

'She is doing Zac Posen and Marc Jacobs.'

'Fuck it,' I say.

'Really?' asks Alexander.

'Marc?' I add.

'OK then,' says Alexander. 'Tell me she can bloody walk.'

'One foot in front of the other,' confirms Aiden with a smile.

This carries on for the next hour and a half. Aiden shows us some plain girl from some Eastern European hell hole, he convinces us of her modelling worth, and we sigh and put her in the show. Thank God Alexander is here doing this with me because I think I might well have lost my temper a long while ago. Some designers get off on the models. They enjoy the screaming glamour of it all. They love the gossip and the high jinks. I just want to book them and get some sort of running order.

It is political and important who you book to open

and close your show. Like ego-driven actors fighting over their billing, the models really care about the order in which they go down the catwalk. It is also an indication of your standing and quite how cutting edge and special you are. If you have a crap model opening and closing your show then you are, by association, a crap designer. And the fashionista picks up on this stuff.

As soon as an editor walks into your show, their fashion antennae are on red alert. Where your show is and at what time will stand either for or against you. The atmosphere you have created. The goodie bags that are on the chairs. Who is doing your make-up. Your hair. Your music. It is all noted and added together. You get points for the celebrities who attend. You get points for the right sort of models. Technically, your show could be deemed a failure even before the first frock has gone down the catwalk.

Fortunately for me, Alexander has an eye for all this stuff and cares just a tiny bit more than I do. He has booked us a well-regarded show producer called Mark who has been in the business for seven years in the US, Milan and the UK. Alexander has chatted him up and has managed to negotiate a good price. Show producers are essential and expensive. They make sure lighting, music and model co-ordinate on the catwalk to give you the best pictures and show possible. But in New York, in addition to the usual flat fee of between $10,000 and $15,000 a show, they also charge 10 per cent of your show spend. So if your space hire, with lights, technicians and music, comes in at about $77,000, you have to pay another $7,700 to the producer. But because it is our first show in New York and he is hoping we will use him again, Mark has agreed to work for the flat fee of $15,000.

Alexander has also managed to strike deals with hair and make-up. He has got the hair and make-up sponsored by Mac and has, using the 'first show' excuse again, managed to get Beverley Blond to do the make-up and James Car to do the hair. Beverley is not quite premier league, which is fortunate, as they would charge something between $20,000 and $30,000 for the show. The majority of that money would be taken by the make-up artist and the rest would be divided up among their team, at about $100 to $150 each. Thankfully, Mac are paying Beverley and her team $15,000 so that they can put their name and logo on the programme. The deal with James is quite similar. With the big boys earning $25,000 a show, we are lucky to have Mac sponsoring James to the tune of $15,000.

'So,' says Aiden, 'you're fine with the girls.'

'Couldn't be happier,' says Alexander.

'That's about $10,000 well spent,' I say.

'Is Lydia opening for you?' asks Aiden.

'I hope so,' I say.

'Because if not, we'll have to have a discussion as to who will open and close. Yulia won't do it if Natasha opens.'

'Oh,' I say. 'I have no idea why anyone cares. I remember hearing a story about Naomi flying in because she heard that someone else was going to close for Valentino.'

'Yeah, well, man, they do,' he says.

'We haven't sorted out the order yet,' says Alexander. 'We're going to do that tomorrow when we fit and 'roid the models.'

'Oh, OK,' says Aiden. 'But if you do have any problems give me a call and I'll deal with the agencies.'

Aiden's mobile goes and he gets up and starts walking around the suite. Alexander and I look at each other, then at the pile of fashionably bland models we have chosen for the show.

'I much preferred it when beauty was back,' says Alexander, leafing through the pile of headshots and vital statistics.

'It was more pleasing, wasn't it?'

'I know.' He sighs. 'I don't like any of these bitches.'

'Yeah, well,' I say, 'Gucci thinks they're great.'

'Look, I said it wouldn't be a problem!' Aiden is pacing up and down the collection rail, running his hands over the clothes, pulling out the occasional jacket or skirt and giving it the once-over. 'Yeah! . . . Right! . . . Fine! . . . Goodbye!' He hangs up. 'Sorry about that. A few problems with the Marc Jacobs show tonight.'

'Oh right,' I say.

'Good collection,' he says.

'Thanks.' I smile.

'I hear McQueen is doing plaid, so you're in good company,' he adds, as he picks up his portfolio. 'Catch you guys later, right? Did someone give you tickets to Luca Luca?'

'Sorry?' I say.

'Luca Luca?' he asks.

'No.'

'Oh, here you go,' he says. 'They aren't front row but you should go. It's always full of celebrities. It's a bit of a scream. Last season I sat opposite Paris Hilton and watched her do her lipstick in the shiny buckle of her Fendi handbag throughout the whole show. Hilarious.'

'See you later,' says Alexander, escorting him to the door. 'And thanks for all your help.'

'Pleasure, man,' he says, closing the door behind him.

'Fuck!' I say.

'What?'

'Did you hear what he said?'

'He said a lot.'

'That McQueen has done tartan.'

'How does he know? McQueen isn't showing for four weeks.'

'Maybe he spoke to a model. How the hell should I know? But we've had the same idea for the collection!'

'And?'

'And fuck!' My heart is racing and my mouth is suddenly dry. 'Fuck, fuck, fuck! We've had the same idea.'

'But that doesn't matter.'

'Yes it does. It makes me look uncool and unoriginal. Like I have copied him.'

'Actually,' Alexander points out with a smile, 'you're the one who is showing first.'

'But . . . I know, you're right. But . . . he'll do it better than me.'

'No he won't,' says Alexander. 'It'll just be different.'

'Better.'

'Different.'

'I wish I didn't know that he was doing it.'

'I know. But you do.'

'I'm going to be obsessing about it now until I see his show in a bloody month, and then I shall be comparing them madly.'

'Calm down.'

'I can't.'

'You can.'

'I can't. Look! My hands are actually starting to shake.'

'You could look at it this way: you'll be next to him in the round-ups.'

'That's true.' I smile at him and tap the back of his hand. He is such a sweet bloke. Alexander always manages to find the silver lining.

'You can see the page: "Tartan is Back", and then you and Lee together making up yet another trend in the pages of spurious trends thought up over coffee in the café off Hanover Square.'

'You're right,' I say, pulling myself together.

'I'm *always* right.' He smiles again. 'Just think of the quarter page in US *Vogue*.'

There's a knock at the door.

'That'll be Beverley,' he says. 'Smile. Let's see if we can really feel it this time!'

Alexander and I have a real thing about make-up. As I am not particularly high-maintenance and Alexander is gay, we both find it extremely difficult to get excited about lipstick. Every make-up artist we have ever used has always made some sort of sweeping pronouncement about what is currently hot. And it's never really that difficult to work out. Every season it's either lips or it's eyes. If it was eyes last season, then this season it will be lips. If it was lips, then it will be eyes. Although I have to say that we were both stumped two seasons ago when it became brows – which we eventually worked out was just a different way of saying eyes. Alexander did once point out rather cruelly that it was never noses. I wanted to laugh so much that I had to leave the room with a pretend coughing fit. Anyway, last season it was eyes, so I am banking on this one being lips.

Beverley walks in with her heavy wheelie bag of make-up while I search for my happy face and my interested-in-cosmetics smile. She is followed by a young model, who must be all of fifteen years old.

'Hello there,' she says, huffing her way through the door.

Round, well padded and English with a large bosom and chunky forearms, Beverley looks more like your favourite sofa than a glamorous make-up artist of almost international repute. She introduces us to Natalya who she says will be showing us a few of her make-up looks. She tells us how much she likes our room then talks us through all the other shows she is doing while unpacking a whole department store of products. She walks over to the collection rack and runs her hands over a few of the satin shirts.

'This pink is amazing,' she declares. 'It is so inspiring. It's clean, it's strong. It's very now. It's very forward as well. And feminine without being girlie. It says, I'm in control. Which is what we are all feeling for 2006/7.'

'Good.' I smile. 'The collection is all about opulence and decadence, but all a bit restrained – a Scottish house party in the forties, full of stifled sex and plenty of buttons.'

'The pink is great,' she says again. 'I think we should have it on all their lips, make it the signature of the show.'

'Really?' says Alexander.

'Oh yah,' says Beverley, who sounds like Liz Hurley, but then they are both from Basingstoke. 'It's lips this season.'

'No?' says Alexander, feigning shock.

'Yah,' says Bev. 'It's lips, big lips, statement lips. It's all about the mouth.'

'Right.' I nod.

'Eyes are nude, nude, nude,' she continues. 'Cheeks are in.'

'As well as lips?' I ask.

'Yah. We're bringing them out with peaches and pinks. You know, healthy. OK then,' she says, sitting down and taking Natalya's chin in her hand. 'I'm feeling nude eyes. You know, like almost not there.'

'OK,' says Alexander.

'I'm feeling a light foundation with a slight shimmer, sort of dewy. Pink cheeks and dark pink glossy statement lips.'

'Interesting,' remarks Alexander.

Bev cracks open her bottles and tubes and lays out her brushes. As luck would have it, Mac has a new glossy pink lipstick that she has been asked to promote, which is perfect for the show. I pretend to look shocked. Alexander tells her how lucky that is. She smears Natalya's fashionably bland face in shimmer foundation, covers her eyes in taupe, and brushes her eyelashes with a transparent mascara which also turns out to be another new Mac product. She rubs rouge into her cheeks and paints a thick shiny layer on her lips.

'The great thing about this,' she says, her fingers working quickly and incredibly accurately, 'is that it's quick and looks great. I mean, your show is early, right?'

Alexander nods.

'Yah, well, you're going to have girls turning up late,

some who haven't been to bed, and some who have been drinking and stuff, and this will cover all that and get them down onto the catwalk quickly. There's not that much to do or that can be messed up. Not that I don't trust my team.' She laughs. 'What hair have you got?'

'James is coming in after you,' says Alexander.

'James Car?'

'That's right.'

'Oh, he's great. I've done lots of shows with him. Didn't he train with Garren?'

Garren is one of the best hairdressers in the world. He is responsible for most of the signature styles on the supermodels. He did Brooke Shields's Calvin Klein ads; he re-styled Karen Elson's hair from long and mousey into a short red bob with no eyebrows, which has become her trademark; and he persuaded Erin O'Connor to lose the long brown hair and cut it short and black, and to grow back her overplucked eyebrows. He has been at the top of the fashion game for the last thirty years and is almost impossible to book, unless you are Steven Meisel.

'Sadly, no,' says Alexander. 'He didn't train with Garren, but I think he was one of the guys behind the Fanny.'

'Oh, I remember that,' says Bev. 'It was a blonde, brushed-forward quiff.'

'That's right.'

'I don't think he did do the Fanny,' I say.

'I think he did,' Alexander counters.

'I liked the Fanny,' says Bev. 'It was very fashion forward. What are you planning for the show?'

'Don't know,' I say. 'I think we'll leave it up to James.'

'Good . . . there you go,' she says, turning Natalya's chin left and right for us to have a look.

I'm not sure what to say. The girl looks like she has run a marathon. Her cheeks are bright pink and her face is shining like it's covered in sweat. The lips, however, look great.

'I think it's wonderful,' says Alexander.

'You do?' I ask.

'Oh yes. Inspired.'

'Well, it's from the collection,' says Bev.

'Maybe if we just tone down the foundation and the cheeks?' I suggest.

'Really?' she asks.

'Well . . .'

'I think it's fine,' says Alexander.

'Fine.' Bev clearly doesn't like the word.

'Fine as in the American use of the word – mighty fine, fabulous,' he says.

'Oh, great,' she says. 'So you're happy?'

'Delighted,' he says, nodding slightly to encourage my reaction.

'It's wonderful,' I add.

'I'm glad you're pleased.' She smiles.

After another seven minutes of platitudes, Bev, her

model and her big bag of stuff are finally ushered out of the room.

'I'm sorry,' says Alexander, shaking his head. 'I just couldn't take any more. We've hired her for her reputation. I know little about make-up and care even less. Let's just let her get on with it.'

'You're right,' I say. 'I was just trying to be a control freak.'

There's another knock on the door.

'Give me strength,' says Alexander as he walks towards the door. 'Hello there!'

James Car walks in dressed head to foot in black and dragging a wheelie case behind him. He is wearing Gucci shades and has an oversize cap on his head. For a man who spends his whole day thinking about and working with hair, James doesn't appear to have much of his own. In fact, when he takes his cap off, he appears to be entirely bald. He has the Californian drawl of a surfer and smokes like a chimney. He has had three cigarettes before he has even managed to get all his hairpieces out. He talks about curly being the new smooth, and partings being very now. He says that 'not done' is the new 'done', but that it actually takes about twenty minutes to get that 'not done', just-got-out-of-bed look for the catwalk. Alexander suggests that we go for something simple. I am worried that as we are the first show some of our models won't get there until half an hour before. So instead of a style, James thinks we should just go 'Beautiful, beautiful,

beautiful.' Which apparently means that it should all be scraped straight back and put in high ponytails all of the same length. He has plenty of pieces for girls with short hair. Alexander and I agree. It's simple, it's chic, it's organized, and we've both had enough. James moves on to another appointment and Alexander and I breathe a sigh of relief. We crack open the bottle of Grey Goose vodka in the mini bar.

'Did we just agree to all our models having a Croydon face lift?' asks Alexander, his lips poised over a long glass.

'D'you know, I think so.'

'We've got a long line of Vicky Pollards coming down the catwalk.' He starts to laugh. 'I just hope they don't get *Little Britain* over here.'

Three hours later and Alexander and I can't face going to the Luca Luca show or the Marc Jacobs party. We have drunk nearly the whole bottle of vodka and had a few lines from the six grams of coke Alexander sewed into the hems of the tartan trousers. I am rather glad that he didn't tell me he was packing drugs into the collection, but with the terrible jetlag we both have I am rather pleased that he did.

Two lines are enough to keep us awake until ten p.m., but not much beyond that. We decide we should have an early night. We have fittings to do and a show to choreograph and a legion of Vicky Pollards to organize.

'Do you know what?' says Alexander, brushing his

teeth, dressed in a pair of endearingly prim striped pyjamas.

'What?' I say as I lie back in bed and take a large sip of vodka.

'I've been thinking that the perfect fashion show would be with one of those dry-cleaning machines. The clothes would travel up the catwalk in time, with the right spaces between them. There would be no falling over, no tantrums. It would be simpler.'

'Yeah,' I agree. 'And so much bloody cheaper.'

18

It's the day before the show, and Alexander, Mimi and I have been on the go since eight a.m. Alexander and I are both tense but upbeat. Mimi's hung over and a little short-tempered. She was up till three hanging out with Roland Mouret, Jefferson Hack, Katie Grand and Luella Bartley. She went on to the Marc Jacobs party where Kate Moss was supposed to turn up, but since she has been publicly bound over to good behaviour, she didn't show.

The party was, apparently, good fun, but not as brilliant as his famous 10 September party the day before 9/11, when the stage flats went down after the show and everyone walked into a backstage full of white balloons. There were champagne and fireworks overlooking the bay. A friend of mine always says it was the quintessential fashion party. He says if Sarah Jessica Parker had been there, she would have held her flute in one hand and in her special breathy Carrie

Bradshaw voice she'd have said something like, 'New York! I love this town. So good they named it twice.' But then I suppose it's impossible for any party to live up to anything like that. However, that didn't seem to bother Mimi. She was willing to give it the full swing of the bat, as it were, and as a result she has a hangover and a cokeover that no amount of bacon sandwiches is going to cure. I have to admit I am slightly annoyed with her as tomorrow is the most important day of my year/life/existence. And I have a stylist who is working at half cock.

This morning is packed with fittings. Then I have a meeting with the show producer, I have a seating plan to organize, and I have a possible preview with Anna Wintour. Her people have phoned and informed Alexander that she may turn up between three and four this afternoon to run her hand over the collection. After some pressure for suggestions to make her visit go as smoothly as possible, we are told that she might like a warm, not hot, café latte from Starbucks and does not like to talk to anyone on the way to the room. She likes to be met downstairs in reception, for someone to keep the lift, for the lift to be empty, and for someone to escort her at all times until she reaches the room. We have, of course, agreed to everything. It would be such a huge stamp of approval to have her visit before the show.

Invitations to preview have also gone out to Glenda Bailey from *Harpers Bazaar* and the editors of *Elle* and

W. Normally they come and coo at the collection, check out the Polaroids of the girls, and see if you have any big models on the wall. They might have a sip of champagne, they'll talk crap for fifteen minutes, and then they'll leave in a flurry of kisses and compliments. If the show is a success, the fact that they have been to a preview means they're first in the queue when it comes to calling in clothes. It says they are a supporter of yours and they are, therefore, hip and marvellous. If the collection is a disaster they will, of course, melt into the background like everyone else.

I have my hand up Yulia's skirt. I'm trying to pull smooth the pink satin plunge top with the puffed sleeves. She's only seventeen, but she seems to be taking my intimacy in her stride. This is her second season.

'How about that?' I ask Mimi, who is sitting on the bed pretending to be alert.

'I think if the dresser pulls it down we should be OK. You know, I just don't think sewing small weights on the bottom of the hem on the front is going to work at this late stage.'

'We've got a seamstress arriving here later,' I say. 'She's $400 for the day, so we can put her to good use if we need to.'

'No, I think it's OK, don't you?' she asks Alexander.

'What?' he says.

Alexander is sitting at a computer desk in the corner of the room trying to finalize our guest list with James, Johnson and West, the PR company who are organizing the invitations and doing the front-of-house meet and greet. We've taken them on to show people to their seats and make sure everyone has a goodie bag. At $7,500 for this service I can't help but think they are a little overpaid. All they provide are a few pretty girls in black suits with clipboards to turn away the hoi polloi and some stamps, invitations and an email address to reply to. They are supposed to help out with the goodie bags but Mac have been total sweeties and filled ours for us. Everyone is going home with the same pink glossy lipstick we are using in the show, a matching nail varnish and a blusher brush. We were thinking of adding more, but then I remembered the last show I went to, the designer for the glamorous girl-about-town, Tuleh, and all I got was an orange bikini that was three sizes too small.

'Are you feeling this?' asks Mimi.

'It looks great,' says Alexander, looking up from his keyboard.

'But are you feeling it?' she repeats.

'I am,' he says.

'You?'

'I am,' I reply, getting off my knees to look Yulia up and down. 'Let's 'roid it.'

'Hang on,' says Mimi, peeling her backside off the bed. 'I need to accessorize her first.' She gets a yellow handbag off the table. It is covered in five or six skull and crossbones keyrings. 'Here,' she says to Yulia. 'If you could just swing it a bit when you walk?'

Yulia nods and obligingly swings the bag a bit for Mimi's approval.

'Great, that's fabulous. Could you walk?'

Yulia nods and heads off in the direction of the door. She is swinging the bag back and forth so hard it looks like she is about to hurl it out of the window into the Hudson.

'Um, no, no, no,' says Mimi, running after her. 'Gently. Relax a bit.' Mimi is clearly of the school of thought that if you speak English slowly to a foreigner then they will understand. Speak quickly and they will not.

'Small?' asks Yulia.

'Yes, yes,' says Mimi. 'Small.'

Yulia walks the length of the room, paris-turns at the end and walks back again. Her walk is fine – a little stiff and laboured, but not the worst I have seen. It's just that her arm is so rigid and the fist she makes on the handle of the bag is so firm she looks afraid that someone is about to steal it from her.

'Oh God,' says Mimi, collapsing into a leather arm-chair. 'This is a nightmare. Shall we just lose the bag, 'roid her and get her out of here?'

'I think that is a great idea,' I reply in a singsong voice, hoping that Yulia hadn't caught what Mimi was saying. 'Thank you, Yulia.'

Yulia poses for her snapshot without the handbag, scowling at the camera. It is hard to believe that she is the face of some £500,000 perfume campaign when she can't actually walk and carry a bag at the same time. But I have lost count of the number of models I have met who find it difficult to multi-task.

As Yulia changes into her typical model daywear of tight jeans, flat shoes, large jumper and strange small hat, Mimi and I compare her developed Polaroid with the others on the table. We have styled and 'roided at least ten girls already this morning and we are trying to work out in which order they should come down the catwalk. This is made slightly more complicated by the fact that some are wearing more than one look. So, not only are we trying to work out which outfits are coming in which order, we are also trying to get some sort of an idea of changing time between them. And this is actually quite tricky.

When we show in London I can more or less rely on the dressers to get the girls out of their clothes and into the next outfit without too many problems. I have used the same dressers for the last six seasons. They are a gang of lovely old girls – most of them are in their sixties – from the East End. They dress for lots of other designers during London Fashion Week and have been doing it for years. They get £70 a show and they can often do four or five in a day. They are all qualified seamstresses so they know their material, they know what to get on first, they look after the girls and are sort of like their mothers or grandmothers. The girls trust them, and they are incredibly efficient under pressure. Over here in New York, they don't seem to have the same sort of system. The dressers are fashion undergraduates or students from the local college who want to earn some extra dollars and feel the fashion buzz. I am not sure how reliable or quick they will be. It is better to err on the side of caution when it comes to timings.

Mimi and I are discussing the order. It's important that we get across the feeling of a Scottish forties house party – opulent, decadent and sexy – with a slight sort of punk twist coming from the skull and crossbone accessories. I obviously have to start and finish with my strongest looks. The rest of the collection is paced, with peaks and troughs working around these two key looks. The only problem is that neither of us can agree which is my strongest daywear look to start the show with. The end look is always a killer dress – the last image you want to sit in the fashion editors' minds as they sit, pen poised, ready to slag you off. I have something black and tailored and tight that ticks that box. The only problem is the opener. Mimi thinks I should go with Yulia and the pink satin button shirt and the tight black secretary skirt.

'She looks like she needs a spanking in that skirt,' observes Mimi.

'And that's a good thing?' I ask.

'Of course.'

'The only thing is that Lydia is opening and closing for us.'

'Let her close for you,' says Mimi. 'Yulia has a big

contract; she looks great in the pink satin. It's the opener.'

'But I've told Lydia that she is opening.'

'For Chrissake,' says Mimi. 'Open with Julia.'

'Yulia.'

'Whatever the fuck her name is.'

'But I've told Lydia—'

'Does Anna Wintour know who Lydia is?'

'She might.'

'Lydia is last season. Hell, she is last year.'

'She is lovely,' says Alexander.

'So's my mum, but I wouldn't open with her,' counters Mimi.

'Actually, yours isn't,' I say.

'What?'

'Your mum isn't lovely.'

'We all know that,' sighs Mimi. 'But Lydia is old hat. She can close the show because she's the muse, the mate. That's fine. But please don't open with her. You'll be old and dead in the water before the first frock hits the end of the runway.'

Alexander and I sit in silence. I don't want to say anything. I know Mimi is right, I just don't want to admit it. I wait for Alexander to make the choice. But he doesn't. After a few seconds of silence he is still tapping his computer keys.

'OK then,' I say.

'Good choice,' Alexander says.

'You can't take everyone with you all the time,' says

Mimi. 'If you want to conquer New York, move onwards and upwards. You have to stay ahead of the curve. She'll understand.'

'Yeah, right.'

'She will.'

'So we're opening with Yulia,' I say. 'The girl who can't walk with a handbag.'

'Give the bag to Lydia,' says Mimi with a smile.

'Fuck off,' I say.

We don't have time to fall out because another extra skinny Eastern European lovely comes walking through the door.

'Natasha,' I say, smiling at the blonde gymslip of a girl. 'Would you like to try this on?'

Mimi and I spend the rest of the morning styling, 'roiding and pinning the models into the thirty-five looks I have for the show. We have put together a running order and are working through the hangers, sellotaping the Polaroid of the model in the outfit to the hanger so that shirts and skirts don't get mixed up and everyone knows what they are doing. On the table is a pile of clothes that need adjusting. Thankfully I have a seamstress arriving in an hour or so to take care of it.

I'm drinking my sixth cup of coffee of the day when Alexander calls up Marc Jacobs's new collection on Style.com. Mimi, Alexander and I go through it, look by look. He's done grunge with a forties twist. It is amazing. Surely another hit. We paw over each design. It feels weird to be here in New York, knowing that we are showing tomorrow, and not to be able to make something similar to send down the catwalk. Normally Trish would be straight down the market grabbing some wool so that we can mock up something. Even now I can feel the temptation.

'Shall we just get some gloves?' ask Alexander, going through the show again. 'Or some fur trim?'

'Oh, I love fur,' says Mimi.

'We'll only get PETA fur protestors on to us,' I say. 'And anyway, half the shops we sell to won't stock fur.'

'Big bags?' says Alexander, still scrolling through. 'We could get into the big bag round-ups?'

'He hasn't got much colour,' says Mimi.

'I know, I know,' I say. 'Turn that thing off. You're just making me nervous.'

'Talking of nerves,' says Alexander. 'While we have a moment, shall we sort the seating plan? I have a list of yeses from James, Johnson and West and I think while we have a moment's calm we should try to sort it out.'

Alexander has been hard at work on the seating for the last ten days. He has drawn a very intricate plan of each chair on a huge sheet of white paper and labelled each section in a different colour. Yellow is for European press, pink is for US press, orange for the retailers, and celebrities are in green. We are hoping that Keira Knightley might show as she is in town for a film. Vanessa Tate has promised that she'll come, and the girl from Goldfrapp is on the list. Mimi is also firming up a couple of her mates. Sophie Dahl has said that

347

she might come. I have also sent an invitation to Candace Bushnell as I love her books and think she is so fabulously New York. But I am trying not to get too involved in the celebrity aspect of it all. The fashion press also don't really approve of celebrities cluttering up their front row. They like to think they are the stars. They have been known to boo celebrities who turn up late. But this does depend on the celebrity. The likes of Nicole Kidman could keep them hanging on for a while. They'd probably pitch tents if they knew Kate was coming. But if you're a B-lister you should know your place and turn up on time.

The front row is so political. Obviously, in fashion terms, the more important you are the closer you are to the catwalk. Editors and fashion directors are front row, their assistants and buyers are second row, and boutiques with orders between £5,000 and £10,000 are at the back, as are students, friends of assistants and liggers.

'OK then, I have *Vogue* here, I have *Harpers* next door, and I have the celebrities together so that they make a better photo op.'

'OK.' I nod. 'Do they get on?'

'I don't care,' says Alexander, sounding a little tetchy. 'I'm organizing a show not a bloody cocktail party.'

'And the goodie bags?'

'Are only on the front row,' confirms Alexander.

'So what happens if Anna doesn't show?' I ask, spotting her pink dot in a prime location.

'Firstly, she will show,' says Alexander. 'If not, I'll put *Vogue Italia* there, move *Harpers* along, and we'll put someone from Neiman Marcus in that place.'

'OK. Just so long as I know where they are. So I can look out for their reactions.'

Some designers are so paranoid about the press that they film them during the show to see if they can read their faces – which I'm sure is one of the reasons why Anna Wintour always wears her shades. There is one designer in particular who checks the film afterwards to see if anyone's yawned so that they can call them afterwards and suggest that perhaps they don't come again.

The balance between the press and the big designers is very fine. Upset it and you can find that your front-row seat suddenly disappears. When TV presenter Lowri Turner famously described Versace's models as looking like 'hookers' she was banned for a season. She was then un-banned, only to be permanently banned by Christian Lacroix. Sometimes, however, the journalistic community fights back. When Bernard Arnault banned Suzy Menkes from all the LVMH shows in Paris after she described Galliano's show for Dior as 'too warlike' in the aftermath of 9/11, the whole industry rallied round. They refused to go to any of his shows in protest, and by the end of the week – the Dior show was on the Tuesday – Arnualt had to back down. The most powerful man in the luxury goods business ended up kowtowing to Suzy. You don't mess with the hacks. But equally, if she'd been a nobody, her invitation would simply have been withdrawn until she learned how to toe the line. Sadly, I don't have that sort of power. I am not an advertiser; I don't have the power to call up a magazine and demand to know why their journalist didn't turn up or write a nice review. I can't ask for editorial compensation. I am not owned by a powerful supercompany. So I have to be nice to the journalists in the hope that they are nice in return.

After a late lunch, Rosa the seamstress turns up with her own machine. Short, middle-aged and shaped like a barrel, she sets herself up in the corner of the room, pops open a huge bag of marshmallows and gets to work.

Ten minutes later Mark the producer arrives. Tall, thin and dressed entirely in black, Mark wears a goatee and black framed glasses. He is tense and twitchy. As he sits at the table his left knee bounces continuously up and down. He is doing ten shows during fashion week and is clearly rushed off his feet.

'I have to say that I'm surprised you are showing in the tents,' he drawls, rolling his own cigarette using brown liquorice paper. 'A young groovy label like yours doesn't normally show in the tents. The tents are establishment. They're Michael Kors, Oscar de la Renta, Carolina Herrera.'

'It was the only place we could get,' says Alexander. 'Next time we'll go somewhere else where we can stamp our personality on the place.'

'Yeah,' he says. 'That can kinda be a pain in the arse too.'

'I know,' I say. 'It's exhausting. Finding the venue, lighting it properly . . .'

'Yeah. I always think that simple is the key. Every time you ask a model to do anything complicated, they fuck it up.'

'They're not all stupid,' I say. 'My best mate is a model.'

'Oh yeah?' he says, getting out his Zippo lighter.

'Lydia Sharp.'

'I know her. She's been around a while.'

'She's closing for us.'

'Oh. Who's opening?'

'Yulia Melekhov,' says Alexander.

'She's cool. She's doing everything. She's supposed to be the new Gemma Ward, or Daria.'

'I heard that,' says Mimi, sounding a little bit too victorious.

'So, what plans do you have for the show?' he asks.

Alexander hands over the show music CD that Damiano burned for us back home. We've been listening to it solidly for the past couple of days, so quite frankly I am happy to see the back of it. He explains that we want the girls to go out as simply as they can. We have no great ideas for choreography. We just want them to go to the end of the runway, turn and return.

'That sounds perfect to me, man,' says Mark. 'Just keep it simple. Last show I did I had girls wandering all over the place. They were supposed to follow different coloured arrows that we painted onto blocks in

Freemasons' Hall. It was a disaster. Not one of them could follow instructions. God, I tell you, when models are stupid they are really stupid. Yesterday I had one from Utah. I said to her, "Are you from Salt Lake City?" She said, "Yes." I said, "Do you believe in polygamy?" She said, "What?" I said, "Are you a Mormon?" She said, "No, I'm intelligent." At which point I gave up.'

Room service arrives with the bottles of champagne we requested for the previews. We've got some dips and bits coming as well, just in case anyone is a bit peckish. Alexander thinks I am mad ordering food as none of these women ever eats. But I just didn't want to look tight.

Alexander finalizes the show details with Mark. They talk through the lighting and the fact that the crew need to show up three hours before the show starts. They shake hands and Mark goes, leaving the room smelling of cigarettes and liquorice. Mimi goes into a panic and starts spraying her Calypso perfume everywhere. There are only ten minutes until Anna is scheduled to arrive and the place smells like a nightclub.

There's a knock on the door. This can't be Anna – she's being met in the lobby. I open the door. It's Glenda Bailey. She's arrived early. I can't tell her to go away and come back later. She comes in. I see the look of panic on Alexander's face. Previews are supposed to be one on one. We can't have the two most powerful editors in the same room at the same time.

Glenda apologizes for being early. She says that

someone had told her the traffic was terrible so she left plenty of time and somehow her driver managed to avoid it all. Dressed in fashion black, her long red hair is loose and her sunglasses are on the top of her head. She puts down her $3,000 handbag, accepts her glass of champagne and walks towards the collection. I am talking so fast and laughing so much I think she thinks I'm on drugs, which I kind of wish I were. Anything to make the next half hour go faster. She asks me lots of questions about the collection. I make up something about being inspired by my Scottish roots.

'I didn't know you were Scottish,' she says in a thick northern accent.

'Oh yes,' I lie. 'My mother's side.'

Alexander talks some guff about fashion week. He asks about the Marc Jacobs party. Glenda says it was fabulous. She says our collection is fabulous. She particularly loves the satin shirts and the tartan trousers. She puts down her half-drunk glass, kisses both my earlobes, and leaves.

'She's gone,' I say.

'I know,' says Alexander, just as stunned as me.

'She stayed fifteen minutes,' says Mimi.

'She did?' I ask.

'Yeah. You were just talking so goddamn fast that you didn't notice or let her get a word in.'

'Was it a disaster?' I ask.

'No,' says Mimi. 'You did well. Although, the Scottish thing?'

353

'I know. I am prone to random lying when nervous.'

Alexander's mobile goes. We all stand and stare at it.

'That's Anna,' he says.

'Well, answer it,' I say.

'Hello?' he says. 'She's downstairs,' he mouths.

As Alexander goes down to meet Anna's car and escort her through the lobby, Mimi and I stand around nervously in line forming a welcoming committee. I feel like we are about to meet the Queen. Which I suppose in fashion terms we are. I have been told the more important you are fashion-wise, the less the entourage. I wonder how many she will bring with her.

'Fuck!' I suddenly say loudly.

'Sssh! What?' whispers Mimi.

'We've forgotten the warm latte.'

'Fuck!'

'Yeah, fuck!'

'Double fuck! I could run downstairs, get one and bring it back,' suggests Mimi.

'Go for it!' I say. 'And run like the fucking wind!'

As Anna comes up in the lift, Mimi runs full pelt down the stairs. I stand to attention as Anna plus an entourage of five walks into the room. It is all I can do to stop myself from curtseying. I feel myself bob up and down as I shake her cold hand. Standing in the flesh, dressed in a fashion black suit with her neat, fringed bob, which is blow-dried every day, she is much smaller than I'd thought. Maybe it's because she is so powerful that I expected her to be taller, but she is tiny for a colossus.

She ignores the champagne and the poorly chosen dips and heads straight for the collection. I am now so nervous that I have gone beyond lying and become mute. Alexander answers her questions. I stand and smile like a moron. She is pleasant about the clothes. Asks questions about my inspiration. Alexander answers. She looks at the Polaroids and says that she also likes the satin shirts and the tartan combination. I let off a burst of loud machine-gun laughter. She and Alexander turn and look at me. At that moment Mimi bursts through the door.

'Anna!' she says. Her cheeks are bright pink and her nose a little runny from being outside in the cold. 'Your coffee!'

'Lovely,' says Anna, not extending her hand.

'I'm afraid it's a little hot,' adds Mimi, putting it down on the table.

'Thank you,' says Anna.

She squeezes both my forearms, wishes me luck for tomorrow, and goes to the door to leave. Alexander moves to escort her downstairs. She smiles and raises a hand. There is no need.

The door has barely shut before Alexander cracks open the vodka.

'Don't think that went well,' I say.

'It could have been worse,' he says.

'How exactly?'

'Give me a minute,' he says, knocking back a stiff-looking shot, 'and I'll think of something.'

By 10.30 p.m. the editors from *Elle* and *W* have failed to show and I have sent Rosa the seamstress home. Alexander, Mimi and I are exhausted. We have been on the go now for more than fourteen hours. The show starts in less than twelve hours and we still have two more models to fit, Lydia and Valentina. Lydia should not be a problem as the clothes were designed around her, and Valentina came in for a pre-fit two days ago. Valentina turns up first. She is tall, blonde and German, and is one of the few models whose name I know in the show. She has been doing Tuleh down in the tents and is on her way out to a party. She is already quite drunk when she walks through the door and she immediately goes to the lavatory to sharpen herself up. When she reappears, she is very chatty indeed. She squeezes herself into the high-waisted tartan trousers which we made slightly larger for her earlier in the week. They seem to hang off her. The fitted shirt is also not as fitted as it should be.

'F-e-erk.' She giggles as she looks down. 'Sorry about that. I've been at the laxatives to lose a few pounds for the shows and they have certainly worked!'

'Yes, they have.' I smile, my teeth gritted. 'Well done you.'

Mimi sets to work with the pins, taking the trousers and the shirt back in. Valentina stands there, rubbing her nose with the back of her hand.

'Is there a drink in this place?' she asks.

'Vodka OK?' asks Alexander, who has had a few himself.

'Don't bother with a glass,' she says, taking the bottle out of his hands.

Watching her standing there swigging from the bottle, I am reminded of a story my mate told me about a Naomi Campbell fitting where she arrived the worse for wear and demanded more booze. There was nothing in the place except for some Metaxa cooking brandy. She drank the best part of the bottle during the fitting. God knows how, but she was all right for the following day's show.

Valentina disappears off into the night with our bottle of vodka, leaving us with the small task of taking her trousers and jacket down a size by hand. Mimi and I settle down at the table with a needle, thread, packet of cigarettes and a glass of champagne. Mimi is spitting feathers about having to re-fit Valentina at the last minute. She keeps calling her selfish and 'fucking annoying'.

'Are you sure we can't kick her out of the show?' she says, her nose in the crotch of the trousers. 'She's not that good any more anyway.'

'Who are you writing off?' asks Lydia, swanning through the door.

'Oh, hi,' I go, already feeling guilty about what I am about to say.

'No-one,' says Alexander.

'Hello!' says Mimi.

'What?' says Lydia, taking a step back. 'Why are you all looking at me?'

'Um,' I say.

'What?'

'I've got something to say . . .'

Lydia takes her demotion well. She says she understands over and over again. The more decent about it she is, the more guilty I feel. She tries on her black dress to close the show. She looks stunning. It's tight and fitted with a plunge front and buttons all the way along the tight full-length sleeves. It falls to the floor and hangs perfectly. I am beginning to think that perhaps I have made a mistake going with Yulia, but I can't change my mind now. Lydia then announces that she is going back to her hotel for an early night. Normally she'd have stayed and gossiped and drunk champagne with us until we'd bagged up the collection and got it all ready around three a.m. She is obviously put out. As she closes the door behind her, I can't help but think that our relationship is over. I am overwhelmed by sadness.

'That went well, don't you think?' says Mimi, snapping a thread of cotton in her mouth.

Neither Alexander nor I reply.

19

It's 5.30 a.m. I've had two hours' sleep and I am so nervous I have thrown up twice already this morning. This is the most important day of my life so far. Today I will either sink or swim. I will either cut it on the international stage or die on my arse. All I can do is smoke, drink coffee and concentrate on slowing my breathing down, otherwise I shall faint.

I'm not the only one feeling the pressure. Alexander's got such bad diarrhoea he's been to our bathroom twice already, each time making it unusable for the next fifteen minutes. Who said the world of fashion was glamorous?

Actually I have to say that even at six a.m. from our cab window, the black-carpeted steps outside Bryant Park have a certain amount of allure. They're normally lined with students, fans, paparazzi, security guards on walkie-talkies and clipboard-toting PR girls; this morning there is something elegant about the lone

Japanese photographer who snaps my puffy face and the hugely fat night guard who checks my pass while Alexander and I stand on the kerb. All week black town cars have been disgorging the fabulous and famous at the bottom of these steps. Somehow I feel like a bit of a chancer standing here, watching my clothes being carted off down a side entrance. My career in the balance. My heart pounding in my chest.

Some efficient woman dressed in black and covered in laminated passes that scream access and importance appears and escorts us through the wide, tented lobby full of champagne bars and small café tables and off out the back to the show tents. Backstage, the place is eerily silent. The black floor, white roof and black and white cotton walls make it appear colder than it actually is. Having said that, it is actually quite chilly. Although I know that in about an hour, when fifteen hairdryers are on the go and you won't be able to move for models, make-up artists, liggers, fans and friends, the place will feel sweatier than a Soho strip club with just about as much naked flesh on show. But at the moment the place is empty and bald. My collection hangs somewhat forlornly on racks down one side of the room. There are banks of chairs and mirrors and lights. There's a wall of plug-sockets for the various hair appliances. There are long tables, hangers, rails and a few large black bins. One will be full of ice and champagne later; another will overflow with paper cups. This really is the calm before the storm.

Half an hour later, out beyond the flats, I can hear the technical crew already at work. I walk out from behind the stage and onto the catwalk. The white runway is covered in black plastic, ensuring that it is pristine for the show. There are three rows of black chairs around the catwalk and there are hundreds more that bank up the side. It is like some latter-day Roman amphitheatre. All we need now are the lions.

Someone turns the lights on. They are so bright and blinding I can't see a thing. A couple of fat guys in jeans and black T-shirts walk past carrying a large piece of white card with my name written on it in oversize capitals.

'You know where that's going, guys?' I hear Mark's voice from out of the shadows. 'No fuck-ups?'

'No, boss,' the fatter of the two shouts back.

I turn and watch them struggle to get my name centre stage. I remember a mate of mine telling me that some *Vogue* reporter once nearly trashed the Givenchy set, just hours before the show started. She was climbing up a ladder to organize a photo when she put her foot through the 'E'. Pandemonium broke out as a hundred fashion staff were despatched to find another 'E'. I can't help thinking that someone must have had one in their pocket.

'To the left, to the left, to the left. Right, right . . .'

Mark is shouting instructions from the middle of the room. I can feel the sweat and tension from here. It is probably best to leave him to it.

I go backstage and at 6.45 the catering staff arrive. Someone is soon charging up a coffee urn. You never get hot drinks back in the UK as one can't afford the bother and expense of one of these. Croissants, fruit, bowls of sweets and chocolate and a pile of sandwiches are being laid out on one of the long tables, ready for anyone to tuck in. There's a collection of Cokes, both Diet and full-fat. There's Gatorade and water too. And some young Spanish guy is emptying carrier bags of ice into one of the black bins, while someone else is unpacking the bottles of champagne. This spread looks good. It looks very generous. I hope all this is included in the price of the tents.

Mimi arrives at seven in a whirlwind of panic. She is wearing dark glasses and her red hair looks like it has spent the night in a skip.

'I am so fucking sorry,' she says. 'My alarm call never arrived.'

'That's OK,' I say. 'We haven't really got going yet.'

'What shall I do?' she asks.

'Organize the clothes. Put them in order. Lay them out on the racks according to each girl . . .'

'Yup, yup, yup.' She's nodding like a dog on the back shelf of a mini cab. 'And put out the shoes and the bags and the necklaces and bracelets . . .'

'Accessories?'

'Those things.' She nods again.

'OK,' says Alexander, coming up to me stinking of

coffee, fags and lavatories, 'I'm going to put the names out on the chairs.'

'Are you sure we should do that now?' I ask.

'Absolutely,' he says.

'Why?'

'Because I can't stand and panic and smoke any more,' he shouts as he walks off out onto the stage, the names of who's who in the fashion world tucked under his arm.

Half an hour later, James Car and Beverley Blond arrive, each with a team of some fifteen people. Bev's team are all in black with 'Mac Professional' emblazoned across the backs of their T-shirts. James's team are all slightly more individual. Some, it should be pointed out, are more individual than others. The group of four men who are all heavily pierced and handcuffed together are perhaps pushing the boat out somewhat. All I can think, as I watch everyone fight for the best positions in this small backstage area, is that they must be very good friends indeed.

There are two and a half hours to go before the show, and some of the models start to arrive. Mimi greets each and every one of them like they are old friends, which I suppose in fashion terms, since we all met yesterday, they are. Dressed in their skinny jeans, large jumper and small hat uniform they are all unkempt and devoid of make-up. Some of them still smell of the B-league bass guitarist whose bed they've just crawled out of. Some still look like they are asleep. Others definitely haven't been to bed. There is one very white-looking girl with a thick Russian accent who stands and shivers in the corner. Is it the coke or the cold? I'm not sure which.

This being New York, we can only smoke outside the tents, so everyone's trips to the open-air smoking area are frequent. I am on my sixth or possibly seventh visit when I bump into Bev. She is huddled around the outdoor heater with two German models and someone who looks like a member of her staff.

'Hi there,' she says.

'Hi.' I smile. 'How's it going?'

'Fine, so fine.'

'Good. I only want to hear fine. I can't cope with anything going wrong.'

'It'll be fine,' she says. 'The collection looks fabulous, the girls are fabulous, the make-up will be fabulous. It's all going to be great.'

'Thanks.'

'Oh, hey, have you met Stacey, my life coach?'

'Um, no,' I say. 'Life coach?'

'Oh yah,' confirms Bev. 'I never travel without her. Everyone's got one these days.'

'Hello,' I say.

'So nice to meet you,' simpers Stacey, shaking my hand like a born-again Christian. 'I'm so liking the atmosphere backstage. It's so very positive.'

'Great,' I say.

'Isn't she great?' says Bev, tapping Stacey on the arm

in such a way that I find myself wondering if she is a lesbian.

Sadly, there aren't that many lesbians in fashion at the moment. We went through a phase a while back when all the girls were sleeping with each other. It was a statement thing. But these days it's babies, dogs or knitting.

Talking of which, we seem to have two mutts back-stage already. Mimi is chatting away to Venetia, who has something small and fluffy on her lap. Mimi is letting it yap bits of croissant out of her mouth. Well, at least someone is eating the food.

It's eight a.m., and there are long-limbed lovelies everywhere. Some of them are fully clothed, some are in thongs and T-shirts, and others are just in thongs. Nearly all the girls are here now, and the place is beginning to resemble a salon for beautiful people. The hairdryers are going at full blast and there are clouds of sickly-smelling hairspray everywhere. Bev's got some pretty girl's chin in her hand. James is brushing out Yulia's hair. At least my opening girl is here. Where's Lydia? I look around. I can't see her anywhere. The awful thing is, she is usually one of the first to arrive. The first to attack the croissants, the first to get her make-up done, the first to prat around while I do press interviews.

'Hi there,' says some stick-thin blonde with dead straight hair. 'I'm Kelly from JJW.'

'Where?' I say. My nerves are increasing, my hands

are getting sweatier and my heart is still pounding in my chest. Anyone would have thought I'd been at the jazz.

'James, Johnson and West?'

'Oh, right.'

'We have a few crews coming down to interview you.'

'Oh, great, OK.'

'Cool,' she says, moving aside to reveal three camera crews standing right behind her. 'This is Fashion File, Video Fashion and CNN.'

'OK,' I say, blinking into their bright lights.

'We've also got Reuters, AP, some guys from *Vogue* doing backstage shots, *W*, WWD, and some girl who is doing a backstage story for *Elle* magazine. Are you busy?'

'What?' I say. 'No. Nothing to do at all,' I add sarcastically.

'Great,' she says. 'Let's do some interviews now.'

And before I have a chance to say I'm joking you stupid cow, she has me up against the mirrors talking about my collection, my influences and my Scottish ancestry. I am repeating myself for the third time when I see Alexander vying for my attention over the well-padded shoulder of the girl from CNN.

'So, your family's Scotch?' asks the CNN girl.

'Um, well, some of it.' I smile.

'Which is why you have plaid in your collection,' she states. She has clearly got the hang of this fashion thing.

'Absolutely,' I lie.

Alexander waves again.

'I'm sorry, I've got to go.'

'Oh, one last question?'

'Oh, OK.'

'I hear you're dressing Vanessa Tate for the Oscars. Any tips on what you'll be putting her in?'

'Oh, right,' I say. 'Something sexy and glamorous and probably long?'

'Great,' she says. 'I just need to do my piece to camera over here.'

'We need you out front,' gasps Alexander.

'What? Why?' I say, my heart pounding.

'We've got a bloody crisis brooding here. It's a fucking nightmare.' He is wringing his hands as I follow him out front.

'What?' I say. 'Is it the lights? The music? Is Anna not coming?'

'No, no, that's all fine . . . This is a total fucking nightmare from hell.' His earnest face is staring at mine. 'We've run out of goodie bags.'

'Sorry?'

'We've run out of goodie bags. What are we going to do?'

'And there was I thinking it was something important.'

'It is,' he insists.

'I think you should leave the front-of-house stuff to the girls from James, Johnson and Thingy,' I say. 'I need you backstage.'

'I haven't done the seating yet,' he says.

'What have you been doing all this time?'

'Worrying about goodie bags.'

'Come on, let's do it together.'

Alexander and I grab a couple of the PR girls and set about sticking names to backs of chairs. We resolve the goodie bag problem by deciding to give them to the press and the US buyers. The UK buyers are sitting over the other side of the catwalk, so hopefully they won't notice. We only seat the front two rows by name; the rest are written down on the list, but their names won't actually be on their seats. The show music is blaring out in fits and starts as they test each of the speakers, and the lighting to go with the show.

'We've got two Anna Wintours!' comes a shout from the other side of the runway.

'Surely everyone knows there is only one Anna Wintour?' I remark with a laugh.

'Fuck? Really?' says Alexander. 'Where's the other Anna Wintour?'

'Oh, I remember putting it back there,' says the PR girl.

'Where?' asks Alexander.

'Row two somewhere?' she mutters.

'Row two? Row two? How old are you? Where are you from? Don't you fucking know who Anna Wintour is?' Alexander's face has gone purple with frustration. 'Who's your boss?'

The poor girl looks terrified. She runs along the

length of the second row. 'Sorry, sorry, sorry,' she repeats. 'Here it is!' She pulls Anna Wintour off the second row and Alexander relaxes.

'Right,' he says. 'No more fucking mistakes.'

Tension still hangs in the room. Alexander can't resist snapping at the PR girl. Mark is shouting at a techie. And I need another cigarette. I leave Alexander with the goodie bags still to do and walk backstage. The smell of cosmetics, hairspray and sweaty girls is overpowering. The area is now so packed there is little room for anyone to move. There are photographers everywhere, snapping the girls' every move. There are film crews shooting the photographers snapping the girls. A couple of bottles of champagne have already been popped. There are cups of the stuff lined up in front of the mirrors. With girls giggling and laughing at one another, with the hairdryers going and the photographers barking out commands and encouragement, it is hard to hear yourself speaking in an interview, let alone the questions themselves.

There's just over an hour to go now and the student dressers are all here, checking their outfits. Mimi is sorting through the accessories for the third time. Some models are already trying on their first looks. Some are chatting into their mobiles. Others are sitting in make-up chairs. I am walking around checking that everyone is here and happy, and that everyone knows what they are doing. Mark is hovering around with a clipboard shouting out the models' names and checking them off his list. Lydia is still not here. Maybe she is so pissed off with me that she isn't going to turn up. She is cutting it fine.

'We're two models down,' Mark says. 'Lydia's on her way.'

'She is?'

'Yeah.' He looks down his list.

'Thank God for that.' My heart actually misses a beat. She doesn't hate me after all.

'She's stuck in traffic,' he says. 'It's Valentina who's the problem.'

'Oh yes?'

'Yeah. I've managed to raise her on the mobile but she says she is stuck.'

'Stuck?'

'Yeah. She's staying around the corner. Do you know—'

'That's done,' announces Alexander, interrupting our conversation. 'Anything else?'

'Oh great,' says Mark. 'Will you rescue Valentina from her hotel room?'

'What?' he says.

'She's stuck.'

'Stuck? How stuck?' asks Alexander.

'I don't know, man,' Mark says. 'She wouldn't say. Only that she couldn't move and that it was slightly embarrassing.'

'Oh, OK,' he says. 'Where's she staying?'

Alexander disappears off to rescue Valentina just as

Lydia arrives. She catches my eye as soon as she enters the room and gives me a cool look as she walks across to sit down in James's chair. I go over to the hair section and start to walk down the line of girls, all of whom are having their locks scraped back into ponytails and being turned into upmarket Vicky Pollards. I talk to each of them in turn. Some of them aren't capable of chatting in English. I am just about to talk to Lydia when she leans forward and picks up her mobile. She pops her large feet up on the side and sits back while James fits a blonde pony hairpiece to the back of her head.

'Fuck off, you bloody bitch!' shouts a girl suddenly. She gets up from her chair and throws her hairpiece across the room. 'You fucking bloody burnt my ear with that thing!'

'I didn't,' replies a member of the hair team.

'You fucking bloody did!' replies the model.

'Hang on, hang on,' says Mark, coming over with his clipboard. 'What's going on?'

'Well,' says one of the members of the chain gang, the other three having no choice but to stand by and listen, 'this bitch here is all twitchy and high and she's picking fights with everyone.'

'Did you burn her ear?' he asks the member of the hair team.

'No,' she replies.

'Then go,' he says to the model.

'What?' says the model, her mouth ajar with shock.

371

'Go,' he repeats. 'You have been surly since you arrived, and I'm not having it. We're all working hard and you are being obstructive.'

'You can't treat me like this. I am the highest-earning model to come out of Eastern Europe.'

'I don't care where you're from, you're history. Now fuck off.' He jabs his thumb over his left shoulder. 'How many looks are you doing?'

'Fuck you,' says the model, picking up her stuff.

'Oh, one,' says Mark. 'Now there's a surprise. Who would like to do this girl's look?' Mark runs his finger up and down the list of names. 'Marina? Anna? Lydia? Lydia, you're the only one.' He looks up and smiles at her. 'OK?'

I look at Lydia. She looks at me. I wouldn't blame her if she told Mark where to get off. But she just smiles and says, 'Sure, anything to help.' And the knot of guilt tightens in my chest.

There are forty-five minutes to go and Valentina is still not here. The backstage area is crammed. People I don't know keep coming up to me, kissing my ears and wishing me luck for the show. I decide the only way to get through the next hour or so is to just keep smiling. There are naked girls everywhere, trying on my clothes, snaking their hips into my skirts. There are dressers ironing clothes and fluffing out skirts and shirts. There are techies coming back and forth from the front of house, checking on the girls, tucking into the food. Two models to my right are complaining that their clothes aren't glamorous enough. It makes me think about Kate, Naomi and Nadja bickering over a silver dress backstage at a Vivienne Westwood show. Kate kept on saying that her rail was missing 'glamour'. Naomi was insisting that as the first supermodel ever to do Vivienne she deserved the dress. Nadja suggested that she was the biggest star and she needed the sequins. In the end Vivienne said that Naomi would look like 'fucking Diana Ross', that Linda was wearing the dress, and that was that. In the end Linda couldn't wear the dress because of an operation she'd just had, so the dress was never worn. I am so tense and tired and nervous I feel like walking up to the two models and turfing them out on their ears. But we are still a model down and the last thing I need is to have to get Mimi onto the catwalk.

Half an hour to go, and Alexander and Valentina arrive backstage. She looks dishevelled and well slept in, and heads straight for the make-up chair.

'What the hell happened?' I ask Alexander as he comes towards me.

'Unbelievable,' he says, shaking his head. 'Found her handcuffed to the radiator with two vibrators up her.'

'Two?'

'I know. Fortunately they'd both run out of batteries.'

'Jesus . . . I don't think I can meet her eye again.'

'I know.' He grins. 'Naughty, dirty girl.'

I look over at Valentina. She has one person doing

her face and two other guys squatting at her feet. I walk over.

'Everything OK?' I ask.

'Sure,' says one of the guys at her feet, a paintbrush of flesh-covered make-up in his hand. 'We're just covering the bruises. I haven't seen marks like these since I did Danielle after she'd had rough sex with a trucker in a lay-by outside Milan. Although she was worse. This girl has whip marks all over her back and welts from the handcuffs.'

'Oh,' I say. 'How long do you think?'

'Ten minutes,' he says.

Valentina looks straight through me and stares into the middle distance. She doesn't say a word.

'We've opened the doors,' says some PR girl in a black pantsuit. 'They're coming in. Twenty minutes to go.'

More and more people are coming backstage now. There are more TV camera crews filming each other. More photographers taking snaps.

'First looks!' shouts Mark from the side of the room.

All the girls start putting the finishing touches to their clothes. Mimi walks around tweaking shirts, smoothing skirts, and adding bracelets and bags. James is holding the largest canister of Elnett hairspray I have ever seen. He appears to be walking around releasing it into the atmosphere like an airhostess sanitizing a plane. I am now mincing my hands. I go from girl to girl, checking them over to see if all the outfits are as they should be. Yulia's walking around in her bright pink shirt and black skirt. I make her stop and I shove my hand up her skirt to pull the shirt down. She just stands there chewing a sweet.

More and more fashionistas come backstage. I see a journalist from the *Telegraph* talking to Mimi. A woman from *The Times* is laughing with Alexander, and the hack from *Elle* magazine is looking at the clothes.

It is now so hot that I can feel myself sweating. I have beads on my top lip. Some of the girls are puffing and pulling their shirts out of their armpits. The music is blaring from the front of house and the noise is building.

Suddenly there is a flash of bulbs and the crowd starts to heave apart. Vanessa Tate is coming towards me, accompanied by Kathy, who appears to be smoking.

'Hi there,' she says, coming over to kiss me. Our moment is shared with the world's media. 'Good luck with the show.'

'Thanks,' I say. 'And thanks for wearing the collection to the show.'

I look her up and down. She is wearing all the clothes Alexander sent her and is looking distinctly Russian.

'I love them,' she says, in a manner that implies she is keeping the lot.

'Great.' I smile, thinking she'll be in for a shock when the bike arrives at eight a.m. tomorrow. 'Enjoy the show.'

'Oh, I will,' she says. 'I'm sitting next to Sophie Dahl.'

'OK, five minutes!' shouts Mark. 'How are we all doing?'

I look around the room. Valentina appears to be nearly ready. Lydia is standing around in a daywear outfit looking fabulous and bored. Yulia looks suitably sour and fashionable, and the thin girl who has been up all night is still shivering.

'OK, line up,' says Mark, getting out his clipboard and running his fingers up and down the list. 'Yulia here, Natasha here, Valentina, Lydia, Gemma, Lily, Agnes . . .' He ticks them off one by one.

At last the backstage area is emptying as people start to take their seats for the show. I go to the very back of the stage and poke my nose through the flats. Fucking hell! The place is packed. It is heaving. There are paps going up and down the runway taking shots of the famous. I can see all the hacks. There's *Vogue*, the *Sunday Times* . . . and I spot the large black-framed sunglasses as I continue to search the crowd. Anna Wintour is here! A huge rush of adrenalin shoots through my body. I've made it! I've made it! I've fucking made it! Anna is here! I've got an Oscar-nominated actress in the front row! I should shoot myself now. Nothing is ever going to be this good again.

The crowd is settling down. They are taking the covers off the runway. The music is teeing up. Not long now. A few minutes. We are only fifteen minutes late.

So much cooler than keeping them all waiting. I turn back to see the girls all lined up in my clothes. Ready to go. The back light comes down. Fuck! I can see all their knickers.

'Shit, shit,' I say. 'Get your pants off.'

The music starts. I am standing at the entrance to the show. Yulia steps forward. I shove my hands up her skirt and pull her G-string off. She steps out of the legs and, head up, walks straight off towards the horde of photographers at the end of the catwalk. Next is Natasha, then Valentina, Lydia, Gemma and Lily. I pull the pants off each of them in turn as they stand waiting to go on. None of them seems to mind. James gives them a quick final spray, I tug at their crotch, and off they go.

I watch the line of girls go down the catwalk, sitting next to a pile of warm G-strings. No sooner have they gone than they are back, collapsing into a panic as soon as they come off stage. The student dressers grab them, pull them out of their clothes, and pour them into something else. They're off and out again. My creations are left in a limp pile on the floor.

There is a shriek of laughter from the audience. I rush to stare through the flap.

'Deborah has broken her shoe,' says Mark.

I look out to see Deborah unmoved, her face staring ahead, walking on the ball of one foot. It is not until she turns the corner to backstage that she reacts.

'Jesus Christ,' she drawls, 'did you see that?'

Her dresser says nothing. There is no time to chat. Instead she puts a new pair of golden sandals on her feet. Deborah steps into a tight satin dress, is zipped up, and walks right back out onto the catwalk, a whole twenty-five seconds later.

Suddenly it is all over. Lydia steps out in the black skin-tight floor-length gown and then Alexander shoves me out, blinking, onto the catwalk. Lydia is carrying a bouquet of flowers. I walk halfway down the runway and bow. The audience applauds, and a line of models files past clapping in time to the music. They do a circuit of the catwalk. Lydia kisses my cheek, and then I follow them all to the back of stage.

Nearly five months of hard work and planning is over in eight and a half minutes. Champagne corks are popping all over the place as models help themselves to their 10.23 a.m. hair of the dog. I have a CNN camera in my face asking for my reaction to the show. There is a surge of people coming backstage, all of whom want to pat me on the back and tell me it was 'fabulous'. I look around for a pair of sunglasses. To no avail. Anna obviously has better things to do. The make-up people are clearing up and packing away their products. Hair have already tidied up. My clothes are hanging like limp rags on their hangers, covered in plastic, some with their Polaroids still attached. Mimi is knocking back the booze. Alexander has his lips around a paper cup. I am talking about myself again as Lydia walks away. She gives me a small wave. I can't respond as I'm mid flow.

'So that's it,' says Alexander, coming over to kiss me for the cameras. 'It's a hit.'

'Are you sure?'

'Oh yeah,' he says. 'I've got a suite booked.'

'Right.'

'Well, we've got some selling to do tomorrow.'

'Cool,' says the reporter for CNN.

The camera is still trained on my face. The bright light shines in my eyes. My heart is beating out of my chest. My mouth is dry. I am so exhausted all I want to do is keel right over. But I smile instead.

'So, what are your ideas for the next collection?'

THE STORK CLUB
by Imogen Edwards-Jones

'There is remarkable courage in the candour that permeates these pages, as well as a sparkling wit which, despite the poignancy of the story, make me laugh out loud'
Mail on Sunday

When Imogen Edwards-Jones was a teenager, she believed that getting pregnant was easy, the inevitable consequence of sex, and that it could ruin her life. Twenty years later, pregnancy could still ruin her life. Although now it was not the threat of what having a baby would do, but of not having a baby at all.

Based on her hugely successful *Daily Telegraph* column, *The Stork Club* is Imogen's very personal, very moving and very funny memoir of her (and her husband's) attempts to conceive. Poked and prodded by endless doctors, pumped full of an exotic cocktail of drugs and forced to try to have sex at the most inopportune moments, Imogen pulls no punches in her account of this gruelling process. On a voyage through despair and elation, she undergoes artificial insemination and IVF, takes endless fertility pills and injects herself with drugs more than a thousand times. Funny and heartbreaking, this is a detailed, poignant account of one woman's journey to motherhood – proof positive that there's light at the end of the darkest of tunnels . . .

'Brutally honest yet often hilarious'
OK! Magazine

'Compelling . . . it made me laugh out loud and cry'
Woman's Own

9780552154383

CORGI BOOKS

HOTEL BABYLON
by Imogen Edwards-Jones & Anonymous

'Something strange occurs to guests as soon as they check in.
Even if in real life they are perfectly well-mannered, decent
people with proper balanced relationships, as soon as they spin
through the revolving hotel doors the normal rules of
behaviour no longer seem to apply.'

All of the following is true. Only the names have been changed
to protect the guilty. All the anecdotes, the stories, the
characters, the situations, the highs, the lows, the scams, the
drugs, the misery, the love, the death and the insanity are
exactly as was told by Anonymous – someone who has spent
his whole career working in hotels at the heart of London's
luxury hotel industry. However, for legal reasons, the stories
now take place in a fictitious hotel known as Hotel Babylon.
More than a decade is compressed into twenty-four hours.
Everything else is as it should be. The rich spend money, the
hotel makes money and the chambermaids still fight the
bellboys over a two-pound coin. It's just another twenty-four
hours in an expensive London hotel.

'Informative, disgusting and utterly fascinating'
Closer

'Reading *Hotel Babylon* is liked mainlining Popbitch'
Metro

'Makes shock revelation after shock revelation'
Daily Mail

'An eye-opener . . . with plenty of tips for the frequent traveller'
The Economist

'Five stars for excess . . . amusing and appalling'
Sunday Telegraph

9780552151467

CORGI BOOKS

AIR BABYLON
by Imogen Edwards-Jones & Anonymous

'A fascinating exposé of life in the sky'
Marie Claire

Do you know the best place to have sex on a plane? Do you
know that one drink in the air equals three on the ground? Do
you know who is checking you in? Who is checking you out?
Do you know what happens to your luggage once it leaves
your sight? Is it secure? Are you safe? Do you really know
anything about the industry to which you entrust your life
several times a year?

Air Babylon is a trawl through the highs, the lows and the
rapid descents of air travel. It catalogues the births, the deaths,
the drunken brawls, the sexual antics and the debauchery
behind the scenes of the ultimate service industry where the
world is divided into those who wear the uniform and those
who don't . . .

'A shocking but fantastic book'
OK! Magazine

'Juicy stuff'
Heat

'Some readers may find a stomach-distress bag essential'
Sunday Telegraph

9780552153058

CORGI BOOKS

BEACH BABYLON
by Imogen Edwards-Jones & Anonymous

How does it feel to live and work in the world's most beautiful and luxurious tropical island resort, surrounded by white sandy beaches and aquamarine seas? How does it feel to be in the lap of luxury when you're thousands of miles from anywhere else? And when the guest are some of the richest and most demanding people in the world, where do you find the energy every day to smile, smile and smile again?

Beach Babylon takes you behind the scenes at a five-star tropical island resort. Do all the stores which take place behind the closed doors of the exclusive spa have happy endings? What do the world's richest people expect from room service during their fortnight in paradise? What does the windsurfing instructor do to keep sane after hours?

In the bestselling tradition of her previous Babylon books, Imogen Edwards-Hones investigates the rivalries and alliances between the staff at a resort where pandering to the guests' most extravagant whims is *de rigueur*. With a cast of millionaires, celebrities, hangers-on and prostitutes, *Beach Babylon* takes you to a world where extreme luxury is the norm and where excess somehow isn't always enough . . .

NOW AVAILABLE FROM BANTAM PRESS

9780593056226

BANTAM PRESS